CAPACITAS

One of the principal tasks for legal research at the beginning of the twenty-first century is to reconstruct the understanding of the relationship between the legal system and the market order. After almost three decades of deregulation driven by a belief in the self-equilibrating properties of the market, the financial crisis of 2008 has reminded everyone of the fundamental truth that markets have legal and institutional foundations, without which they cannot effectively function. The chapters in the present volume are the result of work by a group of legal scholars which began in the mid-2000s, at a time when the shortcomings of deregulatory policies were becoming clear in a number of contexts. The chapters address the question of how the language of contract law describes or conceptualises the market order and the relationship of the law to it. The perspectives taken are, in turn, historical, comparative and context-specific. The focus of the book is on a foundational idea, the concept of *capacitas*, which signifies a status conferred upon citizens for the purpose of enabling them to participate in the economic life of the polity. In modern legal systems, 'capacity' is the principal juridical mechanism by which individuals and entities are empowered to enter into legally binding agreements and, more generally, to arrange their affairs using the instruments of private law. Legal capacity is thereby the gateway to involvement in the operations of a market economy.

Capacitas

Contract Law and the Institutional Preconditions of a Market Economy

Edited by

Simon Deakin and Alain Supiot

·HART·
PUBLISHING

OXFORD AND PORTLAND, OREGON
2009

Published in North America (US and Canada) by
Hart Publishing
c/o International Specialized Book Services
920 NE 58th Avenue, Suite 300
Portland, OR 97213-3786
USA
Tel: +1-503-287-3093 or toll-free: (1)-800-944-6190
Fax: +1 503 280 8832
E-mail: orders@isbs.com
Website: www.isbs.com

Hart Publishing, 16C Worcester Place, Oxford OX1 2JW, UK
Telephone: +44 (0)1865 517530 Fax: +44(0)1865 510710
E-mail: mail@hartpub.co.uk
Website: http://www.hartpub.co.uk

British Library Cataloguing in Publication Data

Data Available

ISBN: 978-1-84113-997-5

Typeset by Forewords, Oxford
Printed and bound in Great Britain by
CPI Antony Rowe Ltd, Chippenham, Wiltshire

Preface

This book is the product of a collaborative initiative, the Capacitas project, which began life in the early 2000s. Its initial impetus was provided by the debate over the report to the European Union on the future of labour law and the transformation of the employment relationship, which was prepared by a group convened by Alain Supiot and published in 1999 under the title *Au delà de l'emploi* (*Beyond Employment*). One of the themes raised in the report was the relevance of economic concepts of 'capability' in framing policy responses to the growing flexibilisation of labour market relations. In the early 2000s, building on this work, a research project entitled 'Social Dialogue, Employment and Territories: Towards a European Politics of Capabilities' (or Eurocap) was launched under the auspices of the EU's Fifth Research and Development Framework Programme. This was an interdisciplinary project involving social scientists from a number of disciplines, including legal researchers, together with representatives of the social partners, civil society organisations and political actors with an interest in the future of European economic integration and social policy. As part of Eurocap, two workshops were convened—in Nantes in 2003 and Cambridge in 2005—to discuss legal aspects of the capability agenda. This work took the form, in part, of a discussion of the implications for legal analysis of Amartya Sen's 'capability approach'. It is very largely thanks to Sen that the concept of capability has achieved a degree of systematisation of the kind needed to make it an essential point of reference in social and economic policy debates. However, for lawyers and jurists, the capability approach is not simply something to be received from the discourses of other disciplines. Legal discourse contains within it ideas which, to some degree, correspond to the economic notion of capability, although the match is not exact. The legal concept of 'capacity', or *capacitas*, which provides the focus for the chapters in this book, is both a much older idea than the contemporary economic notion of capability and also one which is embedded in a particular process of institutional evolution, which has been going on since the late eighteenth century. Charting the evolution of 'capacity' and examining its significance today in a range of contexts is part of the process of understanding how ideas such as 'capability' are operationalised in the very concrete setting of contract law and contractual relations. With that objective in mind, this volume is intended as a contribution to the wider project, of which Eurocap was a part, of the normative realisation of a capability-based agenda for economic and social reform.

Eurocap was an international and multilingual project. Each paper in the present volume appears in the original language (French or English) in which it was written. We are grateful to the publishers and editors of the *European Review of Contract Law* and *European Review of Private Law* for permission to draw on previously published material in respect of chapters 1 and 3 respectively.

We are grateful to the European Union for funding the research on which the book is based; to the Maison des Sciences de l'Homme Ange Guépin and the Centre for Business Research for organising and hosting the workshops in Nantes and Cambridge respectively; to Kate Hansen for her invaluable assistance in the final preparation of the text; and to Richard Hart and his colleagues at Hart Publishing for their encouragement, advice and support.

Simon Deakin and Alain Supiot
Cambridge and Nantes
December 2008

Contents

List of Contributors

Wiebke Brose: Forschungsinstitut für Deutsches und Europäisches Sozialrecht, University of Cologne

Simon Deakin: Faculty of Law and Centre for Business Research, University of Cambridge

Renée-Claude Drouin: Faculty of Law, University of Montreal

Sandrine Godelain: CNRS unit 'Droit et changement social', University of Nantes

Jean Hauser: Faculty of Law, University of Bordeaux-IV (Montesquieu)

Martijn Hesselink: Faculty of Law, University of Amsterdam

Alain Supiot: Institute of Advanced Study, Nantes

Aurora Vimercati: Department of Employment and Industrial Relations, University of Bari

Alain Wijfells: Department of Private Law, Catholic University of Louvain

1

Capacitas: *Contract Law, Capabilities and the Legal Foundations of the Market*

SIMON DEAKIN*

INTRODUCTION: REVISITING THE LEGAL IDEA OF CAPACITY

One of the principal tasks for legal research at the beginning of the twenty-first century is to reconstruct the understanding of the relationship between the legal system and the market order. After almost three decades of deregulation driven by a belief in the self-equilibrating properties of the market, the global financial crisis of 2008 has reminded everyone of a fundamental truth which contemporary economic theory had done much to obscure[1]: namely, that markets have legal and institutional foundations, without which they cannot effectively function. In the coming years there is sure to be a reassessment of the role regulation plays in underpinning economic activity, to which many disciplines can be expected to make a contribution. The chapters in the present volume are the result of work by a group of legal scholars which began in the mid-2000s, at a time when the shortcomings of deregulatory policies were becoming clear in a number of contexts.[2] The chapters

* I am grateful to my fellow Capacitas project members, Wiebke Brose, Renée-Claude Drouin, Sandrine Godelain, Jean Hauser, Martin Hesselink, Alain Supiot, Aurora Vimercati and Alain Wijfells, for many helpful discussions and exchanges, on which I have drawn in writing this chapter. This is a substantially revised version of an article which first appeared in the *European Review of Contract Law* (vol 2, 2006). I am grateful to the editors and publishers of the *Review* for permission to reproduce parts of it here.

1 On which, see the discussion, below, on the modern law and economics movement and the place within it of the work of Becker.

2 The Capacitas project, on which the chapters in this book are based, was part of work funded by the European Union's Fifth Research and Development Framework Programme, Integrated Project 'Social Dialogue, Employment and Territories: Towards a European Politics of Capabilities' (Eurocap), which was completed in 2006. We are grateful to the EU for this support.

address the question of how the language of contract law describes or conceptualises the market order and the relationship of the law to it. The perspectives taken are, in turn, historical, comparative and context-specific, with labour law providing much of the contemporary subject-specific context.

This may seem to some to be a narrowly conceived project. We do not attempt here, for example, to make an empirical assessment of the economic impact of legal rules. Such work can be valuable, but we do not think that it is the only method open to legal scholarship which seeks to throw light on the relationship between the economy and the legal system. On the contrary, if we wish to understand the causes of the recent disorder and breakdown in market systems, we need (among other things) to look again at the micro-foundations of legal thought, and the internal workings of legal doctrine through which the relationship between legal rules and exchange relationships has found expression. Work of this kind can contribute, as we hope to show, to the wider project of intellectual and political reconstruction in the post-deregulatory period that we are now entering.[3]

Our focus is on a foundational legal idea, the concept of *capacitas*, which has deep roots in the civil law tradition and also has a place in the common law through the notion of capacity to contract. Understood broadly, the juridical idea of *capacitas*, or capacity, signifies a status conferred upon citizens for the purpose of enabling them to participate in the economic life of the polity. In modern legal systems, 'capacity' is the principal juridical mechanism by which individuals and entities are empowered to enter into legally binding agreements and, more generally, to arrange their affairs using the instruments of private law. Capacity, in the legal sense, is thereby the gateway to involvement in the operations of a market economy. In its classical form, originating in the contract law of the nineteenth century, capacity was defined negatively, that is to say, by its absence: the very young, very old or very ill were deemed, to varying degrees according to particular contexts, to lack the ability to make legally enforceable contracts. The concept of capacity was therefore a doctrine of selective contract enforcement, which both protected the incapable from exploitation and, equally importantly, protected the market against the incapable.

In his chapter in the current volume, Alain Wijfells traces the historical development of the concept of capacity and relates its emergence, in broad terms, to the rise of a liberal market order based on the principle of freedom of contract, or respect for the autonomy of the contracting

[3] A companion volume to the present one, containing analyses of the capability approach by economists, sociologists, political scientists, legal scholars and philosophers who took part in the Eurocap project, was published in 2007: J De Munck and B Zimmermann (eds), *La liberté au prisme des capacités. Amartya Sen au-delà du libéralisme* (Paris, editions de l'EHESS, 2007).

parties. Legal classification, he reminds us, matters because changes in the categories of legal thought provide an insight into the wider forces at work in a given period. The rise of the idea of capacity in the late eighteenth and early nineteenth centuries was part of a process Wijfells refers to as 'rationalisation', meaning the displacement of heterogeneous legal categories, typical of the hierarchical and status-based organisation of society under the *Ancien Régime*, with relatively homogeneous ones, based on the notion of the equal status of all citizens: 'every single human being—and only the single human being—enjoys capacity', as Savigny put it. From this was derived the legal presumption that all physical persons had full capacity, with the remaining categories of incapacity (relating principally to minors, married women, and the physically and psychologically unable) viewed not as particular types of status but as exceptions to the general rule. These exceptions were expressed increasingly narrowly over time.

Notwithstanding its orientation in favour of freedom of contract, the classical core of contract law gave expression to a theory of the institutional preconditions of a market economy, albeit a rather minimalist one. Incapacity, as a ground for invalidating contractual agreements independently of misrepresentation, fraud or force, was premised on the idea that certain persons did not possess the power to make rational assessments of their own self-interest of the kind required for market-based exchange. The contract law of the nineteenth century also recognised that certain types of transaction could be denied contractual force on the grounds that they infringed particular values which, exceptionally, took priority over the value of freedom of contract. In the common law, these went under the heading of 'public policy', and their effect was to qualify the power to make binding agreements which was otherwise generally vested in physical persons. This body of law therefore offers fragments of a theory of functional limits to freedom of contract: these limits are necessary both to preserve the market against anti-competitive behaviour (as in the case, for example, of the doctrine of 'restraint of trade') and to preserve society itself against the market (for example, the rules against the enforcement of certain illegal or oppressive contracts).

These were no more than fragments, though; the common law notion of public policy was and is an extremely limited one that was frozen in time at the end of the nineteenth century. Social or regulatory legislation has become a far more significant source of contractual regulation. Wijfells sees in the rise of regulatory legislation a process of 'derationalisation', which has led to the fragmentation of the unitary concept of capacity: new forms of legal protection have arisen, representing new interests. In areas such as consumer or employment protection, the law has qualified the notion of capacity, without using the technique of incapacitation to do so. The unitary category of capacity is being eroded by a set of discriminating and differentiating techniques. This poses the question of whether the abstract principle of equality can be maintained in the face of the proliferation of interests claiming protection.

The relationship between social or regulatory legislation and the notion of contractual capacity has always been highly contested: does a law inserting mandatory or default norms into consumer or employment contracts constrain the autonomy of the contracting parties, with negative effects upon the operation of the market, or does it establish a new contractual equilibrium which, by reducing transaction costs and reallocating risks, enhances both efficiency and the integrity of the contractual process? The institutional strand in both legal and economic analysis—a strand represented above all by the legal realist movement and by the economic institutionalist theories which reached their high point in the middle decades of the twentieth century—has long maintained that there is no simple answer to that question; it depends on context, and on an empirical understanding of the conditions under which contracts of different kinds are performed. However, the efficiency of social legislation as a mode of contractual regulation was increasingly put into doubt as deregulatory policy initiatives, many of them finding inspiration in aspects of the 'law and economics' movement, were adopted in many countries from the late 1970s onwards.[4] This occurred at the same time as the unravelling of institutional forms which had been designed for a world of protected national economies and stable economic relationships; the principal example of this was the conceptual 'crisis' affecting the institution of the employment relationship.[5] However, a simple return to private law, through 'deregulation', was never going to offer a sustainable solution to the problem posed by this process of de-institutionalisation. This is because the classical or nineteenth-century core of private law, to which deregulation promised to return us, offered an underdeveloped account of the basis for effective participation in economic life: one in which form (an idealised notion of juridical equality and contractual autonomy) prevailed over substance (a reality of asymmetrical bargaining power and all-pervasive externalities). The problem is epitomised by the poverty of the modern legal concept of capacity and by the conceptual confusion surrounding this notion. Hence we lack, today, a convincing theory of the role of law in enhancing and protecting the substantive contractual capacity of market agents, a notion which

[4] On the political background to the rise 'law and economics' movement in the US at this time, see S Teles, *The Rise of the Conservative Legal Movement: The Battle for Control of the Law* (Princeton, University of Princeton Press, 2008) chs 1 and 6.

[5] See generally A Supiot (ed), *Au delà de l'emploi. Transformations du travail et devenir du droit du travail en Europe* (Paris, Flammarion, 1999).

resembles the economic concept of 'capability'.[6] Re-examining the legal notion of capacity from the perspective of the economist's 'capability approach' has therefore become part of the process of understanding the preconditions for a sustainable market order under today's conditions.

The purpose of this book is to initiate a re-examination of this kind. In this first, introductory chapter, some preliminary questions are addressed, and the contributions made in the following chapters are set out in broad terms. The next section looks at the implicit economic logic of the concept of capacity, explores its links to notions of rationality and assesses the economic functionality of private law rules limiting freedom of contract. The following section then examines in more detail various ways in which the relationship between contractual capacity and regulatory legislation has been expressed in the modern law of contract. The section after that considers the deregulatory critique against the insertion of mandatory norms into contractual relationships. The stage is then set for us to consider the following question: is it possible to identify the elements of a new concept of *capacitas*, one which goes beyond purely formal guarantees of market access, to encompass the conditions needed for effective participation in the complex economic orders which characterise our time?

THE ECONOMIC LOGIC OF CAPACITY, PUBLIC POLICY AND RELATED GROUNDS OF INVALIDITY IN CONTRACT LAW

In civil law systems, contractual capacity is stated to be one of the basic conditions for the formation of a contract.[7] As Martijn Hesselink's chapter in this book explains, in the civil law, 'capacity' has two meanings, one referring to the ability to hold rights (*capacité de jouissance, Rechtsfähigkeit, capacità giuridica,* and so on), the other the ability to exercise them (*capacité d'exercice, Handlungsfähigkeit, capacità di agire,* and so on). Contractual incapacity is almost invariably an instance of the second of these two categories. The capacity to hold rights, which is, in effect, a right to be treated as a legal subject and not as a mere object of legal relations, vests today in all physical persons from the point of birth,[8] as a

6 See A Sen, *Commodities and Capabilities* (Deventer, North-Holland, 1985) and *Development as Freedom* (Oxford, Oxford University Press, 1999). On the potential relevance of the capability approach to understanding capacity-building in the context of European labour markets, see Supiot (ed), above n 5.

7 Eg Art 1108 of the French Civil Code.

8 As Hesselink's chapter points out, there is a human rights dimension to the capacity to hold rights which is recognised to some degree in EU law, in the context, for example, of the rights of minors to benefit from the principle of free movement in Art 18 of the EC Treaty: Case C–200/02 *Man Lavette Chan and Kunqian Catherine Zu v Secretary of State for the Home Department* [2004] OJ C300, 7.

result of the abolition of rules restricting the capacity of certain groups historically denied it,[9] such as married women. This is equally the position in the common law, where the formal distinction between the holding and exercising of rights is, however, of no relevance. In all systems, the remaining grounds of incapacity are now tightly defined; they mostly apply to agreements made by 'minors' (or 'infants'), the very old, and those suffering from mental illness. The question of contractual capacity has been said to be of 'reduced practical significance' in the English law of contract;[10] although not without some theoretical interest, particularly from the point of view of the interaction of contractual and restitutionary remedies, it is essentially treated as a footnote to the main body of the law of contract. The relative insignificance of the subject for English lawyers is compounded by the absence of certain complex rules of French-origin civil law systems, dealing with the circumstances under which lack of contractual capacity can be offset by assistance (*curatelle*) or representation (*tutelle*).[11] These have no equivalent in the English common law, and even some civil law systems, such as the German one, do not recognise the category of assistance.[12] In all systems, the effects of incapacity on a contract also differ according to context: complete nullity is only one option; others include voidability, while alternative remedies in tort or restitution may be available.[13]

The limited and diminishing practical significance of the concept of capacity in modern contract law should not, however, be confused with the issue of its structural significance within contract doctrine. Indeed, there is a case for saying that it is still at the core of what is meant by a contractual obligation. A simple exchange, even between otherwise consenting parties, is not enough to found a contract. It has to be shown, in addition, that each party is able to assess whether the transaction is in their best interests. The law presumes that this may not be so in the case of the young, on the grounds of their immaturity and inexperience, and in those such as the very old or mentally ill who, for one reason or another, may be unable to understand the consequences of their actions.

Put slightly differently, the concept of capacity is based on the view that one of the preconditions for the enforcement of contracts is that individuals possess the capability for rational economic action. One of the elements of the economic concept of rationality is that individuals possess stable preferences, that is, they can rank a given set of outcomes in order of preference. The absence of stable preferences can be under-

[9] E McKendrick, *Contract Law: Text, Cases and Materials* (Oxford, Oxford University Press, 2003) 788.

[10] *Ibid.*

[11] On this, see the chapters by Jean Hauser and Sandrine Godelain in the present volume.

[12] See Hauser in this volume.

[13] For English law see the discussion of McKendrick, above n 9, ch 21.

stood as providing an economic justification for the invalidation of contracts on the grounds of incapacity. In the terms used in law and economics analysis,

> If the promisor's preferences are unstable or not well-ordered, then he is unable to conclude a perfect contract. The law says that such people's promises are unenforceable because they are legally incompetent. For example, children and the insane do not have stable, well-ordered preferences, and as a result, their promises are unenforceable . . . There are also special circumstances in which a person, who is ordinarily competent, may be temporarily incompetent, and during that incompetency she cannot conclude enforceable promises. For example, the ingestion of a prescription drug may make someone drowsy to the point of incompetency so that any promises given while in that state would be unenforceable. Consider a slightly more controversial example: if high pressure tactics are used to confuse a consumer and induce him to sign a contract, a court may be unwilling to enforce it. The consumer's failing is described by some lawyers as a 'transactional incapacity', that is, the incapacity to conduct this transaction rationally under these circumstances.[14]

The effect is that contract law, in one of its core doctrines, views the market as more than just a space within which consensual exchange occurs. Market transactions are exchanges of a particular type, founded on individuals' capacity for independent judgement.

We can go further. The capacity concept is predicated upon assumptions about the need for institutional underpinning of market exchange. One consequence of the doctrine of capacity is to provide protection to the incapable. But the doctrine also protects the market against the incapable,[15] by excluding them from normal participation in exchange relations. They may enter into transactions only with the aid of intermediaries. The doctrines of assistance and representation, formally stated in the civil law and implicit to some degree in the common law rules, are principally intended to enhance the contractual security of third parties and thereby secure confidence in the market as a whole. Thus an inference which may be drawn from the structure of contract law is that legal enforcement of contracts matters, along with its corollary, namely selective non-enforcement. The maintenance of the market order depends upon the legal system being able to take a discriminating view about which contracts to enforce, and how.

To say that this is a foundational assumption of the system of contract law is not, of course, the same thing as saying that it is a proposition supported by empirical observation or by an economic or sociological perspective on law. It is simply another way of describing how the legal

14 R Cooter and T Ulen, *Law and Economics* (New York, Harper Collins, 1988) 237.
15 See Hesselink in this volume.

system views the external effects of its own enforcement mechanisms. However, it is noteworthy that the idea of the law–economy relation which is implicit in the structure of contract law differs markedly from the approach which became predominant in the recent law and economics tradition. Gary Becker's highly influential claim that human behaviour in a wide (in fact, the widest possible) range of contexts can be explained by the three axioms of stable preferences, maximising behaviour and market equilibrium is at the heart of this tradition.[16] From the 'internal' viewpoint of contract law doctrine, Becker's basic position has to be qualified by the understanding that each of these conditions is not a natural state of affairs, but is instead the product of a certain institutional configuration, which is nowhere explained in Becker's account.

In considering that issue, it may be helpful to look more closely at the grounds on which, as a matter of core contract law, enforcement of arm's length transactions is regularly and routinely denied. In the common law systems, a significant set of exceptions to the principle of contractual enforcement takes the form of the doctrine of public policy. This doctrine applies not to contracts which are vitiated by misrepresentation, mistake or coercion, but to agreements which are in every essential respect consensual.[17] A variety of justifications is offered for non-enforcement: these include headings such as 'restraint of trade', 'agreements injurious to good government' and 'agreements contrary to family life'.[18] It is an eclectic and arbitrary-looking list. What, if anything, unites the different categories? If we go beneath the formal language use by the courts, two categories suggest themselves: cases in which the justification for non-enforcement is the protection of the market against itself (or, more

[16] See G Becker, *The Economic Approach to Human Behaviour* (Chicago, IL, Chicago University Press, 1976) ch 1, discussed by A Supiot, *Homo Juridicus: Essai sur la function anthropologique du Droit* (Paris, Seuil, 2005) 116–17. On the centrality of Becker's axioms to the law and economics movement, see E Schanze, 'What is Law and Economics Today? A European View' in P Nobel (ed), *New Frontiers of Law and Economics* (Zürich, Schulthess, 2006). Schanze adds 'institutional choice matters' to Becker's original list, a significant addition, but one which is not altogether easy to reconcile with the more minimalist approach taken by Becker which succeeds in avoiding any explicit reference to institutions.

[17] Agreements which are vitiated by the grounds of mistake, misrepresentation and duress can be quite straightforwardly explained using basic microeconomic insights relating to risk and information (see, eg HG Beale, W Bishop and M Furmston, *Contract: Cases and Materials* (London, Butterworths, 4th edn, 2001), in particular ch 4, setting out the basic position on the economics of contract law, and which is then applied throughout the book in chapters relating to particular doctrines).

[18] J Beatson, *Anson's Law of Contract* (Oxford, Oxford University Press, 27th edn, 1998) ch 9.III, lists the following categories: agreements to commit a crime or civil wrong, or to perpetrate a fraud; agreements which injure the state in its relations with other states; agreements which tend to injure good government; agreements which tend to pervert the course of justice; agreements which tend to abuse the legal process; agreements which are contrary to good morals; agreements which affect the security of marriage or the due discharge of parental duty; agreements which oust the jurisdiction of the court; and anti-competitive agreements.

precisely, against the deleterious effects of consensual exchange); and cases in which the principle is the protection of society against the market.

The doctrine of restraint of trade falls into the first of these categories. This has been called 'a strange beast'; after all,

> its role in contract law is traditionally understood to be that of denying validity to contracts that unduly restrain the freedom of one or both of the contracting parties. The doctrine appears to place non-procedural limitations on freedom of contract and, moreover, to place these limitations because of concerns for the contracting parties' freedom. A concern for freedom is being used, it appears, to limit freedom.[19]

But is it so strange? The doctrine of restraint of trade enables the court to strike down agreements, or parts of agreements, which unduly limit or restrict competition. Thus agreements by employees not to compete with a former employer can only be enforced if they involve the assertion by the latter of a 'proprietary interest' in the form of protection against solicitation of customers or employees, or the maintenance of confidential information or trade secrets.[20] The doctrine has also been used in a variety of contexts to control market entry and exit rules, price fixing, wage regulation and other attempts of market actors to control the competitive process through agreement among themselves.[21] Here, then, is recognition that the principle of freedom of contract has the potential to undermine the competitive process on which the market order ultimately depends for its successful operation. Even if market relations in a broad sense could be maintained in a market partitioned by anti-competitive agreements, the precise and rather fragile conditions needed for a market equilibrium would seem to be particularly vulnerable to this kind of action. Thus the existence of the restraint of trade doctrine involves the recognition, again from the core of contract law (since this is an ancient doctrine), that selective legal enforcement of contracts is a necessity if the market is to function effectively.

Most of the other heads of public policy cannot be explained in this way; rather, they appear to be based on the view that, important as freedom of contract is, there are certain values which take priority over it, and must be protected against it. It is on this basis that the courts will refuse to enforce contracts that are 'contrary to public morals', for example, or which are intended to undermine the government, or which oust their own jurisdiction. Thus the family, the apparatus of government

[19] S Smith, 'Reconstructing Restraint of Trade' (1995) 15 *Oxford Journal of Legal Studies* 565, 567.

[20] Beatson, above n 18, 360–70.

[21] *Ibid*, 358–60.

and the legal system itself are institutions which are not just separate from the market, and operate on a distinctive and separate logic, but also need protection from its potentially destabilising effects.

However, as it stands, the list of grounds of non-enforcement is selective, and arguably outdated. This is the result of the courts' insistence, at the end of the nineteenth century, that the heads of public policy, as they then existed, were a closed set.[22] This position was no doubt influenced by the view, widely held at the time, that the foremost goal of public policy should be to defend the principle of freedom of contract itself.[23] However, it also reflected a perception that regulatory legislation was a more effective and legitimate mechanism than the judge-made common law for regulating contractual relations. In this respect, the English courts of 1890s, for example, were simply anticipating the expansion of regulatory legislation, which began to gather speed around the turn of the twentieth century.

In both these manifestations—protecting the market against itself and protecting other social institutions against the market—the public policy doctrine operates in a manner closely related to the concept of capacity. Across a wide range of consensual contracts, the law refuses to lend its support to contract enforcement. The existence of doctrines at the core of the judge-made law, in the common law systems, and embedded in the civil law codes, which formally limit freedom of contract in the interest of maintaining the market order and the wider social fabric of which it forms a part, is a sign that the market is not a self-constituting order, and that the conditions for its successful operation—including the foundational notions of individual rationality and market equilibrium—are not natural, but institutional, in origin.

THE TRANSFORMATION OF THE CONCEPT OF CAPACITY IN THE MODERN LAW OF CONTRACTS

The diminishing importance of the capacity concept in contract law is part of a dual movement which took place in the course of the twentieth century. The first was the abolition of rules denying capacity to entire groups, in particular married women, a process which was still going on in English law as late as the middle decades of the century.[24] The reduction of the age of majority from 21 to 18 in 1969 removed most of the

[22] *Janson v Driefontein Consolidated Mines Ltd* [1902] AC 484, 491 (Lord Halsbury).

[23] *Printing and Numerical Registering Co v Sampson* (1875) 19 LR Eq 462, 465 (Sir George Jessel MR).

[24] As in the case of the (English) Law Reform (Married Women and Tortfeasors) Act 1935 and the Married Women (Restraint upon Anticipation) Act 1949.

more significant cases of minors' contracts from the scope of the rule.[25] In the civilian systems, in addition to the reforms which saw the removal of the old forms of incapacitation, the doctrine of capacity underwent a series of changes that rendered it both more flexible and more discriminating in its effects. As Jean Hauser shows in his chapter in this book, French law has moved away from using pure age-based criteria for determining the point at which minors cease to be affected by contractual incapacity (much as in English law), and the traditional distinction between classes of incapacity giving rise to representation (*tutelle*) and assistance (*curatelle*) has become blurred over time. The second change was the emergence of new techniques for countering the risk of exploitation in highly unbalanced or unequal contracts—as Hauser puts it, a shift from 'incapacitation' to 'protection'. Where the concept of capacity provided protection to the weak or vulnerable by denying legal enforcement to their contracts, thereby excluding them from independent participation in economic life, statutory regulation inserted mandatory and 'default' terms into contracts for the benefit of parties deemed to be at a disadvantage in terms of bargaining power.

When this process was beginning around a century ago, common law courts initially reacted with extreme hostility to what they saw as a new form of paternalism that undermined the contractual autonomy of the protected party and marked a reversion from contract to status. The English Court of Appeal, in giving a restrictive interpretation to workmen's compensation legislation in a judgment in 1905, noted that

> it presupposes a position of dependence; it treats the class of workmen as being in a sense 'inopes consilii', and the Legislature does for them what they cannot do for themselves: it gives them a sort of State insurance, it being assumed that they are either not sufficiently intelligent or not sufficiently in funds to insure themselves.[26]

In the same year, the language of capacity was used by the US Supreme Court in deciding, in the pivotal *Lochner* case, that statutory restrictions on working time were unconstitutional:

> when the state, by its legislature, in the assumed exercise of its police powers, has passed an act which seriously limits the right to labor or the right of contract in regard to their means of livelihood between persons who are *sui juris* (both employer and employee), it becomes of great importance to determine which shall prevail—the right of the individual to labor for such time as he may choose, or the right of the state to prevent the individual from laboring,

[25] Family Law Reform Act 1969, s 1.

[26] *Simpson v Ebbw Vale Steel, Iron & Coal Co* [1905] 1KB 453; see S Deakin and F Wilkinson, *The Law of the Labour Market: Industrialization, Employment and Legal Evolution* (Oxford, Oxford University Press, 2005) 88 for the background to this case.

or from entering into any contract to labor, beyond a certain time prescribed by the state.[27]

The majority concluded:

> There is no reasonable ground for interfering with the liberty of person or the right of free contract, by determining the hours of labor, in the occupation of a baker. There is no contention that bakers as a class are not equal in intelligence and capacity to men in other trades or manual occupations, or that they are not able to assert their rights and care for themselves without the protecting arm of the state, interfering with their independence of judgment and of action. They are in no sense wards of the state.[28]

The 'substantive due process' doctrine which *Lochner* established was nevertheless held, from an early stage, to have no application to statutes concerning child and female labour.[29] These categories of employment were still overshadowed by the common law doctrine of contractual incapacity:

> history discloses the fact that woman has always been dependent upon man . . . As minors, though not to the same extent, she has been looked upon in the courts as needing especial care that her rights may be preserved.[30]

In time, courts and legislatures arrived at a different justification: all workers were entitled to a basic level of health and safety protection, in order to protect their physical integrity. The germ of this idea was present in *Lochner* itself, in the dissenting judgments. While Holmes's short dissent is the best known among the *Lochner* judgments, the minority opinion of Justices Harlan, White and Day is of particular interest for present purposes. Noting, in passing, that 'there are very few, if any, questions in political economy about which entire certainty may be predicated', Harlan argued that

> It is enough for the determination of this case, and it is enough for this court to know, that the question is one about which there is room for debate and for an honest difference of opinion. There are many reasons of a weighty, substantial character, based upon the experience of mankind, in support of the theory that, all things considered, more than ten hours' steady work each day, from week to week, in a bakery or confectionery establishment, may endanger the

27 198 US 45, 54 (1905).

28 198 US 45, 57 (1905).

29 The doctrine was only abrogated in the 1930s. See generally H Hovenkamp, *Enterprise and American Law 1836–1937* (Cambridge MA, Harvard University Press, 1991).

30 *Muller v Oregon* 208 US 412, 421 (1908). The Court noted (p 418) that the state of Oregon had begun to repeal laws excluding the contractual and personal capacity of married women in the 1870s.

health and shorten the lives of the workmen, thereby diminishing their physical and mental *capacity* to serve the state and to provide for those dependent upon them.[31]

Thus the claim that social legislation possesses a capacity-enhancing effect was present at the very beginning of the debate. In *Lochner*, the issue was phrased in terms of the physical integrity of the individual worker; the evolution of labour legislation from its early-twentieth-century beginnings can be understood as a gradual expansion of the range of interests which the law recognises to be at stake in the formation and performance of the contract of employment. These have been extended, to varying degrees in different systems, to include the economic security, psychological well-being and personal dignity of the individual.[32] Thus laws which provide protection against the risks of interruption to earnings through illness, unemployment and old age (social insurance law) guarantee freedom of association for the purposes of collective action (collective labour law), stabilise the employment relationship against the consequences of economic uncertainty and the arbitrary exercise of employer power (unfair dismissal law), and insert basic labour standards with respect to the wage–work bargain and maximum hours of work can all be understood as underpinning the contractual capacity of the worker. The presence of these norms makes it possible for the individual worker to enter into a contract which is necessarily incomplete and asymmetrical. Such regulatory norms do not 'complete' the contract or render it fully symmetrical, but they do compensate for some of the effects of incompleteness and asymmetry. Far from undermining the unilateral or prerogative power of the employer ('subordination'), they acknowledge its existence and legitimacy. To view labour law in this way is to recognise that it has information-sharing and risk-allocation functions in additional to the more explicitly 'protective' ones which are generally attributed to it.[33] This is not just 'paternalism', nor is it simply 'redistribution', despite the widespread use of such terms on both sides of the long debate concerning the legitimacy of the legislative regulation of contracts.[34] The process of inserting 'social rights'

[31] 198 US 45, 71 (1905). Emphasis added.

[32] See S Simitis, 'The Rediscovery of the Individual in Labour Law' in R Rogowski and T Wilthagen (eds), *Reflexive Labour Law* (Deventer, Kluwer, 1994).

[33] See generally S Deakin and F Wilkinson, 'Labour Law and Economic Theory: A Reappraisal' in G De Geest, J Siegers, and R Van den Bergh (eds), *Law and Economics and the Labour Market* (Aldershot, Elgar, 1999).

[34] See A Kronman, 'Contract Law and Distributive Justice' (1980) 89 *Yale Law Journal* 472; D Kennedy, 'Distributive and Paternalist Motives in Contract and Tort Law' (1982) 41 *Maryland Law Review* 563; A Ogus, 'Regulatory Paternalism: When is it Justified?' in K Hopt, E Wymeersch, H Kanda and H Baum (eds), *Corporate Governance in Context: Corporations, States, and Markets in Europe, Japan and the US* (Oxford, Oxford University Press, 2005).

into the employment contract is one by which labour law re-establishes a contractual equilibrium between the parties.

A similar argument can be made for consumer protection legislation. Laws use a variety of techniques to protect individual purchasers of services or products in their dealings with business entities. Exclusion and limitation clauses may be struck out, and contract terms which are not individually negotiated may be subjected to a proportionality test. In consumer credit contracts, legislation may provide for 'cooling-off periods' or go so far as to require the provision of an independent third-party opinion. The justification for this type of statutory control has gradually shifted over time from a focus on contractual inequality and the absence of 'real' consensus in standard-form agreements[35] to the view that the role of the law is to provide incentives for information sharing and risk-shifting between the parties.[36]

ASSESSING THE DEREGULATORY CRITIQUE OF SOCIAL LEGISLATION

Notwithstanding the arguments which have just been made, a return to *Lochner*-type critiques of legislative controls over contract terms has been a distinct trend since the 1970s, affecting all jurisdictions. How should this deregulatory movement be assessed?

The common thread running through critiques of social and regulatory legislation is the view that the market is a self-equilibrating order, in the context of which legislative norms constitute an 'interference' or 'distortion', preventing the operation of spontaneous forces. Deregulation, by stripping away layers of legislative control, can be expected to restore market mechanisms to their full operation. This view of the market owes much to the main methodological move within recent economic accounts of law, which is to imagine a world of frictionless exchange—a 'zero transaction cost world'—and then to loosen the assumptions underlying the model, in ways which invite a consideration of the sources of market imperfections. The foundational assumptions of neoclassical economics offer no obvious place for a normative order of any kind other than the self-regulating order of the market, which is itself ultimately reducible to the tendency of individuals to engage in maximising behaviour. As we have seen, in Becker's account, individuals are assumed to act rationally, in the sense of maximising their own well-being in the face of constraints, on the basis of pre-given, 'stable' or ranked preferences; likewise, markets are assumed to be clear if they are not interfered with by external forces.

[35] F Kessler, 'Contracts of Adhesion—Some Thoughts about Freedom of Contract' (1943) 43 *Columbia Law Review* 629.

[36] Ogus, above n 34.

The mathematical proofs of the 'fundamental' theorems of welfare economics are generally understood as demonstrating that, in a world of purely competitive markets, the aggregate well-being of all market actors—buyers and sellers—is necessarily maximised.

However, in the 'new institutional' variant of the law and economics literature, these assumptions are relaxed precisely so that a functional relationship between the market system and the legal-normative order can be identified. The environment may be less than perfect: contracts may be complex and hence incomplete, or exchange vitiated by externalities or asymmetrical information, leading to persistent market imperfections, to which contract law responds.[37] The basic behavioural assumptions of the model can be modified through the concept of 'bounded' rationality,[38] or through the use of experimental or psychological evidence for the existence of cognitive biases or traits which, if present in particular contexts, prevent the realisation of equilibrium states.[39] These techniques can be, and have been, used to justify departures from a regime of complete freedom of contract. Such interventions, whether they originate in the realm of 'classical' private law or in regulatory legislation, can be understood as aligning the allocation of economic resources more closely to that of a perfectly competitive market—a 'market-perfecting' agenda. To that extent, the techniques used in the economics of law do not inevitably point in the direction of deregulation.

On the other hand, the presence of market imperfections does not necessarily justify regulation; many such imperfections are thought to be irremediable because the costs of intervention can be expected to outweigh the benefits.[40] Public choice theory dictates that this is particularly likely in the case of legislative intervention, since the political process is thought to be especially vulnerable to the distorting effects of organised pressure group activity. The predominant theory of rule-making in the common law argues that judge-made law, by contrast, contains a self-correcting mechanism, in the form of private incentives for litigation, for the deselection of inefficient (or wealth-destroying) rules.[41] Some analyses have built on this argument to claim that legal systems which rely predominantly on legislation as a mode of rule-making are for

37 This is in essence the explanation offered by Cooter and Ulen, above n 14, ch 6, for the structure of the common law of contract.

38 The implications of bounded rationality, along with market uncertainty and 'asset specificity' or relation-specific investments in transactions, are most systematically set out in O Williamson, *The Economic Institutions of Capitalism* (New York, Free Press, 1985) and *The Mechanisms of Governance* (Oxford, Oxford University Press, 1996).

39 See generally the contributions in C Sunstein (ed), *Behavioural Law and Economics* (Cambridge, Cambridge University Press, 2000).

40 Williamson, *The Mechanisms of Governance*, above n 38.

41 On this contrast between legislative and judicial rule-making, see P Rubin, 'Common Law and Statute Law' (1982) 11 *Journal of Legal Studies* 205.

that reason less adaptable, and hence less efficient, than those which give a greater priority to judge-made law; and this claim, in turn, has been used to argue that civil law systems are inherently less supportive of economic growth than those of the common law.[42] This 'legal origin' claim has nevertheless been contested on both methodological and empirical grounds. It is far from clear, for example, that the characterisation of common law and civil law systems in the most-cited studies in this area is accurate,[43] or that the mechanism by which legal origin (common law or civil law) translates into substantive rules of law has been adequately specified.[44] Nevertheless, it has had a tangible effect on the policy initiatives of the World Bank and of many governments.[45]

One aspect of the recent legal origin literature is a revival of interest in FA Hayek's account of private law.[46] This differs from the modern law and economics synthesis in accepting, at a foundational level, the need for a legal-normative order to underpin market relations. Institutions are no longer viewed as isolated interventions, designed to counteract the effects of market failure. Rather, the 'abstract rules of just conduct'—in essence, the rules of contract, property and tort—are seen as functionally necessary for establishing freedom of disposition and security of transactions in the market place. By contrast, Hayek insists that social legislation, since it has a largely redistributive goal, interferes with market relations in a way that undermines the spontaneous ordering of the market and of society more generally. More generally, Hayek argues that here, as elsewhere, 'attempts to "correct" the order of the market lead to its destruction',[47] suggesting that his schema is even less amenable to legal intervention than the market-perfecting agenda which characterises most contemporary law and economics analysis.

[42] E Glaeser and A Shleifer, 'Legal Origins' (2002) 117 *Quarterly Journal of Economics* 1193.

[43] M Siems, 'Reconciling Law & Finance and Comparative Law' (2007) 52 *McGill Law Journal* 55.

[44] B Ahlering and S Deakin, 'Corporate Governance, Labor Regulation and Legal Origin: A Case of Institutional Complementarity?' (2007) 41 *Law & Society Review* 865.

[45] See R La Porta, F Lopez-de-Silanes and A Shleifer, 'The Economic Consequences of Legal Origins' (2008) 46 *Journal of Economic Literature* 285, 325 (the World Bank's *Doing Business* rankings have 'encouraged regulatory reform in dozens of countries'). For a critique of the use of the legal origin approach in the *Doing Business* reports, see C Ménard and B de Marais, 'Can We Rank Legal Systems According to their Economic Efficiency?' in Nobel, above n 16, who suggest that the *Doing Business* reports 'create an illusion. They pretend to measure the role of legal systems according to their economic efficiency. What they actually do is rank countries according to a set of indexes in which the real properties and specificities of legal systems are almost never captured'. See also the report of the World Bank Independent Evaluation Group, *Doing Business: An Independent Evaluation. Taking the Measure of the World Bank IFC Doing Business Indicators* (Washington, DC, International Bank for Reconstruction and Development, 2008).

[46] See P Mahoney, 'The Common Law and Economic Growth: Hayek might be Right' (2001) 30 *Journal of Legal Studies* 503.

[47] F Hayek, *The Mirage of Social Justice* (London, Routledge & Kegan Paul, 1976) 142.

The main empirical argument buttressing Hayek's account is historical: private law represents the core of a system of contract and property rights which predated the advent of twentieth-century social legislation. In the nineteenth century, Richard Epstein suggests, US labour relations were 'governed by a set of laws that spanned the law of property, contract, tort and procedure'; in other words, a 'common law' of labour relations which could be re-established if the New Deal labour laws of the 1930s onwards were repealed.[48] In the civil law, the concept of the 'private law society' (in the German tradition, the *Privatsrechtsgemeinschaft*) expresses the same idea of a self-equilibrating legal order, which found its highest expression in the nineteenth-century codes.[49] This view of history is, at best, highly selective and, at worst, actively misleading. In nineteenth-century labour and product markets, the police power of the state buttressed the relations of private law: criminal sanctions were used to enforce labour contracts and break strikes.[50] It was this state-based disciplinary power, rather than a pure private law regime, which the social legislation of the twentieth century displaced.[51]

Even if the weakest point of the neoliberal critique of market regulation is the claim that a return to a private law society is possible (let alone desirable),[52] rejection of this claim is not synonymous with uncritical acceptance of the model of social legislation inherited from the middle decades of the twentieth century. Legislation regulating the contract of employment gave expression to a societal compact, in which inequality within the enterprise (the employee's 'subordination' to managerial prerogative) was traded off in return for certain social guarantees (such as protection against risks arising from injury, illness, unemployment and old age). That model was based on assumptions

48 R Epstein, 'A Common Law for Labor Relations; A Critique of the New Deal Legislation' (1983) 92 *Yale Law Journal* 1357, 1357.

49 On the 'private law society', see W Steinmetz, 'Introduction' in W Steinmetz (ed), *Private Law and Social Inequality in the Industrial Age: Comparing Legal Cultures in Britain, France, Germany and the United States* (Oxford, Oxford University Press, 2000).

50 All common law systems, including the US, saw some role for forced labour and the criminalisation of breach of the service contract by workers in the period of industrialisation; see generally D Hay and P Craven (eds), *Masters, Servants and Magistrates in Britain and the Empire, 1562–1955* (Chapel Hill, NC, University of North Carolina Press, 2004). In the civilian systems of continental Europe, a police power to regulate labour contracts operated alongside the private law codes until the middle of the nineteenth century: see B Veneziani, 'The Evolution of the Employment Relationship' in B. Hepple (ed), *The Making of Labour Law in Europe* (London, Mansell, 1986); A Cottereau, 'Industrial Tribunals and the Establishment of a Kind of Common Law of Labour in Nineteenth Century France' in W Steinmetz (ed), *Private Law and Social Inequality in the Industrial Age: Comparing Legal Cultures in Britain, France, Germany and the United States* (Oxford, Oxford University Press, 2000).

51 See Deakin and Wilkinson, above n 26, chs 2 and 3, on the British case.

52 The *locus classicus* of the argument that attempts to create a pure market order have resulted in social catastrophe is K Polanyi, *The Great Transformation: Origins of Our Time* (Boston MA, Beacon Press, 1957), recently reissued (2001) with a new introduction, arguing for its contemporary relevance, by J Stiglitz.

which are perhaps as questionable, albeit for different reasons, as the assumptions made in the Hayekian or neoliberal critique of regulatory legislation. In particular, the employment model of the mid-twentieth century assumed the vertical integration of the enterprise and the traditional division of labour within the nuclear family. The power of the nation state to regulate social and economic relations through legislation was also more or less taken for granted. In all these respects, the employment model was very much a product of a particular mid-twentieth century consensus which is now called into question.[53] The disintegration of the enterprise through mergers and acquisitions, outsourcing and subcontracting; changing family structures; and a perception of the limits to state-based legislative ordering of economic relations together mean that the employment model is less and less able to fulfil its 'cornerstone' role of ensuring social protection while also providing a framework for the governance of work. The current 'crisis' of the regulatory state therefore arises less from its supposed incompatibility with a market economy than from the contingency of the particular circumstances under which certain institutional forms, in particular the employment model, emerged in the course of the twentieth century.[54] Is it possible to renew the employment model and the associated institutions of contractual regulation in a way which aligns them with the today's changed conditions?

CONTRACT LAW, MARKET ACCESS AND THE CAPABILITY APPROACH

The starting point for consideration of this question is to re-examine the concept of capacity, which has been inherited from the private law codes and judge-made common law of the nineteenth century. As we have seen, capacity is the device by which the law accords individuals the power to enter into contracts (among other things). It involves the attribution of a set of legal powers to market actors. The abolition of such traditional grounds of incapacity as sex and marital status has left only age, to a limited extent, and mental incapability as grounds for denying parties the power to make legally enforceable agreements. Thus capacity has come to be defined, in a sense which is both negative and narrow, as the absence of the ability to make reasoned, independent judgments. While this is a vital precondition for the effective functioning of a market order, it can be argued that it is only one of a number of conditions which are necessary in order for the market to operate as an instrument for the creation of

[54] See A Supiot, 'Introduction' in A Supiot (ed), above n 6.
[54] Deakin and Wilkinson, above n 26, 14–18.

well-being in society. That there is a wider set of such requirements—involving institutions for sharing information, allocating risks and compensating for the effects of externalities—is implicitly recognised in the structure of laws inserting mandatory and default terms into contracts. These legal interventions can be seen as enhancing the contractual capacity of market agents, in the sense of endowing them with the resources needed to participate in market exchange in more than a purely formal or procedural sense. To view contractual regulation in this way is to counter the neoliberal critique which views protective legislation as simply carving out exceptions to the general principle of freedom of contract, with the result that contract law is parcellised and its effects fragmented. To enlarge on this counter-critique, it is necessary to locate a more complete conceptual analysis of capacity within a wider legal and economic discussion of the institutional preconditions of markets.

In the 'standard' (in the sense of orthodox or generally accepted) law and economics approach, the operation of markets results in the maximisation of the aggregate wealth or well-being of market actors, because it ensures to the greatest possible extent that the sum total of the preferences or wants of those actors is met. Individual choices cannot fully reflect individual preferences; choices are constrained both by the resources and entitlements with which particular individuals happen to be endowed and, in effect, by the preferences of all other actors. However, aggregate utility can be maximised if full scope is given for free exchange to occur, so that resources will end up in the hands of those who value them most highly. Market-based exchange is the most reliable mechanism for enhancing economic welfare under conditions of scarcity. It is through the act of contracting, unless it is vitiated by factors such as force or fraud, that individuals can express their preferences most consistently with the principle of constrained maximisation. This is the basis for the current orientation of normative law and economics analysis towards freedom of contract and it is also consistent with the negative and narrow version of the capacity concept which has been inherited from the contract law of the nineteenth century.

In this approach, resources, endowments and preferences are all taken as given; that is to say, they are exogenous to the operation of the market mechanism. The assumption of exogeneity is a necessary correlate of the assumption of constrained maximisation. The standard economic model does not concern itself with the process by which preferences and endowments are formed.[55] This is the economic-theoretical equivalent of the idea that contract law is not concerned with the objective value of the

[55] G Stigler and G Becker, 'De gustibus non est disputandum' (1977) 67 *American Economic Review* 76.

consideration given for a promise.[56] Both ideas can be traced back to the period during which notions such as the 'just price' were banished to the margins of contract law.[57]

The more recent introduction into economic theory of the concept of 'capability' introduces a new dimension to this question. Rather than using the language of the maximisation of preferences, the capability approach refers to the 'conversion' of an individual's endowments into various desired end-states or activities, known as 'functionings'. An individual's capability set refers to the extent of their substantive freedom to realise a range of functionings:

> the concept of 'functionings'. . . reflects the various things a person may value doing or being. The valued functionings may vary from elementary ones, such as being adequately nourished and being free from avoidable disease, to very complex activities or personal states, such as being able to take part in the life of the community and having self-respect . . . A 'capability' [is] a kind of freedom: the substantive freedom to achieve alternative functioning combinations.[58]

So far this appears to be no different from the standard economic approach. The difference, for present purposes, comes at the point where the nature of the 'conversion' of resources or commodities into outcomes is being considered. Amartya Sen puts it the following way, using the example of eating as a nutritional and social activity:

> The conversion of commodity-characteristics into personal achievements of functioning depends on a variety of factors—personal and social. In the case of nutritional achievement it depends on such factors as (1) metabolic rates, (2) body size, (3) age, (4) sex (and, if a woman, whether pregnant or lactating), (5) activity levels, (6) medical conditions (including the presence or absence of parasites), (7) access to medical services and the ability to use them, (8) nutritional knowledge and education, and (9) climatic conditions. In the case of achievements involving social behaviour and entertaining friends and relatives, the functioning will depend on such influences as (1) the nature of the social conventions in force in the society in which the person lives, (2) the position of the person in the family and in the society, (3) the presence or absence of festivities such as marriage, seasonal festivals and other occasions such as funerals, (4) the physical distance from the homes of friends and relatives and so on.[59]

[56] R Posner, *Economic Analysis of Law* (Boston MA, Little, Brown & Co, 2nd edn, 1977) 70–71: 'Courts inquire only as to the existence, not the adequacy, of the consideration for a contract. The distinction is important and economically sound.'

[57] PS Atiyah, *The Rise and Fall of Freedom of Contract* (Oxford, Clarendon Press, 1979) 169–77.

[58] A Sen, *Development as Freedom*, above n 6, 75.

[59] A Sen, *Commodities and Capabilities*, above n 6, 17–18.

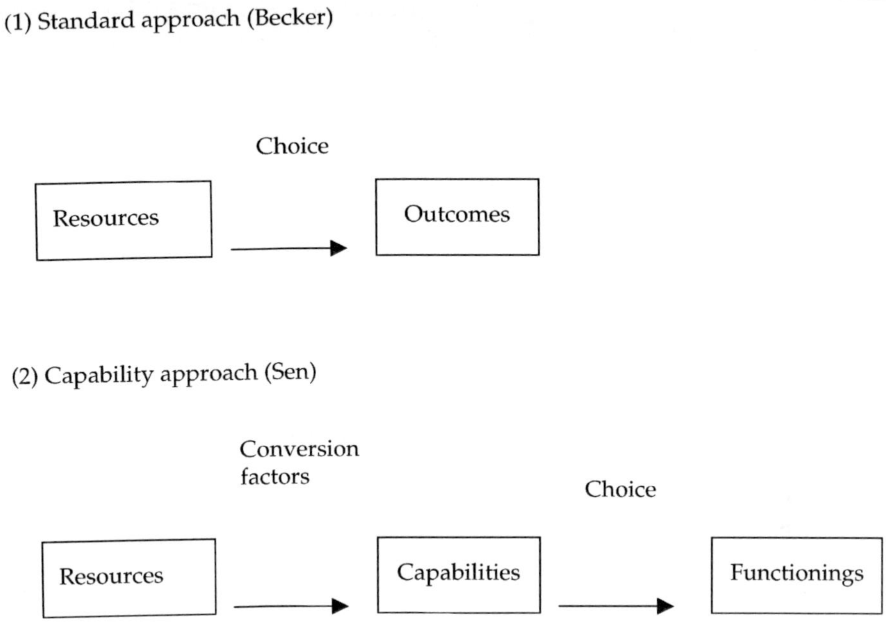

Figure 1 (adapted from J-M Bonvin, 'Capacités et démocratie' in de Munck and Zimmermann, above n 3)

The conversion of endowments and preferences into substantive freedoms—capabilities—precedes choice (see Figure 1). Thus it is not simply a consequence of individuals engaging in 'constrained maximisation'. Instead, the capability approach identifies a range of 'conversion factors' that are necessary for capabilities to come into existence. Conversion factors operate at multiple levels. Thus a person's capability to achieve a particular range of functionings could be determined not just by the characteristics (both physical and social) of their person or even simply by the wider physical and technological environment, but also by the organisational context of their lives (interpersonal networks of the kind which may be based on family, kinship, personal connection, the workplace or membership of an occupational or professional group). Critically, social institutions such as the social norms, legal rules and legal–political forms which play a constitutive role in relation to social and economic activity also play a role.

Thus, in the capability approach, institutional rules do not simply constrain, they also empower. There are further points of difference with the standard approach. The quality of choice is not just a function of the resources with which the individual is endowed or of their power for rational action; it also dependent on the institutional framework in which the relevant exchange is lodged. No doubt an effectively operating contract enforcement system has the potential to enhance individual capabilities in the context of exchange, but it is just one of a number of mechanisms that can achieve this end. It is neither necessary nor sufficient.

What would a contract law system look like if it encapsulated the capability approach rather than the standard approach to the conceptualisation of economic exchange? The answer is that it would look very much like the kinds of contract law regime that are observed in European (and other) systems today—that is to say, regimes in which the classical principles of freedom of contract and *pacta sunt servanda* are complemented by mandatory and default norms of various kinds, mostly originating in legislation. Thus one reason for taking the capability approach seriously in the present context is that it offers a more complete and coherent account of the structure and functioning of the modern law of contracts than that offered by the standard law and economics analysis. This is an account in which the capacity-enhancing role of contractual regulation is recognised as an ordering principle for the law of contracts.

The point has already been made that even in the classical, nineteenth-century core of contract law it is possible find exceptions to the principle of freedom of contract which imply limits to the idea of the self-ordering market, and, indeed, to the idea of a market order which is independent of other social institutions. As we have seen, even the restricted doctrine of public policy in the common law attests to the functional importance of conjoining the market order with complementary social institutions such as the family and the legal system itself; and the body of laws qualifying freedom of contract has grown enormously since the point at which the public policy doctrine was set in its current form around a century ago. As a descriptive or positive matter, there is a far greater volume and variety of laws regulating contractual relations in contemporary societies than the law-and-economics critique allows.

However, this is not the only reason for taking capabilities seriously in the context of legal discussion. As the chapters in this volume show, there is a growing use of legal techniques which reflect a capability-enhancing approach to dealing with issues of asymmetries and externalities in contractual relations. As Aurora Vimercati puts it in her chapter, the core civil law (and common law) assumption has been that persons have the capacity to act, with a number of exceptions based on incapacity for various reasons then being applied. Sen's capability approach, by contrast, is premised on the idea that there is a need for institutions of various kinds to promote the active development of individual capacities. It is possible that the main arenas for putting the capability approach into practice are the political and administrative realms, but the juridicial dimension of the capability approach must not be neglected, since it is here that the fine detail of rights aiming to guarantee the capacity to act often has to be worked out.

Sandrine Godelain's chapter in this volume takes two examples of this process from recent developments in consumer protection law and labour law in France. Once the civil law ceased to see the technique of incapacitation as the main solution to extreme inequalities of resources and information in contracting, it adopted a number of alternative techniques for dealing with highly unequal contracts; in the consumer law field, the doctrines of mistake, fraud and misrepresentation were all deployed to deal with the problems posed by contracts giving rise to excessive indebtedness. However, these interventions were mostly ineffective. A more productive route emerged when lenders were placed under a duty to make an informed assessment of the ability of a consumer to take on large amounts of debt—hence the focus on the financial capacity of the borrower. In labour law, the idea of the professional capacity of the worker, understood as his or her ability to participate in a labour market increasingly characterised by flexibility, multi-tasking and career shifts, has been coalescing around a number of developments in the laws governing the employer's duty to provide training and the state's involvement in employment policy.

Wiebke Brose provides an account of the growing use of capability-related concepts in the German law of dismissal. She shows how an obligation on the part of the employer to protect the employee's capacity for work (*Arbeitsfähigkeit*) is sometimes recognised, along with an obligation not to create a physical or psychological incapacity. However, the language of capacity can also be used in the employer's favour: because the law recognises the principle of the freedom of choice of the employer (*freie Unternehmerentscheidung*) in the matter of economic dismissals, the employer can in effect define at what point he has the 'incapacity' to carry on employing the worker. This principle has been qualified by the idea that the dismissal becomes unfair, under certain circumstances, if the employment could have been maintained had there been retraining at a cost which was 'tolerable' or 'acceptable' for the employer. On the other hand, there is a recent emphasis on the *Leistungsfähigkeit*, or lack of 'performance capacity', of the employee as a ground for redundancy selection. Brose's chapter illustrates the extent to which discussion of capacity has already become contested terrain for labour lawyers.

Aurora Vimercati discusses the concept of capacity in the light of the Italian labour law reforms of the past decade. The emphasis has been on flexibility in the sense of the increased variability of legal norms governing employment and wage security; the principle of the 'inderogability' or mandatory effect of labour law rules, which once formed the core of the Italian approach to the operation of labour legislation, has been significantly undermined. However, very little has been said in the course of these debates about the employer's duty to assist in retraining or human capital formation. This, Vimercati suggests, has been a lost opportunity for Italian labour law: enterprises have been given greater opportunties for short-term labour cost reduction, but few incentives to enhance their competitiveness over the longer term. Labour law, she argues, is all too often called on to be flexible and variable in the context of providing the right incentives for parties to the employment contract, when there is a case for it being 'rigid' and 'precise' when it comes to ensuring the conditions for the real freedom of the individual in a situation of inequality.

Renée-Claude Drouin discusses the concept of capability in the light of the evolution of the International Labour Organisation's approach to the formulation and implementation of labour standards. One of the ILO's founding principles was the need for international action on labour standards to counter destructive competition, but the first social rights were seen as redressing the negative social impacts of the market. In the 1940s, there was a greater emphasis on economic rights as serving social goals, but from the 1980s onwards deregulatory ideas increasingly took hold. Drouin sees the 1998 Declaration on Fundamental Principles and Rights at Work and the 'decent work' agenda which was launched in 1999 as the core of a new approach based on the notion of labour law as capacity enhancing. Referring to the specific use made of capability-related concepts in the 1998 Declaration and in some of the formative documents of the decent work initiative, she argues that labour rights have gone from being seen as means of protecting individuals against the negative consequences of the market, to being the foundation of a dynamic market order.

The market-building role of the capability approach is also discussed by Martijn Hesselink. In the context of the emerging area of European Union contract law, he poses the question: should the internal market be regulated in such a way that an unfair distribution of wealth is precluded from taking place through the enforcement of unfair contracts? He argues that distributional concerns should be embedded in the construction of the internal market. This implies an approach under which highly unbalanced contracts would become unenforceable, a principle which goes further than attempts to codify and restate European contract law have so far achieved. Markets create winners and losers; so the question is, in whose interests should the internal market operate? Internal market law, according to Hesselink, should do more than simply reflect the interests of the rational actor narrowly conceived; it should put in place the conditions for effective participation in market transactions. It should also address the question of externalities. There should be a clearer recognition that contracts giving rise to extremely negative effects for third parties, such as contracts for the sale and distribution of projects involving the exploitation of child labour, should not be enforceable, on the grounds that such agreements contribute to severely undermining the capabilities of third parties to choose the lives they have reason to value.

Hesselink's chapter demonstrates the intertwining of contract law with human rights law that is likely to follow on from the growing uses that are being made of the capability approach. Nowhere, perhaps, is this process more in evidence than at the point where contract law and discrimination law intersect. Discrimination law is the product of a series of legislative interventions which appear very substantially to constrain freedom of contract in the employment sphere (among others).[60] Because the anti-discrimination principle affects all stages of the employment relationship, including hiring as well as the performance and termination of the contract, its regulatory scope is potentially more far-reaching than laws stipulating basic standards for wages and hours or regulating the process of dismissal. The grounds on which discrimination is prohibited have steadily been extended over time, to cover not just race and sex, as in legislation of the 1960s and 1970s, but, as a consequence of recent legislative activity, sexual orientation, religion or belief, age and disability.[61] The anti-discrimination principle is, in many jurisdictions, embodied in constitutional texts, and thereby acquires the additional normative force of a fundamental social right.[62] It has both a collective and an individual dimension: on the one hand, it attacks institutional manifestations of group disadvantage, while on the other hand it profoundly individualises the position of the labour market actor, by insisting that their membership of a particular sexual or racial group (and so on) may not be used as a criterion for determining their access to employment or work-related benefits. In all these respects, discrimination law provides the template for what labour law might become, or is in the process of becoming. As it extends to applicants for employment and certain categories of the self-employed, as well as to employees,[63] discrimination law has already largely overcome the rigid division between employees

[60] See R Epstein, *Forbidden Grounds: The Case against Employment Discrimination Laws* (Cambridge MA, Harvard University Press, 1992).

[61] The most important reference point for this process in European law is the Framework Directive on Discrimination in Employment, Directive 2000/78/EC.

[62] In the context of European law, relevant sources for a constitutional instantiation of the anti-discrimination principle are Art 13 of the EC Treaty and ch III of the Charter of Fundamental Rights of the European Union (2000).

[63] On this, see S Deakin and G Morris, *Labour Law* (Oxford, Hart Publishing, 4th edn, 2005) 631.

and independent workers that has severely limited the effectiveness of traditional protective legislation.[64]

The near universality of the anti-discrimination principle—it is a powerful and pervasive force even in legal systems such as that of the US, which are often (incorrectly) described as having little or no statutory regulation of employment—and its recent extension at a time when most other forms of employment legislation have been in retreat suggest that it is not simply compatible with a 'fluid' or 'flexible' labour market order of the kind which is increasingly recognised to have come into existence with the decline of traditional forms of workplace organisation and collective solidarity; it is fundamental to the contemporary model of labour market flexibility. Discrimination law has extended the scope of the labour market and actively promoted competition over and in relation to employment. It does so by advancing an openly redistributive agenda, in supporting the rights of historically excluded or marginalised groups (such as married women) to participate in employment on an equal basis (in principle) with those previously privileged (such as 'male breadwinners').

Discrimination law stands in the same relation to classical contract law as the capability approach stands in relation to standard law and economics analysis. Becker, again, has expressed the received approach most clearly: discrimination law is unnecessary because the cure for discrimination lies in the market itself. Employers with a 'taste' or preference for hiring men instead of women would pay a price for doing so—unless it was the simply the case all along that in hiring men they were acting rationally. Where unequal pay and job segregation persist, they most likely represent efficient resource allocations.[65] It is perhaps an open question as to why Becker's view, first expressed in the 1950s a few years before the advent of US civil rights legislation[66] and decades before the adoption of European directives on equal treatment in employment,[67] did not have a greater influence on legislators. Was it because of 'rent seeking' by insider groups? Or because classical contract law was widely perceived to be an inadequate mechanism for promoting economic integration of the kind which has accompanied the legal recognition of the equal treatment principle?

The capacity-enhancing function of discrimination law is particularly evident in the case of what is arguably the most advanced type of equal treatment legislation, that is, legislation prohibiting disability

[64] See M Freedland, *The Personal Employment Contract* (Oxford, Oxford University Press, 2003) introduction and ch 1.

[65] G Becker, *The Economics of Discrimination* (Chicago, IL, University of Chicago Press, 1957).

[66] The first and most significant measure was the Civil Rights Act 1964.

[67] The earliest of these was Directive 75/117/EC on equal pay for equal work between men and women.

discrimination. This type of legislation is 'advanced' in the sense that concepts used elsewhere in discrimination law—'direct discrimination', referring to unequal treatment on prohibited grounds, and 'indirect discrimination', referring to group disadvantage arising from institutional practices—have been modified in the context of disability, to produce a 'duty of reasonable adjustment' on the part of the employer.[68] This means that the employer has a responsibility to organise the workplace in such a way as to enable the individual worker to carry out the duties of the post in question, taking their disability into account. The duty is not absolute; the court applies in essence a proportionality test, taking into account the cost and practicability of adjustments and their impact on the ability of the worker to carry out the task. But, even so, the effect is to alter the conceptual framework of discrimination law in ways which point to its potential for enhancing capabilities. The effect of the legislation was described in a recent House of Lords case, *Archibald v Fife Council*,[69] as follows:

> [the Disability Discrimination Act 1995] is different from the Sex Discrimination Act 1975 and the Race Relations Act 1976. In the latter two, men and women or black and white, as the case may be, are opposite sides of the same coin. Each is to be treated in the same way. Treating men more favourably than women discriminates against women. Treating women more favourably than men discriminates against men. Pregnancy apart, the differences between the two genders are generally regarded as irrelevant. The 1995 Act, however, does not regard the differences between disabled people and others as irrelevant. It does not expect each to be treated in the same way. It expects reasonable adjustments to be made to cater for the special needs of disabled people. It necessarily entails an element of more favourable treatment.

The following case, taken from guidance in the form of a code of practice, illustrates the effect in practice of the legislation:

> An applicant for an administrative job appears not to be the best person for the job, but only because her typing speed is too slow as a result of arthritis in her hands. If a reasonable adjustment—perhaps an adapted keyboard—would overcome this, her typing speed would not in itself be a substantial reason for not employing her. Therefore the employer would be unlawfully discriminating if, on account of her typing speed, he did not employ her or provide that adjustment.[70]

[68] See Deakin and Morris, above n 63, 715–20, explaining the structure of the anti-discrimination principle in the context of the Disability Discrimination Act 1995, ss 3A and 4A; see also Wiebke Brose's chapter in this volume, above n 33, discussing a similar point in the context of German dismissal law.

[69] [2004] IRLR 651, para 47.

[70] Disability Rights Commission, *Code of Practice: Employment and Occupation* (London, Disability Rights Commission, 2004) para 6.5.

The effect is striking—rather than requiring the individual to be 'adaptable' to changing market conditions, the law requires that employment practices be adapted to the circumstances of the individual. If disability discrimination laws go further than most forms of social legislation currently do in imposing affirmative duties on employer in the name of market access, they nevertheless exemplify the tendency of the law to grant substantive recognition to new forms of contractual capacity, or, in economic terms, 'capability'. The extension of the labour market in contemporary societies is coterminous with the advance of the capability principle.

CONCLUSION

This chapter has argued that *capacitas*, or capacity, should be thought of as the juridical concept through which the legal system defines the conditions of access to the market by human persons. The various ways in which capacity has been defined, in different periods and in different legal systems, is therefore revealing of the ways in which the relationship between the legal system and the market can be conceptualised. In a narrow conception, capacity is defined as the ability to engage in rational economic action (in economic-theoretical terms, constrained maximisation on the basis of stable preferences). The consequence of the absence of capacity in this sense is the denial to the individual of the normal legal support for the enforcement of contracts. In a wider conception, capacity, or *capacitas*, is the sum total of the preconditions of effective participation in market relations, and the role of the law shifts from the selective enforcement of contracts to the insertion into contracts of mandatory and default terms which serve a variety of functions. These include reallocations of risk and information, which are meant to offset the consequences of unbalanced or asymmetrical contracts. However, contractual regulation also has a wider remit, which is to protect and enhance the capability of the individual, understood as the substantive freedom to realise, through participation in the market, a range of desired end states and activities.

It can be seen from this analysis that the debate over the scope and meaning of the capacity concept is essentially an argument over the nature of the institutional preconditions of a market order. The idea of the self-equilibrating or self-regulating market lies at the core of the predominant approach within the contemporary law and economics movement and of the related deregulatory critique of social legislation. It is also inscribed in a particular judicial attitude to contractual regulation which a century ago found expression in the *Lochner* judgment in the US and in the restrictive interpretation given by the English courts to the early legislation of the welfare state. According to this view, contractual relations rest upon a system of private law whose qualities of autonomy and self-regulation mirror those of the market itself. Social legislation appears, in this context, as an illegitimate interference.

The contrasting view is one in which contractual regulation complements, rather than obstructs, the institutions of private law in providing a framework for exchange relations. In this chapter, examples have been given to illustrate this point from consumer law, employment law and discrimination law, and the later chapters of this book explore these themes in more detail. A law of contracts constructed around the notion that the law has a role in protecting and enhancing capabilities is, it may be argued, in the process of emerging at various points of interaction between private law and social legislation. This would be a law of contracts in which the market was seen not as an end in itself, but as an institution for enhancing the substantive economic freedom of individuals; a law of contracts, in other words, in which the market was adapted to the condition of the individual, rather than the individual being adapted to the demands of the market.

2

Capacity and Capability in European Contract Law

MARTIJN W HESSELINK*

INTRODUCTION

This chapter examines the role of legal capacity in the emerging two-level system of European contract law. It first considers the *acquis communautaire*, then the national contract laws of the Member States and the need for harmonisation. The question whether there is a need for common European rules on the invalidity of contracts concluded by persons who are presumed to be incapable of taking proper care of their own interests raises two further questions. Should persons who have actually concluded a very unfavourable contract not also be protected? Moreover, should contracts which severely undermine the capabilities of other people to choose the lives that they have reason to value be enforceable under European contract law?

LEGAL CAPACITY IN EC LAW

The *Acquis Communautaire*

Until very recently, it seems,[1] the concept of legal capacity was entirely absent from European law. However, in a case from October 2004 the European Court of Justice had to decide whether the legal incapacity of a

* This chapter is reproduced with the permission of Kluwer Law International from M Hesselink, 'Capacity and Capability in European Contract Law' (2005) 11 *European Review of Private Law* 491. I am grateful to the editors and publishers of *ERPL* for permission to reproduce it here.

[1] A search in Eur-lex using the terms '(in)capacity', '(in)capacité', '(in)capacità', 'handlungs(un)fähigkeit', 'handelings(on)bekwaamheid' does not lead to any document where these terms are used in a technical sense.

minor prevents the child's enjoyment of the right that European citizens have to move and reside freely within the territory of the Member States (Article 18 EC). The case concerned the refusal by the UK Secretary of State for the Home Department to grant a long-term residence permit to a very young child (who was an EU citizen). In this case, the Irish government had contended that a young child cannot take advantage of the rights of free movement and residence guaranteed by Community law. This contention was flatly rejected by the ECJ. The Court held[2]:

> [C]ontrary to the Irish Government's contention, a young child can take advantage of the rights of free movement and residence guaranteed by Community law. The capacity of a national of a Member State to be the holder of rights guaranteed by the Treaty and by secondary law on the free movement of persons cannot be made conditional upon the attainment by the person concerned of the age prescribed for the acquisition of legal capacity to exercise those rights personally . . . Moreover . . . it does not follow either from the terms of, or from the aims pursued by, Articles 18 EC and 49 EC . . . that the enjoyment of the rights with which those provisions are concerned should be made conditional upon the attainment of a minimum age.[3]

From the perspective of most legal traditions this is rather an obvious decision. As the Advocate-General in this case rightly pointed out in his Opinion, the capacity to exercise certain rights independently should not be confused with the capacity to hold those rights. Indeed, the mere fact that minors may need another person to exercise certain rights for them implies that they are capable of having rights. See Advocate-General Tizzano[4]:

> The fact that a minor cannot exercise a right independently does not mean that he has no capacity to be an addressee of the legal provision on which that right is founded. The line of reasoning should instead follow the opposite course. Because, according to a general principle which is common to the legal systems of the Member States (and not only to them), legal capacity is acquired at birth, even a minor is a subject of law and, as such, is therefore a holder of the rights conferred by law.

The Civil Codes in some Member States even explicitly underline the 'general capacity' of every person to be capable of having rights and obligations in their first Articles. See, for example, the German Bürgerliches Gesetzbuch and the Italian Codice Civile:

[2] C–200/02 *Man Lavette Chen and Kunqian Catherine Zhu v Secretary of State for the Home Department* [2004] (ECJ).

[3] No 20.

[4] Nos 45–46.

§ 1 Beginn der Rechtsfähigkeit
Die Rechtsfähigkeit des Menschen beginnt mit der Vollendung der Geburt.

Art. 1 Capacità giuridica
La capacità giuridica si acquista dal momento della nascita.

As a result, any person can be an owner, a debtor, a creditor or an heir and can enjoy other private and public law entitlements.[5] With its decision in *Zhu and Chen* the ECJ has now removed any possible doubts that the freedom to move within the territory of the Member States is included in that list as well.

As said, a person's capacity to hold rights and obligations (*Rechtsfähigkeit*, *capacité de jouissance*, *capacità giuridica*), which defines them as a 'legal subject' (*Rechtssubjekt*) as opposed to 'legal objects' (as slaves would be),[6] must be distinguished from the capacity to exercise certain rights independently (*Handlungsfähigkeit*, *capacité d'exercice*, *capacità di agire*), in particular the capacity to bind themselves through a contract (*Geschäftsfähigkeit*, *capacità di contrarre*). Not all citizens enjoy the latter capacity. In most Member States the capacity of minors to conclude binding contracts or to commit similar acts which aim to change their patrimonial position are limited. The same applies to a number of other categories of persons, in particular those suffering from mental illness.[7] The reason for this is, of course, the legislator's suspicion that they may not be sufficiently capable of discerning which engagements are in their own best interest.

However, in spite of the generally protective character of the *acquis communautaire* in the area of contract law today no European Treaty, regulation or directive specifically refers to the concept of the incapacity to exercise certain rights independently.

The CFR Process

In 2003 the European Commission announced that it will develop what it calls a 'Common Frame of Reference' (CFR), which may play several important roles in the near future. First, it may inspire the Commission when revising the *acquis communautaire* in the area of contract law.

5 Contrast the concept of 'mort civile', which was abolished in France in 1854. Cf M Fabre-Magnan, *Les obligations* (Paris, Presses Universitaires de France, 2004) 102.

6 In addition to 'natural persons', 'legal persons' (*juristische Personen*, *les personnes juridiques*, *persone giuridiche*), eg certain collective entities like foundations and (certain types of) companies, can have rights and obligations, ie are 'legal subjects'.

7 In some Member States also persons who have a habit of squandering their property or who are addicted to alcohol (or other drugs).

Secondly, it may provide a basis for an (optional) European Code of Contract Law in the near future.[8]

In all likelihood the general contract law within the CFR will look similar to the Principles of European Contract Law PECL) that were published in 2000 by the Lando Commission.[9] Not only will the CFR be drafted for the European Commission by a Network of Excellence in which the Study Group on a European Civil Code (the successor of the Lando group, which in its work on specific contracts regards the PECL as its general contract law) plays a very prominent role,[10] but also the outline of the structure of the CFR, which the European Commission sketches in the Annex to its most recent communication, looks very similar to the table of contents for the PECL.[11]

However, in contrast to the private laws of the Member States,[12] the PECL contain no rules on legal capacity. Indeed, Article 4:101, the first article on Invalidity (Chapter 4), reads as follows:

> Article 4:101: Matters not Covered
> This chapter does not deal with invalidity arising from illegality, immorality or lack of capacity.

The intention of the Lando Commission does not, however, seem to have been that under their Principles a contract should never be invalid for incapacity. Rather, they regard a lack of capacity to be a matter for the law of persons rather than for contract law.[13] Indeed, in some of their other provisions the PECL presume the (possible) existence of rules which may render a contract invalid for lack of capacity.[14]

One of the main objectives of the European Commission's Action Plan on European Contract Law is to improve the functioning of the internal market. In its Action Plan the Commission argues that different rules on the validity of contracts are among the main obstacles to the proper functioning of the internal market.[15] Moreover, rules on legal capacity

[8] Communication from the Commission to the European Parliament and the Council; A More Coherent European Contract Law; An Action Plan, COM(2003) 68 final, OJEC 2003 C 63/01, 32.

[9] H Beale and O Lando (eds), *Principles of European Contract Law, Parts I and II, Prepared by The Commission on European Contract Law* (The Hague, Kluwer Law International, 2000).

[10] The NoE will be funded under the Sixth Framework Programme. On the SGECC see www.sgecc.net.

[11] See the Communication from the Commission to the European Parliament and the Council; European Contract Law and the revision of the *Acquis*: The Way Forward, COM(2004) 651 final.

[12] See below.

[13] See above n 10, 227 (Comment).

[14] See, eg Art 3:209 in the chapter on the authority of agents and Art 14:305 in the chapter on prescription.

[15] Action Plan, No 25 *et seq*.

may be seen as the rules which determine who has access to the market.[16] In that perspective, it seems that both a CFR and an (optional) European Code of Contracts cannot do without rules on invalidity for lack of capacity.[17]

It is therefore surprising that the 'possible structure of a CFR' which the Commission presents in the Annex to its communication *The Way Forward* does not refer at all to the concept of legal capacity. Indeed, under 'validity' it only mentions the categories of initial impossibility, incorrect information, fraud and threats.

What, then, could European rules on legal capacity (in a CFR, in an (optional) Code of Contracts) look like? Is there a common core in the national laws of the Member States?[18]

LEGAL CAPACITY IN THE LAW OF THE MEMBER STATES

Protecting the Incapable Against the Market

As said, the legal systems of all Member States contain rules which limit the capacity of certain categories of persons to bind themselves to a contract.[19]

The reason for these rules is the desire to protect certain people against their own acts. The underlying idea is that the binding force of contract is in essence based on party autonomy (a person is bound by a contract because he or she has freely agreed to it) and that when this freedom is absent the justification disappears.

16 See S Deakin, chapter 1 in this volume.

17 G Alpa, 'The Meaning of "Natural Person" and the Impact of the Constitution for Europe on the Development of European Contract Law' (2004) 10 *ELJ* 734 forcefully argues that a European Code of Contracts even needs a well-developed concept of the person.

18 For the common core approach to European private law, see M Busanni and U Mattei, 'The Common Core Approach to European Private Law' (1997/1998) 3 *The Columbia Journal of European Law* 339. For criticism, see D Kennedy, 'The Politics and Methods of Comparative Law' in M Bussani and U Mattei (eds), *The Common Core of European Private Law* (The Hague, London, New York: Kluwer Law International, 2002) 131–207.

19 See generally A Heldrich and AF Steiner, 'Legal Personality' in *International Encyclopaedia of Comparative Law, Vol. IV, Persons and Family* (Tübingen, Mohr Siebeck 1995) ch 2; K Zweigert and H Kötz, *Introduction to Comparative Law* (Oxford, Clarendon Press, 3rd edn, 1998) ch 25. For the law in England, see E McKendrick, *Contract Law* (London, Palgrave Macmillan, 5th edn, 2003) ch 16; for France, see M Fabre-Magnan, *Les obligations* (Paris, Presses Universitaires de France, 2004) 102 *et seq*; for Germany, see K Larenz and M Wolf, *Allgemeiner Teil des Bürgerlichen Rechts* (Munich, Verlag CH Beck, 9th edn, 2004), § 6; for Italy, see V Roppo, *Il contratto* (Milan, Giuffrè, 2001); for the Netherlands, see AS Hartkamp, *Mr C Asser's handleiding tot de beoefening van het Nederlands burgerlijk recht; Verbintenissenrecht; Vol II Algemene leer der overeenkomsten* (Deventer, Tjeenk Willink, 12th edn, 2005); J De Boer and C Asser's handleiding tot de beoefening van het Nederlands burgerlijk recht, *Personen-en familierecht* (Deventer, Kluwer, 2002) 786 *et seq.*, 1094 *et seq.* On the history, see M Kaser and R Knütel, *Römisches Privatrecht* (Munich, Verlag CH Beck, 17th edn, 2003) § 14.

The law has long assumed for some categories of persons that they structurally lack the capacity to judge whether a certain transaction is in their own best interest. In particular, two categories stand out: minors and persons suffering from a mental illness.

The way in which the incapable are protected has usually been through invalidity. A contract which is concluded by a person lacking the necessary legal capacity is or may be rendered invalid. The modalities differ a great deal among the Member States—for example, in Germany the contract is void; in England & Wales the contract is also void (in most cases) in the case of minors but voidable in the case of mental illness; in France the contract can be avoided by the court; and in the Netherlands the contract can also be avoided by an extrajudicial declaration.[20] The invalidity can be invoked by the representative of the incapable (for minors, normally their parents; for the mentally ill, often their partner) or, depending on the time limits, by him- or herself after the incapacity has ceased.

Emancipation

In most Member States there has been a marked tendency in the last half century towards limiting the scope of legal incapacity. First, in many Member States the incapacity of married women was abolished in the 1950s. Then, in the 1970s, the age of majority (which marks the end of incapacity) was reduced from 21 to 18 years. Moreover, in many countries exceptions to incapacity were introduced for the transactions that mature minors ordinarily conclude in everyday life. Finally, between the 1970s and the 1990s the incapacity of the mentally ill was limited, and in many countries was substituted with a less categorical system, as a result of new insights in psychiatry.[21] In all cases these law reforms were aimed at the emancipation of those persons who were formerly considered to be incapable. By reducing or abolishing their legal incapacity, married

[20] For Germany, see §105 BGB; for England, see *Re Walker* [1905] 1 Ch 60 (cf McKendrick, *ibid*, for further references); for France, see Fabre-Magnan, *ibid*, 262; for Italy, see 1125 CC; and for the Netherlands, see 3:49 BW.

[21] See notably the reforms in France in 1968, in Germany in 1992 and in the Netherlands in 1994. On the desirability of a law reform in Italy, see Roppo, above n 19, 19, 34.7: the current system '*rischia di tagliare fuori dal traffico giuridico (come dire dalla vita di relazione) interi classi di soggetti, che pure la legge vuole proteggere*. Si teme che ... la protezione dei soggetti "deboli" si traduca in emarginazione e compressione delle *chances* esistenziali' (emphasis in the original). According to Larenz and Wolf, above n 19, § 5, No. 5 the legal capacity (*Rechtsfähigkeit*, but also *Geschäftsfähigkeit*) of a person does not ultimately depend on positive private law; it follows from the fundamental right to human dignity (see, eg Art 1 German Constitution). This means in practice that there is a limit to the extent to which the legislator can interfere with legal capacity. Similarly, Heldrich and Steiner, above n 19, 2–18. Compare C Asser and J De Boer, *Personen-en familierecht* (Deventer, Kluwer, 2002) 791, who refer to Art 8 ECRM. See also Art 6 Universal Declaration of Human Rights (Paris 1948).

women, children and people suffering from mental illnesses were empowered. As a result, their social status was enhanced.[22]

It should be noted that in many Member States, notably the civil law countries, legal capacity is a general concept which is relevant not only in patrimonial law (property, contract, tort) but also in other areas, notably family law. It is in especially the latter area (matrimony, affiliation, succession), rather than with regard to contracts, that the desire for emancipation was strongest, and that paternalism was regarded as intolerable.

Finally, a factor which may have played a role in making the reduced protection, which came with increased capacity, more acceptable is the transformation of general contract law, with the help of doctrines like good faith, away from a classical autonomy orientation into the direction of more solidarity and, in particular, the rise of many protective rules for many types of specific contracts (labour, rent, credit) and of the other, much broader, category of people who are today deemed to be in need of protection when they operate on the market, ie consumers.[23] With some exaggeration one could say that, rather than a decline, there has been a rise in legal incapacity: we are now all regarded as being incapable for some market transactions.[24]

Protecting the Market Against the Incapable

The invalidity of a contract for reasons of incapacity obviously also affects the interests of the other party to the contract. However, traditionally the law has given priority to the interests of the party deemed to be in need of protection. Therefore, the mere good faith of the other party—she thought that she was contracting with somebody who had legal capacity—has never been a bar to invalidity in most Member States.[25]

Nevertheless, the law has taken some care of the interests of trade through measures which are aimed at guaranteeing legal certainty. At first, this mainly took the shape of an often rigid categorical approach. Only certain well-defined categories of persons were incapable, ie minors and persons suffering from mental illness who were declared incapable by a court.[26] Therefore, in theory, anybody could protect themselves

22 On the importance of agency for social change, see A Sen, *Development as Freedom* (Oxford, Oxford University Press, 1999) ch 8.

23 See Heldrich and Steiner, above n 19, 2–19.

24 Compare P Malaurie and L Aynès, *Cours de droit civil, Vol IV, Les obligations* (Paris, Editions Cujas, 9th edn, 1998) No 634, who warn against the risk that extensive pre-contractual duties to inform may 'transformer les agents juridiques en incapables majeurs'.

25 See, eg 1426 CCI. However, in some Member States the case is different where the minor has deliberately concealed his age through manoeuvres (see, eg 1426 CCI).

26 The latter requirement (court intervention) does not exist in Germany. See § 104 II.

against the risk of invalidity for incapacity—they only had to always ask for identification and to regularly follow the official publication of the relevant court decisions.

Moreover, some legal systems have always had a rather limited protection of the incapable, thus taking more account of the interests of the other party. For example, under French law a contract can be annulled by a court for the lack of capacity of a minor only in the case of economic disadvantage (*lésion*): *minor restituitur non tamquam minor, sed tanquam laesus.*[27]

Also, the rules which are present in many Member States and which exclude from invalidity contracts which are normally concluded by a person of the same age or which are necessary[28] may be explained, as shown above, by a wish to treat minors and people who are mentally ill as much as possible like any other person. However, they may also be explained in terms of the need to protect legal certainty in trade: the market needs the certainty that ordinary transactions and/or contracts which actually (ie 'objectively') are in the best interest of the otherwise incapable contracting party will be enforceable in law. Indeed, for example in the Netherlands, the law reform which introduced the legal presumption of the incapable persons' representatives' permission for ordinary contracts was preceded by case law on the subject. However, the relevant cases did not concern minors who contested their parents' avoidance of a contract that they had concluded. Rather, they involved counterparties who contested the invalidity.[29]

Finally, the legal systems which make a contract concluded by a person who lacks capacity void rather than voidable[30] effectively also favour the interests of the other party, who can invoke the invalidity of the contract if she regrets having agreed to it.

Actual Incapacity

What if a person who concluded a contract did not belong to one of the categories of legal incapacity but claims to have been actually incapable (temporarily or permanently) of proper judgement at the time of

[27] See Art 1305 Cc. Compare classical Roman law regarding *minores* (younger than 25). Cf Kaser and Knütel, above n 19, § 14, II.

[28] See, eg in France 389–3 Cc, in Germany § 110 BGB (pocket money paragraph), in England the concept of 'necessary goods or services' (for the sale of goods see, eg s 3(3) Sale of Goods Act 1979) and in the Netherlands 1:234 (3) BW.

[29] See, eg HR 23 January 1987 *RvdW* 1987, 38, where a 17-year-old person, who received unemployment benefit, refused to pay the rent for the apartment where she lived independently. See also the English cases on necessary goods or services, eg *Nash v Inman* [1908] 2 KB 1, where a tailor sued a minor (a Cambridge undergraduate) for payment of 11 fancy waistcoats.

[30] See, eg § 135 II BGB.

concluding the contract? In some legal systems in such cases (*incapacità naturale*) the law declares the contract annullable under certain circumstances.[31] Typically, the party that wants to annul the contract on this ground must prove in each specific case that his good judgement was affected and that the contract was detrimental to his interests.

However, in such cases the law generally provides protection to the other contracting party in good faith.[32] The reason for this is that, unlike legal incapacity, actual incapacity cannot always be easily recognised by others.[33]

Harmonisation

Negative Harmonisation

If, indeed, all European citizens enjoy the four freedoms no matter what their age (as said, this seems to follow from the *Zhu and Chen* case), this raises the question whether some national rules that limit the right to exercise those freedoms by declaring contracts concluded by some categories of citizens invalid may themselves be invalid. In other words, are some of the national rules on legal capacity an inadmissible infringement of the four freedoms?

In principle, these rules seem to be safe. They seem to be the kind of rules that are protected by the 'rule of reason' that the ECJ has developed in a line of cases since *Cassis de Dijon*[34]: in the absence of Community harmonisation, reasonable, non-discriminatory measures can be taken by Member States to protect certain interests.

Still, there might be some doubt as to whether some of the national rules are not disproportionate. This may especially be the case for those rules, eg in Germany, which declare contracts concluded by an incapable person to be void, with the effect that the other party can also invoke the invalidity,[35] and (to a lesser extent) the rules which, unlike the French, also allow for avoidance in cases where the contract does not harm the interests of the incapable person.

[31] See, eg 105 II BGB, 428 CCI, 3:34 BW.

[32] See, eg Arts 428 CCI, 3:35 BW. For England, see *Imperial Loan Co v Stone* [1892] 1 QB 599.

[33] See, eg a Dutch case where a man had sold his farm because at the time of concluding the contract he was under the impression (as a result of schizophrenia) that it was possessed by ghosts and where the buyer objected that the seller had seemed to be completely capable of good judgment (HR 11 December 1959, *NJ* 1960, 230 (Eelman/Hin)).

[34] See P Craig and G De Burca, *EU Law; Text Cases and Materials* (Oxford, Oxford University Press, 3rd edn, 2003) 638 and, with a specific focus on private law, JW Rutgers, 'The Rule of Reason and Private Law or the Limits to Harmonization' in JH Jans and AAM Schrauwen (eds), *The Rule of Reason* (Groningen, Europa Law Publishers, 2005).

[35] See above, p 36.

Positive Harmonisation

If the European Commission is going to include rules on legal and actual incapacity in the CFR and/or in an (optional) European Code of Contracts—and, as said, there seems to be no reason why it should not—then it will have to balance the three concerns which have been discussed here: the concern for protection, the concern for emancipation and the concern for the interests of other market participants. The best way of dealing with such policy choices seems to be a democratic rather than a merely technocratic process.[36]

SUBSTANTIVE FREEDOM OF CONTRACT

European Contract Law and Social Justice

As shown above, in all Member States the main reason for rules on legal incapacity has been a wish to prevent certain categories of persons, who are deemed to lack sufficient judgement, from concluding contracts which might harm their economic interests. The ultimate justification for such a policy seems to lie in some idea of social justice: it would be unfair to keep a person to a (detrimental) contract if that person had no substantive (as opposed to formal) freedom of contract.[37]

Fair Prices in the Internal Market

If social justice is indeed the main justification for rules on legal incapacity, the question arises why the validity of contracts should only be challengeable when they are concluded by persons who, as a category, are presumed not to be capable of properly taking care of their own interests when committing themselves to a contract.

What about individuals who actually did 'freely'—ie in the absence of a 'defect of consent' (information asymmetry)—conclude a contract which both objectively (ie because it strongly deviates from the market price) and subjectively (with hindsight they regret their commitment) was (grossly) against their best interest?

Or, to put it differently, if even in France—a Member State with a relatively low degree of protection for lack of capacity—a minor is

[36] See MW Hesselink, 'The Politics of a European Civil Code' (2004) 10 *European Law Journal* 675.

[37] On social justice in European contract law, see Study Group on Social Justice in European Private Law, 'Social Justice in European Contract Law: a Manifesto' (2004) 10 *European Law Journal* 653.

protected not as a minor but as a *lésé*, why should not other persons who conclude a (very) imbalanced contract also be protected merely for that reason?[38] Should the internal market not be regulated in such a way that an unfair distribution of wealth is precluded from taking place through the enforcement of unfair contracts?[39]

To (re)introduce a fair price requirement into the internal market would mean an important change in principle.[40] In all likelihood, however, the results would not be all that revolutionary. Rather, it would lead to much more transparency. Today, many doctrines are 'forced' in their application, as many courts, when confronted with a very unbalanced contract, frequently do their very best to find some sort of defect of consent or other market failure: 'a rational party would never have consented to such an unbalanced contract, therefore there must be a defect in consent', courts frequently seem to argue. In other words, in practice courts do care for social justice. The many applications of the doctrine of good faith across Europe show a variety of examples of this.[41]

Therefore, it seems a good idea to explicitly provide in a European Code of Contracts that very unbalanced contracts are not enforceable (or, technically, can be avoided/annulled).[42] Indeed, such a rule currently exists in the Scandinavian countries. Article 36 of their Contract Act says[43]:

38 See also MW Hesselink, 'Fair Prices in the Common Market; On Commutative and Distributive Justice in European Contract Law' in G Alpa and R Danovi (eds), *Diritto privato europeo; Fonti edn effetti; Materiali del Seminario dell'8–9 novembre 2002* (Milan, Giuffrè Editore, 2004) 245–54, on which this section is partly based.

39 Against distributive justice in contract law, see CW Canaris, *Die Bedeutung der iustitia distributiva im deutschen Vertragsrecht* (Munich, Verlag der Bayerischen Akademie der Wissenschaften, 1997).

40 On the history of the *iustum pretium* doctrine, see J Gordley, *The Philosophical Origins of Modern Contract Doctrine* (Oxford, Oxford University Press, 1991); R Zimmerman, *The Law of Obligations* (Oxford, Oxford University Press, 1996) 255 *et seq*. In favour of the introduction of a *iustum pretium* or similar requirement in Dutch law, see JM Smits, *Het vertrouwensbeginsel en de contractuele gebondenheid* (Arnhem, Gouda Quint, 1995) 233 *et seq*; FW Grosheide, 'Iustum Pretium. Enkele opmerkingen over de contractuele gebondenheid' (1996) 6227 *Weekblad voor Privaatrecht, Notariaat en Registratie* 435. Contrast T Hartlief, 'Iustum pretium: op weg naar een rechterlijke toetsing van de rechtvaardigheid van het contractuele evenwicht?' in T Hartlief and CJJM Stolker (eds), *Contractsvrijheid* (Deventer, Kluwer, 1999) 239–53.

41 See MW Hesselink, 'The Concept of Good Faith' in A Hartkamp *et al* (eds), *Towards a European Civil Code* (The Hague, Kluwer Law International 2004) 471–98.

42 In the same sense T Wilhelmsson, 'Varieties of Welfarism in European Contract Law' (2004) 10 *European Law Journal* 712, 732. Recently, Brigitta Lurger has even proposed a European constitutional right to contractual relationships which are at least 'somewhat fair'. See B Lurger, *Grundfragen der Vereinheitlichung des Vertragsrechts in der Europäischen Union* (Vienna, New York, 2002) 294, 'das "soziale" Grundrecht auf einigermaßen faire Vertragsbeziehungen, die eine einseitige schwerwiegende Verletzung der wirtschaftlichen Interessen einer der Parteien verhindern'. See further MW Hesselink, 'The Horizontal Effect of Social Rights in European Contract Law' (2003) 5 *Europa e diritto privato* 1, 1–3.

43 See R Nielson, *Contract Law in Denmark* (The Hague, Kluwer Law International, 1997), 128 *et seq* and 382 *et seq*.

> (1) An agreement may be amended or set aside, in whole or in part, if its enforcement would be unreasonable or contrary to principles of fair conduct. The same applies to other legal transactions. (2) In applying subsection 1 of this provision, consideration shall be given to the circumstances at the time of the conclusion of the agreement, the content of the agreement, and later developments.

On the basis of this article, the price may also be policed.[44] The Scandinavian experience shows that such a very broad general clause is not unworkable in practice.

The PECL are insufficient in this respect. On the one hand, on the basis of Article 4:110, the *Inhaltskontrolle* is limited to unfair terms 'which have not been individually negotiated', while section 2 excludes application to terms which define the main subject, in a fashion very similar to the Directive on unfair terms.[45] On the other hand, in Article 4:109 (Excessive Benefit or Unfair Advantage) the PECL have adopted a double requirement of (1) some sort of weakness and (2) excessive advantage. In other words, under this rule a combination (or rather: accumulation) of procedural and substantive unfairness is required[46]—neither suffices in isolation.[47] This seems a rather harsh rule. The UNIDROIT Principles of International Commercial Contracts are more generous in this respect. Article 3.10 (Gross disparity) says that 'a party may avoid the contract or an individual term of it if, at the time of the conclusion of the contract, the contract term unjustifiably gave the other party an excessive advantage', without any further requirement. Procedural unfairness is only one of the factors which a court should take into account.[48]

Markets, Freedom and Capabilities

One of the main aims of the European Commission's Action Plan on contract law is to improve the smooth functioning of the internal market.[49] With regard to the main instrument that the Commission is planning to use for this purpose, the CFR,[50] it says[51]:

44 See T Wilhelmsson, 'Private Law in the EU: Harmonised or Fragmented Europeanisation?' (2002) 10 *European Review of Private Law* 77, and PECL, Art 4:110, Note 4.

45 See Art 4(2) Dir 93/13/EEC on unfair terms in consumer contracts.

46 See Art 4:109.

47 Art 4:109, Comment B. A similar approach was earlier adopted in Italy (Art 1448 CC) and in Portugal (Art 282 CC).

48 See Art 3.10(1)(a)–(b): '. . . Regard is to be had, among other factors, to (a) the fact that the other party has taken unfair advantage of the first party's dependence, economic distress or urgent needs, or of its improvidence, ignorance, inexperience or lack of bargaining skill; and (b) the nature and purpose of the contract.'

49 See especially Action Plan Nos 26 *et seq*.

50 See above, pp 33–35.

51 Action Plan, 59.

> This frame of reference should meet the needs and expectations of the economic operators in an internal market which envisages becoming the world's most dynamic economy.

In order to attain this aim, the CFR should be based on the guiding principle of freedom of contract[52]:

> In this context contractual freedom should be the guiding principle; restrictions should only be foreseen where this could be justified with good reasons.

At first sight, the introduction of invalidity for lack of capacity and for gross disparity into a CFR and, subsequently, into a European Code of Contracts might seem to be in sharp contrast with the idea of freedom of contract, which may be regarded as the cornerstone of a market economy. However, on closer examination much depends on the definitions of a market and of freedom.

Economists have long demonstrated that economic growth (in terms of (per capita) Gross National Product) per se does not necessarily make everybody in a society better off[53]; indeed, it can often make the least privileged worse off. In the words of Joseph Stiglitz, the idea of 'trickle-down economics' is a fallacy.[54] Given this fact, distributive concerns must always be a part of a policy aimed at enhancing the functioning of a market. A market creates winners and losers: for whom should the market function better?

What is the aim of the European internal market? The European Union, which aspires to having a social market economy,[55] may well ask itself whether the ultimate (or at least an important) aim of the internal market should not be to contribute to enhancing the possibilities for its citizens (and others; I will come back to this) to choose the lives they have reason to value.

In several publications the economist and philosopher Amartya Sen has developed a theory of social justice in which the idea of substantive freedom plays a central role. According to Sen, legislators and other policy makers should aim to ensure that people have the capabilities to live the lives that they have reason to value.[56]

Of course, the most fundamental policies which can (instrumentally) contribute to giving people substantive freedom to choose the lives they want are probably to be found in the areas of the health service,

52 Action Plan, 62. See also 92–4.

53 See Sen, above n 22, 14: 'economic growth cannot sensibly be treated as an end in itself'. Amartya Sen was a Nobel laureate in 1998.

54 See JE Stiglitz, *Globalization and its Discontents* (London New York, Allan Lane, Penguin Press, 2002) 78. Joseph Stiglitz was a Nobel laureate in 2001.

55 See Art I-3 Treaty establishing a Constitution for Europe (TCE).

56 See, eg Sen, above n 22.

education, security, etc.[57] The different market transactions which a person is free to choose (in the utilitarian perception, 'preferences') may be seriously limited if he or she is poor or ill, or belongs to a minority who are systematically discriminated against or even attacked. Or—to give a less dramatic example—the capabilities of market actors to make informed choices crucially depends on the education that they have received. Nevertheless, it still makes sense to examine how contract law can contribute to improving the capabilities of people.[58]

Therefore, if indeed the aim (or at least one of the aims) of the internal market is to improve the capabilities of people to choose the lives they have reason to value, then the question arises how European contract law can contribute to attaining that aim.

Rules on legal capacity and on gross disparity in a CFR and in an (optional) Code of Contracts seem to be options which should at least be considered. Not only do they provide safety nets which can create confidence in new entrants in the market (and thus enhance economic growth), they can also directly contribute to the substantive freedom of individuals by preventing their economic situation from being seriously undermined as a result of an extremely unfavourable bargain.[59] As Sen explains, the idea of safety nets does not necessarily contradict the idea of a market economy.[60] Indeed, even the possible champion of free markets, Adam Smith, was in favour of the invalidity of loan agreements for usury.[61]

Frankly, European rules on legal capacity should go further than mere protection against 'objectively' unfavourable (*lésion*) or abnormal contracts. Why should a person in a vulnerable position have the average lifestyle or living standard imposed upon him or her? If it is normal today for a child of 14 to have a mobile phone and if a child has bought such a phone for the normal market price, does that mean that the freedom to make a different choice for their child should be taken away from its parents?

[57] On 'instrumental freedoms' (ie freedoms which tend to contribute to the general capability of people to live more freely), see Sen, above n 22, 38 *et seq*.

[58] This capabilities approach was embraced by the Supiot report on the transformation of labour and the future law in Europe. See A Supiot (ed), *Au delà de l'emploi. Transformations du travail et devenir du droit du travail en Europe* (Paris, Flammarion, 1999). More generally, on the important role that the law, including contract law, has play today in people's lives, see A Supiot, *Homo Juridicus. Essai sur la fonction anthropologique du Droit* (Paris, Seuil, 2005) esp ch 3.

[59] On the role of 'social rights' including the right to a minimum wage, compare S Deakin, *Renewing Labour Market Institutions* (Geneva, International Institute for Labour Law Studies, 2004) ch 3.

[60] Sen, above n 22, 123 *et seq*.

[61] See the reference in Sen, above n 22, 124.

Validity rules of contract law tell us a great deal about the kind of market that the legislator in a given system aspires to.[62] Will the European internal market only be a market for persons who correspond to the model of what many economists call a 'rational agent', ie a person who will always only conclude contracts which are in his or her own best interest as long as he or she is fully informed and the other party does not have a dominant market position (ie in the absence of 'market failures')?[63] In other words, can the regulation of the European market through contract law be limited to a set of rules for cases where consent is flawed as a result of information asymmetry (see many recent EC directives which aim to protect consumers) or the abuse of a dominant position (see Article 82 EC) combined with a set of ('non-mandatory') 'default' rules for standard situations? It seems that a European social market which is aimed at improving capabilities should also do so through providing safety nets to protect citizens against exploitative market actors.

The classical argument against a fair price rule is that such a rule will lead to great legal uncertainty: how can a seller anticipate whether a judge will consider the price that he charges to be extremely unfair? However, the question can be inverted: why should a seller be excused from not knowing basic standards of fairness in his society? Social scientists have shown in empirical research that legal certainty depends more on the existence in a given society of generally accepted social norms than on formal rules.[64] If such shared norms exist in a certain market, it seems to be the responsibility of the participants in that market to be aware of these norms. If, on the contrary, a shared understanding of minimum values and norms of fairness and social justice does not yet exist in the internal market, this would be very worrying indeed. It would mean that the minimum requirements for a functioning market are absent.[65]

[62] See S Deakin, chapter 1 above. See also U Mattei, 'Hard Code Now!' (2002) 2 *Global Jurist Frontiers* 1. However, the importance of 'default rules', which are often de facto mandatory, should not be underestimated. See MW Hesselink, 'Non-mandatory Rules in European Contract Law' (2005) 1 *European Review of Contract Law* 43.

[63] Critical of such a very narrow definition of rationality is A Sen, *Rationality and Freedom* (Cambridge MA, The Belknap Press of Harvard University Press, 2002) 4–6: 'Rationality is interpreted here, broadly, as the discipline of subjecting one's choices—of actions as well as of objectives, values and priorities—to reasoned scrutiny . . . This can be contrasted with a narrowly formulaic view of preference and choice which is quite common in some parts of economics, such as the view that a person must be seen as pursuing only what she takes to be her self-interest (without any role being given to other objectives and ignoring all values other than narrowly self-interested reasons). That view, in effect, amounts to seeing people as "rational fools", who are unable to see the difference between various distinct concepts, such as (1) personal well-being, (2) private self-interest, (3) one's goals and objectives, (4) individual values (including, as Arrow puts it, "values about values"), or (5) diverse reasons for what one may sensibly choose.' See also Sen, above n 22, 270.

[64] See H Collins, *Regulating Contracts* (Oxford, Oxford University Press, 1999) pt 3, with many further references.

[65] See Sen, above n 22, ch 11.

EXTERNALITIES

If at least one of the aims of European contract law is to contribute to social justice through enhancing substantive freedom, it is inconceivable that the concern for justice will be only limited to those who are already the most privileged on our planet.

This raises the question whether a contract which is mutually beneficial to the contracting parties but which severely undermines the well-being and capabilities of others should be enforceable at all. Some examples include contracts for the sale and distribution of products (eg sneakers) which are produced by means of child labour or under circumstances amounting to near slavery (sweatshops), or other severe violations of fundamental rights,[66] rights which the European Union regards as universal.[67]

Under some European legal systems, contracts, the performance of which will foreseeably lead to an immoral result—and this may be said today for the sale of a pair of sneakers on the high street—are invalid for immorality.[68] The same would apply, it seems, under the PECL[69]:

> Article 15:101: Contracts Contrary to Fundamental Principles
> A contract is of no effect to the extent that it is contrary to principles recognised as fundamental in the laws of the Member States of the European Union.

Obviously, usually neither the buyer nor the seller has an interest in flagging up the immoral character of their contract.[70] However, in the same jurisdictions, a court often has to raise the immorality of a contract

[66] For some documentation see, eg N Klein, *No Logo* (London, Flamingo, 2000), especially ch 10.

[67] See the Preamble to the Nice Charter of Fundamental Rights of the European Union (later pt II of the TCE): 'Conscious of its spiritual and moral heritage, the Union is founded on the indivisible, *universal* values of human dignity, freedom, equality and solidarity'. See also the preamble to the TCE: 'Drawing inspiration from the cultural, religious and humanist inheritance of Europe, have developed the *universal* values of the inviolable and inalienable rights of the human person, freedom, democracy, equality and the rule of law'. Compare Article III-292 (1) TCE: 'The Union's action on the international scene shall be guided by the principles which have inspired its own creation, development and enlargement, and which it seeks to advance in the wider world: democracy, the rule of law, the *universality* and indivisibility of human rights and fundamental freedoms, respect for human dignity, the principles of equality and solidarity, and respect for the principles of the United Nations Charter and international law' (emphasis added).

[68] For example, in Dutch law. See Asser and De Boer, above n 21, ch 12.

[69] O Lando, E Clive, A Prüm and R Zimmerman (eds), *Principles of European Contract Law, Part III, Prepared by the Commission on European Contract Law* (The Hague, Kluwer Law International, 2003).

[70] This may be different in cases where the immoral production method was not (and could not have been) known to both parties. In such a case a buyer may be willing to cancel the contract for non-conformity. See T Wilhelmsson, 'Varieties of Welfarism in European Contract Law' (2004) 10 *European Law Journal* 723, 731 note 44.

of its own motion.[71] In other words, if a seller (or principal) brings proceedings against a buyer (or distributor) for ordinary non-performance (ie the buyer or distributor did not pay), the court should dismiss the claim if the contract was indeed invalid because of the immorality of its object (ie its foreseeable result).

The question here is not whether there exist any better, more effective and efficient ways of combating child labour and sweatshops; rather, the questions are whether immoral contracts should be enforceable under European contract law and whether a contract is immoral when the performance will foreseeably lead to the violation of fundamental rights. Obviously, these questions have nothing to do with the legal capacity of minors but all to do with their capabilities.

CONCLUSIONS

So far, the concept of legal capacity is absent in the *acquis communautaire* on contract law. This article argues that a common frame of reference and an optional European code of contracts cannot do without rules on legal capacity.

In the national contract laws of the Member States the main aim of the invalidity of contracts for incapacity has been the protection of persons against the consequences of a misjudgement of their own interests. This raises the question why the law should only protect persons who belong to a limited number of categories (typically minors and those who suffer from a mental illness) who are presumed not to be able to take proper care of their own interests. This article argues that under European contract law a person who has concluded a contract that is actually (extremely) unbalanced deserves equal protection. Such a 'fair price' rule would contribute to substantive freedom of contract as it would facilitate access to the market.

Finally, this article questions whether European contracts should be enforceable if they contribute to severely undermining the capabilities of other people (eg child workers in sweatshops) to choose the lives they have reason to value.

[71] In the Netherlands, see Art 25 Rv.

3

Rationalisation and Derationalisation of Legal Capacity in Historical Perspective: Some General Caveats

ALAIN WIJFFELS

Rationalisation and derationalisation should not be understood here by the standards of a general (present-day) legal theory. It is not suggested, when those terms are used in the present paper, that they refer to any supposedly general, absolute or timeless model of rationality, whether in legal science or otherwise. The processes of rationalisation or derationalisation are envisaged here within a specific historical context, namely that of eighteenth-century *Vernunftrecht*. The model of rationalisation which the Law of Reason (taken here as a broad, mainstream current of continental-European legal thinking during the eighteenth century) tried to work out consisted of bringing into homogeneous and general (and therefore to some degree abstract) classes or principles, notions and rules from hitherto heterogeneous legal categories or entities, ordered, whenever possible, according to a unitary and consistent principle of classification. That definition is probably not comprehensive, but it expresses the general drift of the method. It should be linked with corresponding attempts to conceive and formulate the natural sciences during the same era. The classifications by Linnaeus and others, for example, may be seen as fitting counterparts—in fact, most often as models—for what legal scholars of the Law of Reason were aspiring to. The Law of Reason—usually still referred to in scholarly textbooks and literature as the 'School of Natural Law', though, of course, it was axiomatic to rationalist philosophy that the structure and functioning of Nature and Reason were essentially congruent—was a necessary stage and a prerequisite for the modern codification era of the late eighteenth century and early nineteenth century. However, its effects and impact should be acknowledged well beyond the area of private law and civil law codifications: it also affected legal thinking and more or less rationalistic constructions with regard to the sovereign state, criminal law, tax law and many other traditional or less traditional branches of the law—indeed, the tutoring of these branches was often the work of the Law of Reason.

Derationalisation, accordingly, is also to be envisaged as a specific historical process: it is the dismantling of that classical rational model, which had become particularly visible by the end of the twentieth century and which is still today an ongoing process. Observing the current phenomenon, it becomes obvious that this dismantling has the effect of creating new, apparently increasingly heterogeneous legal categories and entities, which correspond to new dominant values and interests.

Derationalisation has therefore acted as a widescale deconstruction of the classical paradigm of Western legal science upon which modern national codifications were built. The paradigm still prevails in most of today's legal curricula, textbooks and legal literature. Legal studies which tend to challenge the paradigm still have a way to go before they can hope to have a significant impact on mainstream legal methods. On the other hand, the practical effects of derationalisation are already affecting many aspects of legal practice, and one may wonder whether approaches worked out and experimented on in the context of major law firms and lobbying groups, all of which tend to influence a legally defined decision-making process, are not in some way anticipating an overhaul of legal studies by now long overdue among legal academics.

The derationalisation process, clearly visible less than two centuries after the classical rationalisation process had reached its high-water mark, also raises the more general question of the very possibility and usefulness, or, in terms of scientific theory, of any long-standing validity, of any method resting on general categories and a general classification of the law. Historically, the question is whether or not, or possibly to what extent, such a classification matched values and interests which reflected determinant social, economic and political factors of the time. In terms of legal theory, the question is whether or not such overarching categorisation and principles may or may not fulfil methodologically any significant purpose.

A good example of the current controversies around these questions is the by now popular discussion surrounding the principles of corporate governance, for instance when the classical hierarchical model of government and administration (and therefore 'rational' model in the sense set out above) is being challenged by alternative concepts of governance, such as the network model. That the derationalisation process is thereby not an entirely conscious process of deconstruction may be clear when one looks at some of its most striking effects on our polities. In public law, for example, the latter part of the twentieth century has witnessed how the theoretical quasi-monopoly of state sovereignty has receded with the re-emergence of heterogeneous political legitimacies. Correspondingly, the courts' systems in most Western European countries have seen the classical pyramidal organisation of the courts overgrown with the creation of numerous special-interests courts and tribunals. Tax law, another example, no longer encapsulates all the duties which are levied—as a cursory look at one's paysheet in any country may testify.

Legal capacity may well have undergone a similar fate of rationalisation (in the sense of conceptualisation as a general, homogeneous category) in the wake of the Law of Reason and positivistic legal science during the codification era, and of derationalisation (in the sense of a conceptual fragmentation) in our own era of legal pluralism. Graphically, the course of the historical development can be summarised as in Figure 1.

For the present-day jurist, the hypothesis of such a development raises an additional question, namely whether or to what extent the new categories remain linked (and, if so, for what purpose?) as they develop autonomously.

As a general historical contribution, the following pages will mainly deal with the pre-rationalisation period, ie some aspects of capacity before its conceptualisation as a general rational category. The materials

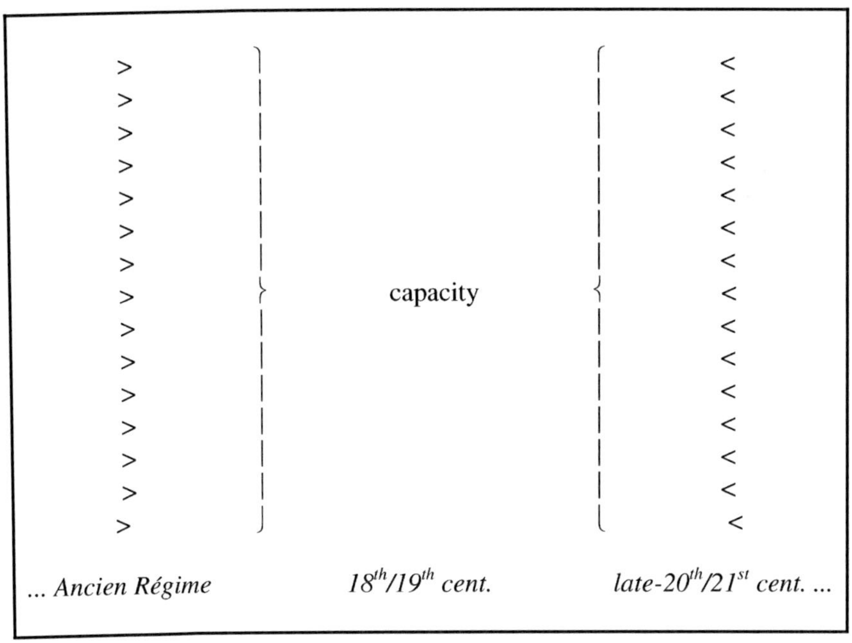

Figure 1

used to illustrate some broad lines of development are principally drawn from the early-modern *ius commune* (or civil law) tradition and, for the *ius proprium* tradition, from the customary and statutory laws of Northern France and the Southern Low Countries. It may be recalled that whereas the customary expression of a rule was often specific and plastically descriptive in its formulation, considering directly the interests at stake, the 'learned law' often tended to find a more general and abstract expression of a principle. The difference should nevertheless not be overstated, as the *ius commune* tradition itself was in many ways practice-orientated and did sometimes include policy considerations in its reasoning.

Two examples, outside the law of contracts but nevertheless relevant for recognising capacitating and incapacitating devices in law, may help to consider more specifically the general mechanism of rationalisation: firstly, the concept of property as it was eventually encapsulated in the definition of Article 544 of the (French) Code civil (Cc); and secondly, the general principle of liability in tort formulated in Article 1382 Cc. In both cases, the general dialectical movement referred to here above in the schematic diagram may be recognised, showing first a movement of concentration of originally different and independent rules into one rational concept or notion, then subsequently the fraying of that concept and the emergence of distinct, increasingly autonomous strands. The examples may be said to be particularly telling because in both cases doctrinal rationalisation resulted in formulaic articles of the civil code, which, paradoxically, have so far survived their deconstruction since the nineteenth century.

Under the law of the *Ancien Régime*, the structure of real estate was such that the question 'Who is the owner?' was comparatively less relevant. Indeed, the so-called system of dual ownership and the differentiation between *domaine direct* and *domaine utile* had developed in such a way that, by the eighteenth century, legal authorities had, paradoxically, assimilated the holder of the latter as the true 'owner', or *propriétaire*. Far more relevant than ownership were the various property rights which could be vested on a particular land, and which included both public and private duties, service charges and many other rights which could be exercised *in rem*. These rights *in rem* (or, in French, *droits réels*) would all weigh economically on the property and affect its value. Correspondingly, these various interests in the property reflected vested rights, values and privileges protected by the system of *Ancien Régime* society. The French Revolution and the 1804 Civil Code both enfranchised and refocused real property: the enfranchisement meant that the law of property tended to suppress as much as possible any 'outside' interests resting on the property; it is in that sense that the revolutionary motto of 'abolishing feudal rights' went much further than putting an end to feudal property rights in the strict legal sense, but included in its programme several other interests which, in legal terms, were not feudal in nature at all. At the same time, the new law set out to concentrate as much as possible all powers (*uti et abuti*) into the hands of the proper owner. The rationale of Article 544 Cc was clearly ideological, intended to neutralise interest groups who had benefited from the old, divided structure of property. The new definition of property also expressed an agenda of economic policy which wanted to introduce land more fully into a market economy and thus to enhance, one expected, its productivity. Article 544 Cc defined ownership entirely in terms of land and property law, outside the areas of personal status and obligations, where capacity was 'slotted' according to the classical systematisation. Nevertheless, it should be clear that the 'absolute power' of the new-style owner was not totally unrelated to legal capacity in a wider sense. Apparently, Article 544 Cc considered the relationship between the owner and his property without any reference to any other person *in concreto*. Such a definition would seem to have given the owner full rights to use his property, to neglect it, to torture or abuse it, or to destroy it. However, the final clause of Article 544 could also be understood to have implied a reference (if only potentially) to other persons *in abstracto*, or the commonwealth.

After 1804, the law of property reflected the gradual emergence of concurrent interests which were legally protected so as to affect the full enjoyment of the property. Once again, these concurrent interests now show great diversity. In private law, they may be linked to neighbourhood, to the protection of tenants, to the protection of a 'family residence', etc. In public law, they have arisen as the result of planning restrictions, environmental protection, the protection of values associated with cultural heritage, etc. Whatever the interests, their legal recognition results in restricting the owner's capacity *utendi et abutendi*. These restrictions of his capacity not only affect his individual and private relationship with the property (eg not being allowed to replace a particular type of windows in his Grade II house), but also his handling of the property in relation to other people (eg avoiding excessive disturbance to neighbouring properties).

In the current legal tradition, one tends to regard real property with respect to restrictions of proprietary rights, but it should be obvious that these restrictions create in effect degrees of incapacity with regard to the legal owner. In fact, the mutual effects between property rights and capacity may be recognised at all stages of legal history. To take but one example from Nuzi, a Sumerian city around the second millennium BC: there appear to be no surviving records of land conveyances to non-relatives, which has led some scholars to assume that such conveyances were prohibited; however, the records of the same city show evidence of adoptions, particularly adoptions including a conveyancing clause: typically A would adopt B and convey to him the ownership of some specified land, while B would give A (in consideration?) some valuable commodity (eg a certain quantity of copper). Archaeologists have discovered that the same person, probably some businessman, appears as the adopted party in some 130 contracts. One may infer that the adoption was the standard means to create a capacity which otherwise seems to have remained outside the scope of the rule governing real property.

The second well-known example of rationalisation as the concentration of various rules into one general and codified principle is Article 1382 Cc. The predominant historiography on tort liability may nevertheless be somewhat misleading, as it has tended to emphasise too exclusively the thread of doctrinal *Dogmengeschichte*, reconstructing the intellectual progress through doctrinal works of the civil law tradition which eventually led to the formulation of a general, overarching principle of tortious liability. That picture is somewhat different from the one offered through *Ancien Régime* legal practice, and the mainstream legal literature primarily intended for legal practitioners, where, right until the end of the *ancien droit*, the most common approach consisted in considering different categories, or at least situations, which gave rise to a non-contractual, Aquilian or quasi-Aquilian liability. In that literature, these situations were largely dealt with as heterogeneous cases of liability, ie without a common or overarching rationale or principle. Moreover, those heterogeneous categories of standard situations reflected each time particular interests or particular professional categories. Indeed, even the general phrase 'liability' (in the case of legal literature in French, *responsabilité*) as an overarching concept was comparatively rarely to be found in titles of books, of sections within a large work, in indexes, summaries or as an entry. On the other hand, historiography finds it easier to trace the general notion of liability through the influence of the 'School of Natural Law' as the intellectual mould which eventually produced the rule expressed in Article 1382 (the following articles of the code reflecting to some extent the unfinished process of rationalisation and some categories of special situations characteristically dealt with in pre-codification law). In any case, it is remarkable to see that at first, during the early nineteenth century, the rule may perhaps have been perceived more as a principle of natural law or as a moral principle of natural justice rather than a general rule of law on a par with the general theory of contracts: at any rate, the full potential of Article 1382 Cc remained for many years overshadowed by the rules governing contractual liability. Even so, even tortious liability was nevertheless affected by notions of capacity. Thus, the requirement of a wrong (*faute*) would exclude infants or the insane. For the latter, the condition of *mens rea* in criminal law seems to have played a part *mutatis mutandis*, but both before and after the enactment of the Cc, it appears that the question of tortious capacity (ie the faculty to incur tortious liability, in the German sense of *Deliktsfähigkeit*) could sometimes be dissociated from the actual liability to pay damages or compensation.

Even before the twentieth century, the limitations of such a 'perfect' general rational principle as the sole statutory authority became apparent. By then, the general principle was in fact splintering into distinct categories of tortious liability which increasingly developed according to their own dynamics and proper needs. Here, again, several examples may illustrate the point, whether one considers the various distinct categories of professional liability, the development of strict (non-fault) liability, but also developments where the links with the structure of Article 1382 Cc become even more tenuous, as in the case of the *principe de précaution*.

The political, economic and ideological agenda which may have prevailed for Article 1382 in 1804 is not as clear as for Article 544. Perhaps the various categories of tortious liability in pre-revolutionary law were not deemed to affect any major interests which might have called for the special attention of the lawmaker. The *usus modernus* had not, it seems, developed a general concept of *Deliktsfähigkeit*, but the formulation of Article 1382 Cc was nonetheless in line with the general tendency to express a uniform, equal status to all, in this context with regard to the capacity of acting tortiously. On the other hand, the post-1804 tendency and current developments express more clearly the emerging interests and values which have justified the often spectacular extension of the applications of Article 1382, which mean in effect the extension *in concreto* of *Deliktsfähigkeit* in a wide range of different situations or categories. That may be seen as a paradox, insofar as methodologically, the general formulation of Article 1382, albeit originally introduced as an expression of rationalisation, now appears to fuel its own diversification and, hence, derationalisation. At present, Article 1382 continues to serve as a general rationale and justification for the development of fresh categories of tortious liability. At the same time, this tends to obfuscate the policy considerations behind these extensions (at least in those legal systems, such as France, where policy considerations still fail to be explicitly incorporated within the legal argument and thinking on issues of liability).

Having looked at two examples of a codified principle which 'rationalised' an originally heterogeneous array of rules by conceptualising and formulating a general principle under which all those rules—and other situations—could be subsumed, but which have both since 1804 increasingly been exposed to a derationalisation process in the sense that the general principle has largely been broken up in order to meet and protect fresh interests, one may now address the question, from a historical perspective, whether such a rationalisation (and, as an antithesis, a derationalisation) process may be recognised with regard to the legal notion of 'capacity'. The answer to that question, as indeed the question itself, is not as straightforward as it may seem. The difficulty for the legal historian consists in avoiding a reduction of his analysis to conventional categories of persons with no, or with a limited, legal capacity; on the other hand, the historian will also have to avoid the pitfall of imposing too strongly a nineteenth-century conceptual labelling inspired by the since then prevailing abstract *Dogmengeschichte* to particular sets of rules which developed in a *sui generis* way according to his own, distinct rationale.

That difficulty becomes immediately apparent when approaching the question through the customary law tradition. For even when considering distinct categories *ratione personae*, it often appears that there is no precise boundary between capacity and incapacity. Even within recognisable categories, the distinction between capacity and incapacity (borrowing the modern terminology) may strongly differ *ratione materiae*. In other words, if one assumes that, in law, the distinction between capacity and incapacity reflects capacitating and incapacitating strategies which are meant to protect particular interests (be they persons, types of transactions, objects of transactions or any other type of interest), that protection nonetheless will not always adopt the form of a capacitating or incapacitating legal rule. The examples set out above on property have already illustrated the point. The case of children and young persons (hereafter outlined from the old—ie pre-1795—Belgian customary and statutory law)[1] may contribute to elaborate on the complexity of the capacity/incapacity distinction. 'Majority' was originally acquired when a person had reached nubile age, which for girls was usually set between 11 and 14 years and for boys between 14 and 16 years. However, the effect of majority on one's capacity depended on the system of parental authority, which varied considerably from one region to another. Normally, a person who had reached majority would be able to contract marriage, would be criminally liable, might carry arms, could (under some conditions) sue, act as a witness, take an oath, etc, but the age of majority and the end of parental authority did not coincide in all the customs. In many cases, someone who had reached the age of majority might still remain under parental authority and would only acquire full capacity in law when that authority had ended. This could occur (i) when either parent died (as in Brabant, Hainaut, large parts of Flanders), when the surviving parent died (Liège) or upon the father's death (as in

[1] The following paragraphs are mainly borrowed from P Godding, *Le droit privé dans les Pays-Bas méridionaux du 12ᵉ au 18ᵉ siècle* (Bruxelles, Palais des Académies, 1987), the standard reference on ancient Belgian private law, which I used for many years in my course on legal history.

Gallican Flanders); (ii) through marriage; (iii) by acceding to some office (such as priesthood, or being elected an alderman); or (iv) by explicit emancipation. Moreover, from the fifteenth century onwards, one notes that, particularly in the cities, the age of majority was raised—up to 18, 25 or even 28 years—which meant that until he had reached such an age, a person under the city's laws would remain incapable of effecting certain transactions (such as selling or mortgaging immoveable property). On the other hand, an underage child who was also under parental authority might remain incapable not only of performing certain acts and transactions, but also of enjoying certain rights (eg of holding goods of his own). The important point is that the incapacity could depend on both the person's age and the nature of the act or transaction.

Infants were generally fully incapable. More relevant was the position of young persons in those regions where the age of majority did not entail the end of parental authority. There, incapacity was not unqualified beyond infancy. In some regions, moreover, a special regime prevailed: in Brabant, for example, a child under parental authority would not have any property of his own; when he came of age he could make contracts but would only be personally liable, as he held no property which might be seized by creditors. Special rules also applied to young persons *in statu pupillari*: when they reached the age of majority, they could sometimes remain under the authority of their guardian. The guardian's authorisation was therefore necessary when they wanted to enter a contract, but several local laws nevertheless accepted the validity of contracts entered into without the guardian's authorisation if the contract improved the ward's position. In most cases, however, when a ward came of age, the guardianship was ended. Minors were usually barred from procedural acts; the system of *dormition des actions*, which ensured that the period of limitation regarding the minor's rights was suspended, was intended to protect his interests. Alternatively, the minor could be represented by a parent or ward.

More noteworthy than the position of minors and young persons under parental authority was the limited capacity allowed to persons who had come of age and whose guardianship had been ended, or who had been emancipated and were therefore no longer under parental authority. Such youngsters should normally have been fully capable, yet local authorities regularly took steps to protect their interests (mostly, the interests of the family property) by restricting their capacity to dispose of, or to establish property rights on, their land. A statute in Brussels of 1383 stated that no child could dispose of his land without the consent of four close relatives until he had reached the age of 28.

One also notes a great divergence for other acts, either because the interest to be protected was not so clearly defined as landed family property, or because there were conflicting legitimate interests which could claim protection. The capacity to make a will, for instance, was recognised by several customs for comparatively young persons (eg when the old medieval age of majority, ie after puberty, had been reached, or when the person had been allowed to marry), but the capacity apparently also depended on other rules: for example, no will could be made if, according to the local custom, the child under parental authority could not have property of his own.

Emancipation might occur for a variety of reasons. Sometimes, it was used in order to enable the young person to engage in trade, or to administer his own property. In some areas, emancipation was controlled by the local authorities, who were supposed to check whether the person had the necessary qualities. Some customs did not allow emancipation until the youngster had reached a minimum age; this was particularly the case in those customary systems where the age of majority did not automatically entail emancipation. The effect of emancipation was, in principle, to make the person fully capable in law. Inevitably, one encounters several qualifications to that rule: for example, a typical restriction was sometimes imposed, once again, with respect to real property (immoveables), so that even the emancipated youngster could not dispose of interests, or vest an interest on his real property. Likewise, in some Flemish customs, some forms of emancipation only allowed the young person to dispose of his income.

Conversely, one should remember that the laws also made provisions for situations where, under judicial or administrative control, the effects of minority could be extended, eg in the case of an immature individual.

The second conventional example of a 'protected class' was that of women, especially married women, or, in the old English legal phrase, the 'femme covert'. The status of a married woman varied greatly from one region to another: a clear example that the interests at stake were not perceived unanimously. Generally speaking, there was not, during the medieval and early-modern period, a general sense in the Low Countries that a woman had necessarily to be incapacitated in law. After all, the region had experienced several rulers who were women. In feudal law, some Belgian customs admitted that a fief could be held by a woman. Urban laws often reflected the participation of women in trade and their position in businesses, a reality which tended to allow more generally a greater degree of equality in women's legal status. During the early-modern period, in other areas of social life, too, there existed a tendency that fitted within the global change of social climate at the time and which has been dubbed, in a different context, as the *Grand Renfermement*: for women, it often meant that their incapacity was now emphasised and their capacity was restricted to particular situations or operations. In public law, women were barred from public offices (except, for dynastic reasons, at the highest political level) and sometimes they were not admitted as witnesses in court proceedings.

A single woman's status during the later Middle Ages would depend on the regional custom. In some areas (Flanders, Hainaut, Liège), she could act on her own (in Liège, if she was a widow, she would need a guardian); in Brabant, the *mamboer*, a guardian entrusted to assist her, was the rule. For the early-modern period, the customs were not always sufficiently explicit, but it seems that the differences inherited from the Middle Ages lived on. Yet, even under the regime of customs which required the assistance of a guardian or the control of aldermen, some acts could still be accomplished by the woman alone: this was typically the case for entering an ante-nuptial contract, making a bequest or drafting a will. Other acts were barred: typically, this would be the case for acting as a guardian herself, or for the acts which were deemed to fall under the prohibition of the Senatus-Consult Velleianum (namely the intercession in favour of a third party).

The married woman's status also varied according to regional custom, but in addition, significantly, it underwent a much deeper change during the transition from the medieval to the early-modern period. For the Middle Ages, no customary system appears to have imposed a general incapacity. There were instances where the woman required her husband's assistance for disposing of her immoveables, but one also comes across several examples of a married woman acting by herself—it was not unusual for a noblewoman to use her personal seal. In early-modern times, by contrast, a generally accepted principle of incapacity came to prevail. Even then, however, the incapacity suffered several exceptions, including the faculties (i) to carry on as a public businesswoman (separately from her husband); (ii) to sue in different types of proceedings (matrimonial causes, separation, criminal proceedings); (iii) to make a will (a faculty sometimes qualified by the requirement of the husband's authorisation); and (iv) to enter into all transactions and legal actions related to the day-to-day management of the household. A legally separated wife in theory regained a fuller capacity. In effect, the capacity of a married woman would also have depended to a great extent on the prevailing system of (customary or conventional) family property under which she was married.

Other categories of persons conventionally identified as being (at least partly) incapable, but whose position is often less documented than minors and women, were disabled persons (whether the disability was physical or mental), to whom so-called 'prodigals' were somehow assimilated; members of religious orders (particularly regarding their capacity to inherit, or to receive gifts) and mainmorte corporations (particularly ecclesiastical corporations and institutions); illegitimate children;

foreigners; and serfs and other 'unfree' persons, though, by the late Middle Ages, the latter category largely belonged to the past.

The *ius commune* tradition[2], one would expect, may have offered a more uniformly conceptualised approach to legal capacity. However, it does not seem that *ius commune* doctrines developed a general concept around legal capacity. *Ius commune* authorities were in any case confronted with the fact that on some issues, such as those related to immoveables, one's personal status was not primarily the decisive criterion, but rather the *lex rei sitae*. According to the German legal historian H Coing, only when an overarching notion of 'legal subject', ie of a legally defined person, had been worked out, a construction which was tributary to the notion of an abstract capacity, did it become possible to subsume individuals and organisations (corporations) under such a general concept. That, in turn, implied that such a concept of person had reached a certain degree of uniformity and equality. Such a condition was not fulfilled under the *Ancien Régime*, in which society was based on social groups which were not on an equal footing with each other. *Ius commune* could not ignore the prevailing legal pluralism *ratione personae* as one of the distinctive and constitutive features of society. Against the theoretical notion of a 'status naturalis', the *status civilis* was characterised by its 'accidental' or 'relative' nature, and was hence a decisive factor in the diversity of status. It was only the Law of Reason which introduced a general notion of person as a subject of right and duties, and it was only by operating an abstraction of the particular status that it paved the way to a concept of general freedom and equality of all human beings. That idea was expressed in 'civil' codes, ie the citizens' codes, from the early nineteenth century onwards—late-eighteenth-century codifications, such as the Prussian ALR, would still differentiate between subjects. By the nineteenth century, however, legal capacity had become one of the essential attributes of a person as a legal subject, as an expression of the individuals' free and equal status. Von Savigny (quoted by Coing) wrote that

> all law exists in order to guarantee the moral freedom which belongs essentially to every human being. Therefore, the constitutive concept of person or subject in law must coincide with the notion of 'human being'. Every single human being—and only the single human being—enjoys capacity.

Some discriminations nevertheless remained. At the beginning of the nineteenth century, slavery could in some cases still be enforced through the application of foreign law. Matrimonial law, when not fully

[2] The following paragraphs follow H Coing, *Europäisches Privatrecht, I, 1500 bis 1800, Älteres gemeines Recht* (München, CH Beck, 1985) and *II, 1800 bis 1914, 19. Jahrhundert* (München, CH Beck, 1989).

secularised, could still entail specific or discriminating incapacities. Foreign citizenship was a typical ground for discrimination, unless a system of reciprocity prevented it. Some systems, such as that of the 'civil death' in France, organised incapacities based on a criminal conviction. And, of course, the traditional categories of partly or fully incapable persons 'by nature' or otherwise were also to be found in the codified law: persons under age (with various differentiations depending on age, the impact of the transaction on the youngster's patrimony, etc), the mentally ill and married women. In many countries, the status of corporations was ambiguous: whereas commercial companies were encouraged, the ghost of a revival of the *Ancien Régime*'s mainmorte played an inhibitive role. Nonetheless, the general picture seems to show that, for physical persons, the general approach consisted in looking at these categories as exceptions to the general principle, namely that persons were normally deemed legally capable *ratione personae*. The categories of exceptions were on the whole fairly conventional and did not substantially change the position of those persons compared to their status under the old law, though for some categories (eg persons under age, married women) the incapacity was sometimes attenuated to some degree.

Perhaps the most significant change since the nineteenth-century codifications in that respect has been the emergence of new protected interests, for which one of the instruments of legal protection has been the creation or extension of incapacities. Conversely, however, some of the traditional categories of legally incapable persons have seen their incapacity abolished (married women) or reduced (adolescents under age). Furthermore, the examples set out above with regard to Articles 544 and 1382 Cc show that the 'dismantling' of a central concept (ownership, tortious liability) does not always follow the pattern of creating exceptions to the rule: sometimes, a different, external approach may take place, such as (with respect to Article 544) the prohibition of certain clauses or practices, or (with respect to Article 1382) via insurance techniques. Similarly, with regard to legal capacity, the protection of interests does not necessarily take the shape of an incapacitating device. A typical example is consumers' protection, as there is no legal incapacity of either the seller or the buyer to make a contract regarding defective goods, but, to some extent, the economic result for the contracting parties is not dissimilar to that of a protective incapacity.

Again, the examples of Articles 544 and 1382 Cc also remind us that the derationalisation process is still under way. Indeed, in spite of the erosion which has affected both principles, they remain, at least partially and imperfectly, a reference in their respective areas. Similarly, *capacitas* in its classical and rationalised sense also remains an operational concept and reference in current legal methods. Derationalisation means not that the rational construction and principle have been suppressed and possibly replaced, but that the concept is applied and is operating in a context which no longer respects its coherence and systemic role. As a result, the principle and concept are increasingly less fit to govern the methods of legal argumentation and reasoning in their proper field and context.

The classic, egalitarian concept of legal capacity has therefore evolved into a more differentiating and discriminatory technique, partly by introducing legal incapacities in the conventional sense, often on an ad hoc basis. The discriminations may be either positive, ie protecting particular interests because of a perceived imbalance and in order to redress substantive equality, or negative, ie protecting particular interests against other competing interests. At present, it is questionable whether a general and abstract principle of equality still prevails. Instead, equality appears to be approached more frequently through the principle of non-discrimination on certain grounds. That approach implies a potential conflict with directly or indirectly incapacitating forms of protection of interests, for protecting interests consist not only in restricting formal equality, but also in restricting formal freedom. Any rethinking of capacitating and incapacitating techniques in law will therefore have to take into account the extent to which the principles of freedom and equality remain essential values of a societal organisation, and whether these may have to yield to other values and priorities in shaping society and the international community. Considering the general tendency of the past two centuries, the historian might expect that, as a general concept, legal capacity will continue to break apart in the ongoing process of protecting particular interests, especially in an increasingly globalised world which has so far provided no institutional framework for achieving general freedom and equality similar to that which the late-eighteenth and early-nineteenth-century nation-state could pretend to achieve within its limited territorial boundaries.

4

Revisiter la notion juridique de capacité?

JEAN HAUSER*

La capacité juridique c'est l'aptitude à exercer ses droits, aptitude mentale ou physique mais c'est en réalité la rencontre de la théorie des droits subjectifs ou des libertés et de la réalité du sujet qui les exerce. En un sens la capacité est un mode d'individualisation de l'attribution des droits à partir d'un jugement particulier sur la possibilité de les exercer.

Si l'on considère les droits individuels, point de vue à notre époque fort répandu, on peut en imaginer les destinataires à partir d'une pyramide. Sa base, la capacité est la règle et l'incapacité l'exception, est en principe constituée de tous les individus vivants[1] dont on présume qu'ils peuvent exercer les droits que l'organisation politique leur attribue. On pourrait admettre qu'avant même cette présomption d'attribution par le système juridique, il existe ce qu'on appelle une 'capacité naturelle' sur laquelle, pour reprendre la même image, reposerait cette pyramide.[2] Ses étages sont ensuite plus ou moins larges selon que l'aptitude du sujet diminue.

* S'agissant d'une étude conceptuelle générale, on a supprimé toute référence à des écrits nationaux ou étrangers qui eussent été très nombreuses. Pour une bibliographie plus complète, J Hauser, 'La notion d'incapacité' (2000) 164 *Petites Affiches* 3s et, pour les incapables mineurs, du même auteur, 'Du discernement à une famille réduite à la procédure' (1999) 84 *Petites Affiches* 11s. Sur le droit des incapacités en général en droit français, J Massip, *Les incapacités* (Defrénois, 2002). Pour la jurisprudence, chroniques régulières de J Hauser à la revue trimestrielle de droit civil (Sirey-Dalloz) et de T Fossier, *Revue Droit de la famille* (LITEC) et T Fossier et JM Plazy, *Semaine juridique notariale et immobilière* (LITEC).

1 Ce qui, on le sait, n'a pas été le cas, et de loin, dans l'histoire.

2 Cette capacité naturelle se traduit dans tous les régimes de protection soit par des actes que personne ne peut faire à la place de la personne protégée, notamment pour ceux qui touchent sa personne, ce qui apparaît très protecteur mais finalement peut ne pas être sans risque car certains de ces actes seraient fort intéressants pour la personne protégée. Il ne faut donc pas, pour des raisons théoriques et souvent idéologiques, étendre trop cette catégorie qui doit demeurer une sorte de 'sanctuaire' de la personne.

Le but poursuivi par ces diminutions qui peuvent aboutir, si le sujet est hors d'état d'exprimer un consentement, à le priver de toute forme de décision, a été, contrairement à ce qu'on pourrait penser, assez variable dans l'histoire. Certes, la protection de l'individu n'a jamais été étrangère à la diminution de sa capacité mais, très souvent, l'idée de sa mise à l'écart pour des raisons d'ordre public a été avant tout invoquée. Cette idée n'a disparu qu'avec l'évolution des conceptions médicales et sociales sur l'insanité d'esprit. La dominante de l'intérêt de la personne n'est plus contestée et la majorité des systèmes juridiques ne fait plus référence à l'incapacité mais à la protection. Il demeure tout de même que, sans hypocrisie, pour assurer cette protection on diminue en pratique l'exercice des droits, sinon leur jouissance.

Le soubassement philosophique d'une intervention du droit dans ce domaine étant ainsi précisé, l'effort des juristes doit se porter sur la procédure de déclenchement de la protection (ou de l'incapacité), étant acquis à peu près partout[3] que cette procédure doit, en tout premier lieu, être respectueuse des libertés et des droits fondamentaux de la personne. La difficulté évidente est que, comme toute individualisation de la norme, il faut faire confiance à ceux qui appliquent le droit, ce que les systèmes continentaux, au moins certains, n'acceptent pas toujours.

A vrai dire il faut alors introduire une distinction importante. Le défaut de capacité des mineurs ne pose guère de problème puisqu'il peut être cadré par des conditions d'âge, encore que, on le verra, la détermination n'en est pas si simple. Il n'en est évidemment rien pour les majeurs et il reste inimaginable, malgré l'allongement de la durée de la vie, qu'on fixe un âge au delà duquel on ne serait plus pleinement capable.[4] Il faut donc s'en remettre à des décisions individuelles. Mais, de nouveau, il y aurait lieu—ce que les systèmes juridiques font rarement—de distinguer entre deux catégories de personnes majeurs protégées, distinction d'autant plus essentielle en notre temps que l'incapacité due au grand âge est devenue un problème. Pour certaines personnes la notion même de majorité ou de minorité n'a pas eu de sens si leur capacité a été atteinte dès l'origine. L'origine de la protection ne peut donc leur être qu'extérieure. Pour d'autres, et l'on en revient à l'âge, leur capacité n'a décliné que pour des raisons ordinaires. Or, la réponse juridique peut être ici très différente pour plusieurs raisons.

Si donc l'adaptation moderne du concept d'incapacité (I) peut s'opérer par une redéfinition des techniques en intégrant la capacité dans

[3] Ce qui n'est pas forcément évident et permanent, les systèmes autoritaires ayant souvent utilisé l'internement psychiatrique ou la privation de droits pour contrer leurs adversaires politiques: qui est contre moi est un incapable!

[4] Est-il pour autant totalement inconcevable d'imaginer qu'un jour il faudra peut-être y songer? Le droit français des accidents d'automobile a retenu l'âge de 70 ans au delà duquel la victime d'un accident de la circulation ne peut plus se voir opposer même sa faute inexcusable (L 5 juillet 1985, art 3).

l'ensemble de l'action du sujet, il n'est pas non plus exclu qu'on puisse anticiper sur cette incapacité (II).

I. ADAPTATION DE LA CAPACITÉ PAR UNE REDÉFINITION DES TECHNIQUES

Si le remplacement du mot incapacité par le mot protection apparaît souvent plus formel que réel, trois évolutions sont plus prometteuses dans la perspective de cette étude:

- la remise en cause, pour les mineurs, du critère purement chronologique
- la remise en cause pour les majeurs de la répartition entre les deux grands systèmes de la représentation et de l'assistance
- l'insertion du concept d'incapacité dans l'ensemble du commerce juridique

Remise en cause du critère chronologique pour les mineurs

L'idée d'une pré-majorité en fonction de l'âge ou des actes à accomplir s'est développée très rapidement à partir des années 1960 jusqu'à conduire à un tableau très diversifié, et d'ailleurs très désordonné, puisque la question n'a jamais été reprise dans son ensemble mais toujours traitée par la voie parallèle de textes spéciaux dont l'objet était autre. Reste que, dans l'ensemble, il s'agit bien de donner au mineur la capacité de faire les actes dans lesquels il a les moyens de sa liberté soit en raison de son âge, soit en raison de l'acte considéré.

L'individualisation selon l'âge

L'apparition systématique au fil des textes de l'âge de treize ans au delà duquel le mineur est considéré comme ayant le moyen de sa liberté est très caractéristique. Le changement de nom, l'adoption et bien d'autres actes sont maintenant soumis à cette progressivité chronologique et si d'autres domaines n'y sont pas (actions d'état par exemple) c'est parce que les réformes n'ont pas touché ces domaines.

A ce seuil chronologique certains textes—et certaines jurisprudences—préfèrent la référence à la notion de 'discernement', notion non juridique qui consiste en fait à renvoyer au juge le soin de déterminer si le mineur a les moyens de sa liberté.[5]

[5] Le critère de la Convention internationale des droits de l'enfant laisse au juge un très large pouvoir d'appréciation.

La méthodologie préférable pourrait consister à construire de grandes catégories d'actes dans lesquelles l'aptitude du mineur pourrait progresser.

L'individualisation selon l'acte

A vrai dire la méthode n'est pas nouvelle et on a toujours admis que certains actes personnels étaient possibles si la lucidité du mineur était suffisante qu'il s'agisse du mariage par exemple (même s'il faut des autorisations) ou encore de la reconnaissance d'enfant. L'aptitude sur son corps ou ses dérivés pourrait être la première que l'homme peut acquérir?

Pour autant, en droit moderne, la réponse n'est pas toujours des plus faciles. Faut-il laisser la mineure qui accouche seule choisir la déclaration sous anonymat[6] puis consentir, encore seule, à l'adoption: est-elle tout à fait responsable et a-t-elle les moyens de sa liberté?

Elle est encore plus douteuse quand on entre dans les décisions de nature thérapeutique ou biologique et si la loi du 4 mars 2002 laisse aux parents la capacité entière sur les décisions thérapeutiques, d'autres textes se replient de nouveau sur le consentement au dessus de 13 ans.

Dans le domaine patrimonial la référence aux 'actes courants' nourrit une réflexion plus générale sur le concept de 'capacité naturelle' qui concernerait alors tous les incapables: les actes liés à la qualité d'être humain social et qu'on pourrait toujours faire . . .

Cette individualisation à perte de vue a bien pour but de concilier protection et responsabilité à tel point que les techniques elles-mêmes pourraient être rediscutées. Le mineur est actuellement soit représenté, soit capable pleinement. L'échelon intermédiaire de la seule assistance n'est pas utilisé dans l'incapacité des mineurs en considération de ce que la situation est provisoire et qu'elle repose sur l'exercice d'une autorité des parents qui se concilierait mal avec une simple assistance. Il est facile d'imaginer que l'évolution des idées pourrait utilement conduire à revenir sur ce point d'autant que la technique de l'assistance est assez à la mode dans la catégorie des majeurs.

La remise en cause de la répartition représentation—assistance pour les majeurs

L'individualisation de la responsabilité de l'individu protégé en fonction de ses moyens est traditionnellement illustrée, en droit français, par la dualité représentation ou simple assistance à laquelle correspondent en gros la tutelle et la curatelle dans le régime né de 1968. Mais la loi permet

[6] Ce que permet le droit français non sans discussion.

d'aller beaucoup plus loin dans cette adaptation laquelle est très utilisée et la réforme du 5 mars 2007 amène à poser, à cette occasion, une question centrale pour notre sujet d'aujourd'hui.

L'adaptation de la distinction représentation—assistance

Notons que certains systèmes étrangers, poussant jusqu'au bout l'euphémisme, ont renoncé à la représentation pour ne plus retenir que l'assistance (droit allemand).

Dans le système né de 1968 de nombreuses nuances—parfois trop utilisées, parfois pas assez—tempèrent cette dichotomie.

a. Dans la sauvegarde de justice—qui n'est pas une incapacité et permet seulement d'annuler plus facilement les actes passés par le protégé—il est possible de désigner exceptionnellement un mandataire qui sera chargé d'effectuer certains actes. Le cas pratique du vieillard en état de se gérer lui-même mais en difficulté avec la gestion de ses revenus et de ses comptes est typique et maintenant très fréquent, trop fréquent puisque la Cour de cassation est obligée de réagir régulièrement à ce glissement vers un régime simple.... mais ainsi dévoyé.
b. Dans la curatelle où la personne est seulement assistée, il est possible—et très utilisé—de prévoir une curatelle dite aggravée dans laquelle certains actes seront exceptionnellement soumis à représentation en fonction de leur nature ou de leur gravité. Par contre l'allégement est rarement utilisé, ce qu'on peut regretter.
c. Dans la tutelle inversement il est toujours possible—mais également peu utilisé—de prévoir une tutelle allégée sur certains actes dont la possibilité sera restituée à la personne protégée. Conçue à l'origine comme une technique visant à préparer la réinsertion de certains majeurs dans la capacité ordinaire elle reste rare car elle nécessite un gros investissement judiciaire.

L'apparition d'un nouveau système d'adaptation

La curatelle sous ses différentes formes est actuellement en croissance pour deux raisons, le grand âge et les difficultés économiques. C'est ce second point qui présente un intérêt majeur pour notre sujet.

L'un des cas d'ouverture de la curatelle—classique—demeure la prodigalité qui correspondait et correspond normalement à une véritable maladie mentale, classée et connue. Or on assiste à un dévoiement considérable en liaison avec l'explosion du surendettement, les commissions de surendettement poussant à la mise sous curatelle pour éviter une rechute. Ce dévoiement pose des problèmes de principe et appelle une solution.

a. Problème de principe

Il est profondément anormal d'utiliser une technique du droit des incapacités dans un tel cas sauf à admettre qu'il existerait des incapacités sociales et il est également contre-productif d'utiliser un régime judiciaire aussi complexe pour ce type de cas. On aperçoit bien entendu la réponse préventive dans le droit de la consommation, les obligations imposées aux banquiers, les limites de la publicité, les limites du crédit mais les résistances économiques sont considérables . . . Faut-il accepter qu'à notre époque, entre la personne capable pleinement et la personne incapable, il y aurait une personne vulnérable[7] qui appellerait un traitement juridique et social, civil et pénal spécifique? On peut aussi soutenir que toute personne capable doit pouvoir se protéger elle-même mais ce serait condamner bien des branches du droit privé, et notamment le droit du travail?

b. Solutions?

A vrai dire il existe déjà des réponses partielles mais dont le fonctionnement ne répond pas vraiment au problème. La tutelle aux prestations sociales sur les avantages vieillesse de la loi de 1966 et la tutelle aux prestations sociales, enfant de la même loi, répondent, en partie, pour les prestations visées seulement, à cette difficulté d'une gestion 'ciblée' de certains revenus.

La question a été de créer en 2007 un système plus large de mesures d'accompagnement que la loi nomme 'mesure budgétaire et sociale' ou 'mesure de gestion financière et sociale' qui permet bien—évitant d'entrer dans une incapacité inadaptée—de tenir compte de cette situation particulière. Elle suscite des débats de principe . . . et des débats sur son financement!

Ainsi revisiter la capacité par une adaptation individualisée des techniques se produit lentement mais sûrement en prenant en considération moins le résultat—ce qui était le cas—que l'origine même de la difficulté d'exercer une capacité, au fond en privilégiant la personne sur l'objet. La réforme française ajoute d'ailleurs au code civil un titre préliminaire sur la personne de l'incapable où sont envisagés des points aussi concrets que celui du maintien du logement, déjà prévu, ou encore, plus nouveau, du maintien des comptes bancaires à l'identique sauf nécessité ce qui apparaît en pratique un point très sensible pour la personne dont la capacité diminue.

[7] Le congrès des Notaires français en mai 2006 à Strasbourg a choisi précisément d'étudier les 'personnes vulnérables'.

c. L'insertion du concept d'incapacité dans l'ensemble du commerce juridique

La définition classique induit nécessairement une frontière claire entre le sujet capable et le sujet incapable, soit parce que l'âge détermine cette frontière, soit parce qu'elle dépend d'une décision judiciaire. On en déduit, au moins dans la plupart des systèmes continentaux, que le droit des incapacités est une branche particulière du droit civil. A vrai dire cette frontière n'a jamais été vraiment respectée. Dans le code civil lui-même le sujet est aussi traité au titre du droit des obligations[8] comme si la seule capacité était celle de faire des actes juridiques. Le droit des incapacités ou certaines parties spécialisées comprennent néanmoins, en dehors même des régimes d'incapacités, des textes tout à fait généraux prévoyant des possibilités d'annulation sur la seule constatation d'une insanité d'esprit au moment de l'acte.[9] Or, ces possibilités globales, sont de plus en plus utilisées par la jurisprudence française, essentiellement pour assurer une protection générale du grand âge, en dehors de toute ouverture d'un régime de protection. Les ayants droit des personnes âgées qui n'ont pas utilisé l'ouverture d'un régime de protection, parfois par négligence mais aussi souvent par délicatesse, ont de plus en plus recours, a posteriori, à l'argument de l'insanité d'esprit pour faire annuler des actes qui leur sont préjudiciables. Cette nébuleuse qui doit plus au droit des obligations qu'au droit des incapacités se double désormais d'un volet de droit pénal conduisant à incriminer les abus de faiblesse ou d'influence. On peut alors hausser le problème au niveau d'une protection plus générale contre les inégalités qui permettrait d'établir un continuum mais on entrerait cette fois dans l'ère des discussions idéologiques.

Mais on peut aussi songer à une autre direction qui rendrait en partie à la personne le soin de décider ou de prévoir les conditions même d'exercice de sa liberté et donc de sa responsabilité.

II. ADAPTATION DE LA CAPACITE PAR UNE ANTICIPATION DES EVENEMENTS

Le champ de la capacité ou de l'incapacité a traditionnellement été exclu, en droit français, du domaine des actes juridiques de prévision pour plusieurs raisons. Au premier rang se présente le principe

[8] C'est à l'art 1123, donc au titre des obligations, que le code français prévoit que 'toute personne peut contracter, si elle n'en est pas déclarée incapable par la loi'. Le projet de réforme affirmerait le principe dès les premiers arts du code.

[9] C civ art 489 posant un principe général pour faire un acte; art 489-1 prévoyant l'annulation éventuelle d'un acte après la mort de l'auteur; art 901 posant le même principe pour faire une donation ou un testament.

d'indisponibilité des droits relatifs à la personne et la méfiance du Code civil envers les opérations de prévision portant sur des droits futurs. Ce n'est qu'exceptionnellement que la volonté peut avoir un effet sur ces situations et on ne trouverait guère que l'émancipation des mineurs pour illustrer cette exception dans notre sujet, encore faut-il remarquer qu'elle ne peut avoir lieu qu'à l'initiative des parents et non du mineur lui-même (à rediscuter) et qu'elle suppose une décision judiciaire de contrôle.

Pour le reste l'organisation même d'une éventuelle incapacité est légale ou judiciaire et la place de la volonté de l'intéressé est quasi-inexistante.

Il y a à cela d'autres raisons. L'incapacité des majeurs a été largement conçue en fonction du majeur atteint ab initio pour lequel une participation quelconque était inconcevable. Pour le majeur atteint par la suite, essentiellement par l'âge et la dépendance, l'incapacité et son régime juridique devaient beaucoup à la protection des héritiers et du patrimoine familial plus qu'à une vision personnaliste et humaniste de la protection du vieillard.

Or le changement des idées, de la composition des familles, des patrimoines familiaux conduit à reposer la question à l'instar d'un certain nombre de droits étrangers dont le droit québécois ou encore le droit allemand. Il est vrai que cette question se poserait peut-être plus simplement si nos techniques de gestion de patrimoine étaient moins obérées par une définition du patrimoine dépassée et contestable. Mais il ne s'agit pas seulement de patrimoine mais aussi de personnes . . .

Là encore—et cette fois uniquement de lege ferenda—les esprits évoluent et l'idée que l'individu lui-même pourrait participer par anticipation à l'organisation d'une éventuelle future incapacité n'est plus inconnue. Désigner celui ou ceux qui vous assisteront voire vous représenteront éventuellement, aller plus loin en prévoyant le contenu même de cette protection qui pourra être progressive et limitée. Ce serait bien ici 'indexer la politique des incapacités sur le temps long de la vie des hommes'.

Prévoir son assistant ou son représentant

En réalité la demande est ancienne mais, s'il est possible pour les parents de désigner un tuteur par testament sur un mineur, cette possibilité n'existait pas pour un majeur soit que les parents ne le puissent pas sur un enfant handicapé devenu majeur soit que la personne capable ne puisse pas prévoir à l'avance qui sera son tuteur ou son curateur. Ce traitement d'ordre public de la capacité ou de l'incapacité confinait à l'absurdité quand on est en présence d'un enfant atteint d'une maladie dès sa naissance et hors d'état d'assumer une quelconque capacité. Le seuil majoritaire est artificiel et pourtant il conduit à un changement juridique dans le système de protection, les parents administrateurs légaux jusque là devienne tuteurs datifs, même si la plupart du temps on ouvrira simplement une tutelle sous forme d'administration légale.

Mais il en résultait l'impossibilité de désigner à l'avance le tuteur en cas de décès des parents. A côté d'une possibilité de désignation éventuelle par la personne elle-même il convenait de prévoir, lors de la réforme en cours, la possibilité d'une désignation a futurum par les parents quand la cause de l'incapacité est sans remède.

Prévoir son régime d'incapacité

On pouvait aller plus loin encore dans la personnalisation en permettant une véritable organisation générale. Au fond, à l'instar de l'organisation de sa succession par le moyen des libéralités, on doit pouvoir gérer son éventuelle future incapacité par le moyen d'un acte notarié permettant de prendre en main l'avenir de sa 3ème ou 4ème vie . . . La technique du mandat conditionnel n'a rien de révolutionnaire et elle doit simplement être adaptée à une utilisation qui dépassera le seul cas de la gestion des biens pour atteindre les personnes. Elle pourra d'ailleurs être modulée selon le processus contractuel classique en offrant plusieurs possibilités en fonction de l'état et de la capacité des personnes considérées avec, bien entendu, les contrôles nécessaires et la possibilité d'un recours judiciaire si le système prévu s'avère inadapté ou contraire aux intérêts de la personne au moment de sa mise en œuvre. C'est donc le regard que porte la personne sur ce que pourrait être l'avenir proche de ses capacités qui ferait ainsi l'objet d'une prévision.

La complexité des sociétés modernes et l'allongement de la durée de vie pourraient bien remettre en cause l'opposition simple entre capacité et incapacité. Etre doté d'une capacité ne serait plus forcément être capable d'exercer ses droits. Le primat de la protection des libertés restant essentiel, il restera à trouver un juste équilibre entre une protection étouffante et une liberté suicidaire. C'est peut-être à la façon dont elles protégent leurs personnes vulnérables qu'on reconnaîtra en notre siècle les sociétés développées?

5

Le concept de capacité dans le droit des contrats français

SANDRINE GODELAIN

INTRODUCTION

1. Selon l'article 1108 du Code civil, la capacité est l'une des conditions de formation du contrat.[1] Elle se définit comme l'aptitude à avoir et à exercer des droits.[2] On distingue en général en droit français deux degrés de capacité juridique.[3] La capacité de jouissance, que toute personne physique possède, s'analyse comme l'aptitude à avoir des droits.[4] Quant à la capacité d'exercice, elle correspond à l'aptitude de mettre soi-même en œuvre les droits dont on dispose.

Malgré l'existence d'un principe de capacité contractuelle, la définition de la capacité dans les contrats a été délaissée. Et c'est sur la délimitation de la notion d'incapacité que le droit civil s'est focalisé.[5]

1 Art 1108 du Code civil: Quatre conditions sont essentielles pour la validité d'une convention:

Le consentement de la partie qui s'oblige;

Sa capacité de contracter;

Un objet certain qui forme la matière de l'engagement;

Une cause licite dans l'obligation.

2 G Cornu, *Vocabulaire juridique* (PUF collection Quadrige, 3ème édition, 2002).

3 H Perinet-Marquet, 'Contrats et obligations: capacité de contracter' *J-Cl civil* 1123–25-1 fasc 8; G Roche, 'Incapacités juridiques' in *Encyclopedia Universalis* (éd Encyclopedia Universalis France, 1995) 1034; L Topor, 'Etat et capacités des personnes' [1990] *Répertoire civil Dalloz* 40.

4 Par exception, il existe encore aujourd'hui quelques incapacités de jouissance spéciales ne faisant obstacle pour l'individu qu'à l'existence d'un droit spécial et dans des conditions particulières. Tel est le cas de l'art 1125-1 du Code civil qui rend le personnel médical incapable de conclure un acte avec les patients dont il s'occupe. De la même manière, l'art 1596 du Code civil rend le tuteur incapable d'acheter les biens du tutélaire dont il assure la gestion des biens. Voir R Le Guidec, 'Vente: capacité des parties' [1997] *Jurisclasseur civil* 1594.

5 J Hauser, 'La notion d'incapacité' (2000) 164 *LPA* 3.

2. Il existe ainsi, selon le Code civil, deux catégories principales d'incapables: les mineurs et les majeurs protégés.[6] Ces individus sont, par principe, présumés incapables et l'ensemble des actes qu'ils pourraient conclure est dépourvu d'effets juridiques. Ce sont donc des incapables de droit. L'article 489 du Code civil complète ce dispositif et prévoit la possibilité de prononcer ponctuellement l'incapacité d'un contractant compte tenu des circonstances dans lesquelles cet individu a conclu l'acte.[7] Tel est par exemple le cas de l'individu qui signe un contrat alors qu'il est ivre. Dans une telle hypothèse si l'incapacité au moment de la conclusion de l'acte est prouvée, elle annihile les effets juridiques de cet acte. On parle alors d'incapacité de fait.

Que l'incapacité de protection soit ponctuelle ou continue, elle emporte les mêmes effets juridiques et permet d'annuler le contrat. De plus, l'incapacité de contracter a toujours la même finalité: protéger le contractant vulnérable compte tenu sa faiblesse psychologique (immaturité pour le mineur et trouble mental pour le majeur protégé).

3. Il convient toutefois de noter qu'il existe une autre catégorie d'incapacités en droit français. Cette catégorie, nommée incapacité de défiance, s'appuie sur une distorsion dans la logique du droit des incapacités. Elle se fonde sur une dissociation entre le contractant frappé d'incapacité et celui qui a besoin d'une mesure de protection.[8] La finalité de l'incapacité de défiance n'est pas de protéger l'incapable, mais au contraire de se protéger de l'incapable. Un tel détournement de l'incapacité de contracter se justifie par l'unique recherche des effets juridiques de l'incapacité, à savoir la possibilité de remettre en cause le contrat.

Un tel procédé a pour conséquence de révéler l'existence d'une distension entre l'incapacité et la vulnérabilité du contractant.

4. Cette rupture du lien entre incapacité et vulnérabilité se vérifie aussi au sein de l'incapacité de protection. Nous avons vu que l'incapacité contractuelle s'enracine dans la présomption ou la preuve de la vulnérabilité psychologique du contractant. Cette vulnérabilité, qui fait obstacle à la liberté de contracter de l'individu, rend nécessaire, à des fins de protection, la limitation de la capacité contractuelle de celui-ci. Mais la théorie des incapacités peut générer un décalage entre l'incapacité de

[6] Art 1124 du Code civil: Sont incapables de contracter, dans la mesure définie par la loi:

Les mineurs non émancipés;

Les majeurs protégés au sens de l'art 488 du présent code.

[7] Art 489 al 1 du Code civil: Pour faire un acte valable, il faut être sain d'esprit. Mais c'est à ceux qui agissent en nullité pour cette cause de prouver l'existence d'un trouble mental au moment de l'acte.

[8] M Fabre-Magnan, *Les obligations* (PUF Thémis collection droit privé, 2000) 2645, § 102; P Malaurie and L Aynes, *'Droit civil: Les personnes, les incapacités' par P Malaurie* (Defrénois, Collection droit civil, 2004) 213 § 507.

droit et la capacité de fait[9] du contractant. Une telle réduction injustifiée de l'exercice de droits contrevient alors à la dignité humaine du contractant.[10]

Aussi est-il possible de constater que certaines mesures d'assouplissement dans le droit des incapacités contractuelles ont été adoptées. Ainsi, une distinction fondée sur la gravité de l'acte juridique s'est développée. Les incapables peuvent conclure valablement certains contrats en application de la théorie des actes de la vie courante.[11] La validité d'actes relatifs à la personne et conclus par un incapable est également reconnue si la preuve du discernement de l'individu au moment de la conclusion de l'acte peut être rapportée.[12]

De manière générale, la réforme du droit des majeurs protégés démontre l'étiolement du lien entre l'incapacité et l'idée de protection. La protection du contractant peut aussi se faire par un soutien de la capacité contractuelle.[13]

5. C'est pourquoi l'équation entre l'incapacité et la protection du contractant n'est plus vérifiable. Il semble désormais possible de protéger le contractant vulnérable sans le rendre incapable de contracter. L'essor de la notion de capacité dans les contrats est ainsi assuré par le rôle qui peut lui être attribuée dans la protection de la partie faible au contrat.

Le développement de la notion capacité contractuelle peut être recherché dans les différents types de contrats où la vulnérabilité d'une partie au contrat est inhérente à la relation contractuelle. Le développement de la notion de capacité dans les contrats est ainsi assuré par le rôle qui peut être confiée à cette notion dans la protection de la partie faible au contrat.

Le contractant est ainsi vulnérable dans ses relations de consommation. Il l'est aussi en tant qu'acteur de production. Nous examinerons donc l'émergence de deux nouvelles acceptions de la

9 F Betaillole-Gonthier, 'La capacité naturelle', Thèse, Bordeaux IV (1999).

10 E Paillet, 'La dignité de la personne majeure protégée' in *Mélanges C Bolze, Ethique, droit et dignité* (Economica, 1999) 283–99.

11 JC Montanier, 'Les actes de la vie courante en matière d'incapacité' (1982) I *JCP* 3076; P Conte et JC Montanier, 'Les actes patrimoniaux du mineur non émancipé' (1986) *JCP* éd N Doctrine 401; J Stoufflet, 'L'activité juridique du mineur non émancipé' in *Mélanges P Voirin* (LGDJ, 1967) 782 s.

12 Par le biais de l'intégration de normes internationales conclues par la France, la notion de discernement s'est développée dans notre législation. Ainsi les arts 388–1 et 388–2 du Code civil, depuis la loi du 8 janvier 1993 reprend la condition de discernement pour que l'enfant soit auditionné par le juge lors des procédures qui le concerne. Notons que cette nouvelle rédaction est en fait une transposition de l'art 2 de la Convention internationale sur les droits de l'enfant de New York en date du 20 novembre 1989: 'Les Etats parties garantissent à l'enfant qui est capable de discernement le droit d'exprimer librement son opinion sur toute question l'intéressant'.

13 T Fossier, 'L'objectif de la réforme du droit des incapacités: protéger sans jamais diminuer' (2005) n° 38076 *Defrénois* 3; JM Plazy, 'La réforme du droit des majeurs protégés annoncée' [2005] *Revue Lamy droit civil* 29.

capacité dans les contrats: la capacité financière et la capacité professionnelle.

L'ÉMERGENCE DE LA NOTION DE CAPACITÉ FINANCIÈRE DANS LES CONTRATS

6. Dans notre société de consommation, acquérir ne constitue plus une simple satisfaction des besoins mais participe de la réussite de l'individu dans la société.[14] Consommer est un facteur d'intégration sociale. Afin d'accroître cette aptitude à consommer, notre société a développé des techniques d'anticipation de revenus qui prennent la forme de crédits ou de cautionnement. Ces techniques provoquent un endettement.[15] Si l'endettement n'est pas mauvais en soi, il le devient lorsque le contractant (qu'il soit emprunteur ou caution) ne peut plus faire face à ses dettes. On parle alors d'endettement excessif. Cet endettement excessif est en fait le résultat d'une mauvaise évaluation de la solvabilité du contractant, (c'est-à-dire de l'actif) ou la conséquence d'une mauvaise appréciation du montant de l'endettement (c'est-à-dire du passif). La capacité financière peut dès lors se définir comme le point d'équilibre entre la solvabilité et l'endettement du contractant. Si l'équilibre est rompu, le contractant est en situation d'endettement excessif. En d'autres termes, il est incapable financièrement.

La détresse financière dans laquelle se trouve plongé le contractant incapable de faire face à ses dettes a nécessité la mise en place de certaines mesures de traitement.

7. Ces mesures de traitement de l'endettement excessif se révèlent inefficaces (A). Le recours à la notion de capacité financière semble présenter un intérêt dans cette lutte contre l'endettement excessif (B).

L'inefficacité des mesures traditionnelles de traitement de l'endettement excessif

8. C'est dans le droit des obligations que des solutions pour combattre l'endettement excessif ont été recherchées. Ces solutions se sont fondées d'une part sur la contestation de la validité du contrat constitutif d'un endettement excessif. La seconde voie empruntée par le droit positif a consisté à traiter l'endettement excessif qui empêche l'exécution du contrat.

[14] T Revet, 'L'argent et la personne' in *Archives de philosophie du droit, Tome 42. L'argent et le droit* (Paris, Sirey, 1998) 43.

[15] B Oppetit, 'L'endettement et le droit' in *Mélanges en hommage à A Breton et F Derrida* (Dalloz, 1991) 307.

Quant à la remise en cause de la validité du contrat

9. Avec plus ou moins de réussites, des tentatives de contestation de la validité du contrat qui génère un endettement trop important ont été lancées. La théorie des vices du consentement est la méthode la plus élémentaire pour se dégager du contrat. C'est pourquoi certains contractants ont invoqué une mauvaise appréciation de la situation financière pour contester l'intégrité de leur consentement. La jurisprudence relative aux problèmes d'intégrité du consentement pour la caution fournit une parfaite illustration des problèmes de mise en œuvre de la théorie des vices du consentement en matière d'endettement excessif.[16]

10. En ce qui concerne le vice de l'erreur, la jurisprudence a notamment tenté d'appliquer l'article 1110 du Code civil pour anéantir certains contrats de cautionnement. Comme pour toute erreur, la caution doit rapporter la preuve d'une inadéquation entre la croyance qu'il avait au moment de la conclusion du contrat et la réalité.[17]

La caution peut invoquer une erreur sur sa propre solvabilité pour obtenir la nullité de son contrat de cautionnement.

Elle peut aussi affirmer que la solvabilité de l'emprunteur constitue une qualité essentielle et déterminante de son consentement à la conclusion du contrat de cautionnement.

Comme pour toute erreur vice du consentement, la caution doit prouver que l'erreur sur sa solvabilité, ou l'erreur sur la solvabilité de l'emprunteur a été déterminante, que c'est une erreur commune et qu'elle présente un caractère excusable.

Face à la complexité des preuves à rapporter, l'erreur sur la solvabilité ne permet qu'exceptionnellement la remise en cause du contrat.

11. C'est pourquoi certaines cautions ont tenté de démontrer que leur mauvaise appréciation de la situation financière résultait d'une erreur provoquée, c'est-à-dire d'un dol.

L'erreur peut être provoquée par des manœuvres frauduleuses, telles que des mensonges, ou par une réticence d'information.[18] L'application stricte des conditions énoncées à l'article 1116 du Code civil en matière de cautionnement a pour conséquence de rendre inefficace la théorie du dol dans le traitement de l'endettement excessif. C'est pourquoi, les juges ont tenté d'assouplir les différentes conditions du dol dans cette matière.

La première tentative d'assouplissement des conditions du dol a consisté à étendre le domaine de la réticence dolosive. La gravité de

16 D Garez, 'Les vices du consentement de la caution' [2001] *Gaz Pal* doctrine 1044–46.

17 Y Picod, 'L'erreur de la caution sur la solvabilité du débiteur, prise en considération' *D* 2003, somm comm 1617–18.

18 P Chauvel, 'Cautionnement et réticence du banquier' in *Mélanges en l'honneur de J Stoufflet* (PU Clermont-Ferrand, LGDJ, 2001) 33–49.

l'information passée sous silence s'est atténuée. A l'origine seule une réticence dolosive quant à la situation irrémédiablement compromise pouvait donnait lieu à l'annulation du contrat de cautionnement sur le fondement de l'article 1116 du Code civil. Puis la jurisprudence a admis que le silence sur la situation désastreuse, ou encore sur la simple situation obérée pouvait être analysée comme une réticence dolosive.[19]

Le deuxième axe d'extension de la théorie du dol porte sur le caractère excusable de la non connaissance de l'information pour la caution. Alors que la jurisprudence opposait à la caution le fait qu'elle connaisse ou qu'elle aurait pu connaître la situation d'insolvabilité de l'emprunteur compte tenu leur relation, les juges ont affirmé que la réticence dolosive rend toujours excusable l'erreur provoquée.[20]

Le dernier assouplissement des conditions du dol aurait pu résider dans une nouvelle définition des personnes pouvant être l'auteur de la réticence ou des manœuvres frauduleuses. Il serait ainsi possible de considérer que le dol émanant de l'emprunteur, tiers au contrat de cautionnement, puisse entraîner la nullité de ce contrat. Toutefois, la Cour de cassation a réaffirmé récemment que seul le dol émanant du cocontractant peut être source de nullité du contrat.[21]

12. Pour conclure, on doit considérer que la théorie des vices du consentement strictement appliquée ne peut être efficacement mise en œuvre pour régler les problèmes d'endettement excessif.

Le traitement des situations d'endettement excessif en cas d'inexécution du contrat

13. L'analyse des techniques juridiques mobilisées pour enrayer l'endettement excessif nuisible à la bonne exécution du contrat, révèle une absence de cohérence dans le droit positif, du fait de l'éparpillement de la règle juridique.

14. Il existe ainsi en matière de contrat de crédit et ou de contrat de cautionnement une véritable concurrence entre les dispositions du Code civil et celles du Code de la consommation. Pour le contrat de prêt comme pour le contrat de crédit les dispositions du droit civil ont été complétées par le droit de la consommation. L'emprunteur comme la caution voient le régime juridique applicable à leurs relations contractuelles modifiées avec leur qualification de consommateur et celle de professionnel de leur contractant.

[19] Cass civ 1, 10 mai 1989, JCP éd G 1989, II, 21363, n° 7 et 8, n Legeais.

[20] Cass civ 3, 21 février 2001, Bull civ 3, n° 20, p 17; D 2001, p 2702, n Mazeaud; JCP éd G 2002, II, 10027, n Jamin; RTD civ 2002, p 353, obs Mestre et Fages.

[21] Cass com 13 novembre 2002, D 2003, jurisp, p 684–87, n Roman.

15. Pour ce qui est de la législation portant sur le contrat de prêt, aucune règle ne prévoit le problème d'insolvabilité de l'emprunteur. La protection mise en place par le droit de la consommation s'appuie pour sa part sur le formalisme informationnel. Cette législation considère qu'un consommateur parfaitement informé ne saurait s'engager dans une relation contractuelle qui le mène à un endettement excessif.

La place de la solvabilité dans les mesures encadrant le contrat de cautionnement semble plus précise. Mais si le Code civil s'intéresse à la solvabilité de la caution, ce n'est que dans le but de protéger le créancier en lui ménageant une garantie efficace.[22] L'objectif du Code de la consommation est au contraire de s'intéresser à la solvabilité de la caution afin d'empêcher que celle-ci ne contracte un engagement excessif ou qu'elle ne puisse se défaire d'un engagement excessif.

Alors que la situation financière de la caution est prise en compte dans le contrat de cautionnement, aucune allusion n'y est faite pour l'emprunteur dans le contrat de crédit. C'est donc la juge qui a tenté de combler les interstices laissés par le législateur.

16. L'emprunt et le cautionnement sont sources de risques potentiels pour ceux qui les souscrivent. L'exigence de protection s'impose donc pour les emprunteurs et la caution. La jurisprudence a exploité deux fondements destinés à contrecarrer les effets de l'endettement excessif.

Pour contrebalancer la supériorité économique et informationnelle du créancier prêteur, les juges ont décidé de rééquilibrer le contrat par un renforcement des obligations de celui-ci. La découverte par les juges d'un devoir de conseil à la charge du créancier prêteur permet de limiter les effets du contrat lorsque celui-ci provoque un endettement excessif pour l'emprunteur ou la caution.[23] Ainsi, selon les juges, si un emprunteur potentiel ou une caution a pu conclure un contrat qui provoque un endettement excessif c'est que son contractant (un banquier en général) n'a pas remplit son devoir d'information. Ce devoir de conseil oblige non seulement le banquier à transmettre des informations à son client mais aussi à l'orienter vers un choix favorable pour ce dernier, y compris si c'est de renoncer à conclure le contrat.[24]

Le constat d'un endettement excessif est analysé par le juge comme la preuve du manquement à son devoir de conseil du banquier,

[22] Art 2018 du Code civil: Le débiteur obligé à fournir une caution doit en présenter une qui ait la capacité de contracter, qui ait un bien suffisant pour répondre de l'objet de l'obligation, et dont le domicile soit dans le ressort de la cour royale [cour d'appel] où elle est donnée.

[23] D Legeais, 'L'obligation de conseil de l'établissement de crédit à l'égard de l'emprunteur et de sa caution' in *Droit bancaire et financie: Mélanges AEDBF-France II* (éd Banque, 1999) 257–70.

[24] M Fabre-Magnan, *'De l'obligation d'information dans les contrats. Essai d'une théorie', Préface de J Ghestin* (éd LGDJ, collection Bibliothèque de droit privé Tome 221, 1992) 385 § 471.

manquement de nature à déclencher la responsabilité de celui-ci.[25] Si ce fondement juridique est efficace pour traiter l'endettement excessif subi par un emprunteur ou une caution ayant la qualité de consommateur, en dehors d'un rapport contractuel entre consommateur et professionnel sa mise en œuvre semble plus délicate. Les juges ont donc recherché un fondement juridique susceptible de traiter de manière globale le problème de l'endettement excessif.

17. Les juges ont tenté de combattre le principe même de déséquilibre contractuel en instaurant un principe de proportionnalité dans le cadre de l'opération d'endettement. Ce principe, qui est apparu dans l'article L 313-10 du Code de la consommation, fait obstacle à l'exécution du contrat de cautionnement si celui-ci constitue un engagement disproportionné et qu'il a été conclu entre une personne physique et un banquier, c'est-à-dire un professionnel.[26] Le principe de proportionnalité a été généralisé à toutes les cautions par la Cour de cassation avec l'arrêt Macron.[27] Après quelques hésitations de la jurisprudence quant au domaine d'application du principe de proportionnalité,[28] c'est finalement le législateur qui a réaffirmé toute l'étendue de ce principe dans la loi Dutreil.[29] Le droit de la consommation est ainsi devenu le droit commun du contrat de cautionnement. Cette généralisation du principe de proportionnalité en droit interne forme également un écho du droit communautaire. La Commission européenne a, le 11 septembre 2002, validé l'article 9 de la

[25] Cass civ 1, 27 juin 1995, Bull civ 1, n° 287, p 200; RTD civ 1996, p 385, obs Mestre; D 1995, p 621, n Piedelièvre: 'La présentation d'une offre préalable conforme aux exigences de l'art 5 de la loi du 13 juillet 1979 ne dispense pas l'établissement de crédit de son devoir de conseil à l'égard de l'emprunteur'.

[26] Art L 313-10 Code de la consommation: Un établissement de crédit ne peut se prévaloir d'un contrat de cautionnement d'une opération de crédit relevant du chapitre Ier ou II du présent titre, conclu par une personne physique dont l'engagement était, lors de sa conclusion, manifestement disproportionné à ses biens et revenus, à moins que le patrimoine de cette caution, au moment où celle-ci est appelée, ne lui permette de faire face à son obligation.

[27] Cass com 17 juin 1997, Bull civ 4, n° 188, p 165; RTD civ 1998, p 100 et 157, obs Mestre et Crocq; JCP éd G 1998, I, 103, n° 8, obs Simler; D 1998, jurisp, p 208, n Casey.

[28] C'est notamment l'arrêt Nahoum rendu par la Cour de cassation en 2002 qui a semblé limiter le champ d'application du principe de proportionnalité en rejetant l'application de ce principe pour les cautions intégrée (caution appartenant à l'entreprise cautionnée): Cass com 8 octobre 2002, Bull civ 4, n° 136, p 152; RTD civ 2003, p 125, obs Crocq; D 2003, jurisp, p 414, n Koering; JCP éd G, 2003, II, 10017, n Picod. Voir aussi: D Bakouche, 'La proportionnalité dans le cautionnement à l'épreuve de la loi et de la jurisprudence (2004) 5 *Contrats-conc-consom* 7; F Guerchoun, 'Le principe de proportionnalité en matière de cautionnement' (2004) 72 *LPA* 12.

[29] Art L 341-4 du Code de la consommation: Un créancier ne peut se prévaloir d'un contrat de cautionnement conclu par une personne physique dont l'engagement était, lors de sa conclusion, manifestement disproportionné à ses biens et revenus, à moins que le patrimoine de cette caution, au moment où celle-ci est appelée, ne lui permette de faire face à ses obligations.

Proposition de Directive relative aux crédits à la consommation qui adopte en la matière le principe de proportionnalité.[30]

18. Cette généralisation du recours au principe de proportionnalité ne saurait effacer toutes les incertitudes de la matière. Non seulement le principe de proportionnalité interroge quant à l'efficacité du cautionnement, mais il ne règle pas les problèmes de variations de sanctions en matière d'endettement excessif.[31] L'absence de cohérence dans le traitement de l'endettement excessif nécessite la recherche d'un régime juridique cohérent qui assure la sécurité juridique. La notion de capacité semble constituer un support intéressant.

L'intérêt de la notion de capacité financière dans la lutte contre l'endettement excessif

19. La capacité financière est une expression qui a parfois été utilisée par certains membres de la doctrine française.[32] Elle fait également partie de la terminologie employée par les juges de la Cour de cassation.[33] Les apports de cette notion dans le traitement de l'endettement excessif doivent être recherchés.

20. La définition de la capacité financière d'un contractant suppose la connaissance de l'actif comme du passif de cet individu. Afin de réduire les risques d'endettement excessif, les techniques ayant pour but de prévenir l'excès se sont multipliées.

La prévention du risque d'endettement excessif peut se faire notamment par une meilleure connaissance de la solvabilité (c'est-à-dire de l'actif) du contractant.

21. Le banquier français a mis en place à cet effet un ensemble d'outils qui se révèlent critiquables et peu fiables.[34] L'objectif de ces instruments est

30 Art 9 de la Proposition de directive COM(2002) 443: 'Lorsque le prêteur conclut un contrat de crédit ou de sûreté ou augmente le montant total du crédit ou du montant garanti, il est censé avoir estimé préalablement, par tout moyen à sa disposition, que le consommateur et, le cas échéant, le garant seront raisonnablement à même de respecter leurs obligations découlant du contrat'.

31 La formulation proposée par l'art L 313-10 du Code de la consommation n'identifie pas clairement la sanction encourue en cas de disproportion. La doctrine a proposé une multitude de sanctions: nullité du contrat, rescision pour lésion, inopposabilité du contrat, caducité de l'obligation de la caution, déchéance. La jurisprudence préfère accorder des dommages intérêts à la caution en considérant que le préjudice né de l'excès de l'endettement pour la caution est consécutif d'une faute.

32 JL Rives Lange et M Contamine-Raynaud, *Droit bancaire* (Précis Dalloz, 6ème éd, 1995) 670, note 3; A Piedelievre, 'Les modifications apportées à certains cautionnements par la loi du 31 décembre 1989' (1990) 1 *Gazette du Palais* 158.

33 Cass Civ 1, 10 mai 2005, pourvoi n° 03–14446, RLDC juillet-août 2005, n° 741, p 35–36.

34 MC Barret Barney, 'Les différents systèmes d'enregistrement des crédits dans les Etats membres de l'Union européenne' [2003] *D aff* 1082.

de sélectionner parmi les candidats à l'emprunt ou au cautionnement ceux qui présentent le maximum de garanties financières.

L'évaluation du risque d'endettement se fait par la centralisation des renseignements dans des fichiers. Certains de ces fichiers sont dits 'négatifs' car ils ne retracent que les incidents de paiements. D'autres fichiers dits 'positifs' constituent un répertoire de l'ensemble des crédits en cours. Ces fichiers donnent une information sur le passif réel du contractant mais ne donnent aucun élément d'appréciation quant à la solvabilité du candidat à l'emprunt.

C'est pourquoi une seconde méthode, dite de 'crédit *scoring*', a été développée par les banques. Il s'agit d'une analyse statistique des informations délivrées par le candidat sur demande de la banque. Ces différentes informations sont traitées par un logiciel qui délivre une appréciation de la capacité financière du candidat sous la forme d'un coefficient de garanties de remboursement du candidat.

Ces différentes méthodes d'évaluation des risques d'endettement ne remplissent pas leur objectif. Les fichiers ne présentent qu'une information parcellaire et le crédit scoring ne permet pas de donner une image réelle de la capacité financière du candidat.

22. Pourtant les tentatives de prévention de l'endettement excessif par une évaluation des risques semblent relancer par le droit communautaire. L'Union européenne qui poursuit une politique de développement des mesures de prévention face au surendettement, a énoncé dans un projet de Directive européenne certaines mesures destinées à réduire les dangers d'incidents de paiements.[35] Ces mesures renforcent le contrôle de la capacité financière du consommateur au moment de la conclusion d'un prêt, sont regroupées dans le principe du prêt responsable.[36] Elles mettent à la charge du banquier un certain nombre d'obligations destinées à vérifier la capacité financière réelle du candidat à l'emprunt. Placée au cœur du dispositif de prévention des risques d'endettement excessif, la notion de capacité financière améliore l'efficacité des mécanismes de prévention, en offrant une représentation fidèle de la situation financière de l'emprunteur.

23. La notion de capacité financière constitue également une solution dans le traitement de l'endettement excessif. La capacité financière peut se définir comme l'aptitude qu'a un individu à exercer des droits pécuniaires compte tenu de ce dont il dispose et de ce qu'il peut avoir avec ce qu'il a. Cette capacité s'analyse comme un rapport évolutif entre l'actif et le passif du patrimoine d'un contractant. Lorsqu'un contractant

[35] Proposition de directive du 11 septembre 2002 en matière de consommation en matière de crédit à la consommation, JOCE C 331 E/222 du 31 décembre 2002

[36] B Stauder, 'Le prêt responsable' *in Etudes de droit de la consommation, Liber amirocum Jean Calais-Auloy* (éd Dalloz, 2004) 1029–47.

ne peut plus faire face à ses obligations pécuniaires au moyen de son actif, il doit être considéré comme incapable financièrement. Seul le caractère excessif de l'endettement génère une situation d'incapacité financière. C'est pourquoi la réduction pour excès semble être la technique juridique la plus adéquate au traitement de l'excessivité de l'endettement.

24. Il convient pour terminer cette étude de la capacité financière de rendre compte des conséquences de l'admission de cette nouvelle acception sur la définition de la capacité dans les contrats. Nous avons constaté qu'en droit civil ce qui justifie la mise en place d'une incapacité contractuelle, c'est la nécessité de protéger un contractant vulnérable compte tenu sa faiblesse psychologique. Cette définition de l'incapable, partie vulnérable dans sa relation contractuelle, permet d'envisager d'intégrer dans la définition de l'incapable celui souffrant de vulnérabilité économique, tel que l'endetté. Mais nous avons également constaté que la protection du contractant vulnérable peut se faire en terme de soutien de ses capacités plutôt qu'en terme d'incapacité. Dès lors la notion de capacité contractuelle semble offrir un cadre juridique intéressant pour la mise en place de mesures de protection destinées au contractant vulnérable. La vulnérabilité du contractant se vérifie également lorsqu'il produit, c'est-à-dire lorsqu'il travaille. C'est pourquoi il nous faut à présent étudier le développement de la notion de capacité professionnelle dans le contrat de travail.

LE DÉVELOPPEMENT DE LA NOTION DE CAPACITÉ PROFESSIONNELLE DANS LE CONTRAT DE TRAVAIL

25. En tant qu'acteur de production le salarié se trouve en situation de vulnérabilité dans la relation contractuelle qu'il partage avec son employeur. La législation travailliste s'est construite autour de la nécessité de protéger le travailleur puisque celui-ci est soumis, dans le cadre de son contrat de travail, à un lien de subordination qui fait de lui une partie faible au contrat. L'origine de la faiblesse du travailleur s'est modifiée et la législation du travail a dû évoluer, notamment en adaptant sa terminologie.

Il convient de déterminer comment est apparue la notion de capacité professionnelle avant d'en établir les effets normatifs.

L'apparition de la notion de capacité professionnelle dans le droit positif

26. Avant de rendre compte de l'apparition de la notion de capacité

professionnelle dans notre législation nationale et dans la législation communautaire, il convient d'étudier le contexte qui a permis l'émergence de cette nouvelle notion.

Le contexte d'émergence

27. La nécessité de faire appel à une nouvelle notion est directement liée aux nombreuses évolutions que le droit social doit intégrer. C'est en premier lieu le marché du travail qui a connu ces dernières années de profondes mutations.[37] La mondialisation, les délocalisations qui en résultent, ainsi que les différentes révolutions technologiques, ont modifié les secteurs d'activités aujourd'hui porteurs d'emplois en France. Et le développement d'un chômage structurel et durable a fait disparaître l'idée de plein emploi. Ce sont également les relations de travail qui se sont modifiées. La subordination, élément caractéristique de la relation contractuelle unissant l'employeur à son salarié, a changé de nature. Ce n'est plus la manière dont est exécuté le travail qui lie le salarié à son employeur mais la seule atteinte d'objectifs. Enfin, c'est la place du travail dans la vie des hommes qui s'est modifiée. A l'origine simple moyen d'acquisition de revenus, le travail est désormais aussi perçu comme un instrument d'intégration sociale compte tenu du caractère structurant qu'il présente pour chacun.[38]

28. Face à l'ensemble de ces mutations, la législation du travail a vu son objet évoluer. A l'origine le droit du travail est né de l'exigence de protéger l'intégrité physique des travailleurs. Face aux risques physiques encourus par le salarié lors de l'exécution de son contrat de travail, le législateur a institué, à la charge de l'employeur, l'obligation de respecter un certain nombre de mesures d'hygiène et de sécurité. A cette sécurisation du lieu de travail s'ajoute l'exigence d'une vérification de l'aptitude physique du travailleur au moment de l'embauche et tout au long de la relation de travail.[39]

Mais au-delà de la sécurité physique, c'est aujourd'hui la sécurité professionnelle des travailleurs qui constitue l'objectif des normes travaillistes.

[37] 'La sécurité de l'emploi face aux défis des transformations économiques', Rapport n° 5 du CERC, *Bulletin social Lefèbvre*, avril 2005, 283–90.

[38] R Castel, 'Travail et utilité au monde' in A Supiot (ed), *Le travail en perspectives* (Paris, LGDJ, collection droit et société, 1998) 15–22.

[39] Art R 241–48 I al 1 du Code du travail (trav): Tout salarié fait l'objet d'un examen médical avant l'embauchage ou au plus tard avant l'expiration de la période d'essai qui suit l'embauchage. Art R 241–49 I C trav: Chaque salarié bénéficie d'examens médicaux périodiques, au moins tous les vingt-quatre mois, en vue de s'assurer du maintien de son aptitude au poste de travail occupé. Le premier de ces examens a lieu dans les vingt-quatre mois qui suivent l'examen d'embauche prévu à l'art R 241–48.

Avec la banalisation du risque de chômage, le législateur a dû mettre en place un certain nombre de mesures pérennisant la relation de travail pour celui qui en a une ou favorisant l'aptitude à trouver un travail pour celui qui en cherche un. L'ensemble de ces mesures de protection peut être rattaché à la notion de capacité professionnelle, ce qui explique son apparition dans notre législation.

L'apparition de la notion

29. La notion de capacité professionnelle se développe concomitamment dans la législation française et dans le droit communautaire.

Dans la législation française, la notion de capacité professionnelle est apparue dans certains textes qui réglementent l'accès à des professions. Ainsi l'individu qui veut exercer une activité de transports ou une profession agricole doit faire la preuve de sa capacité professionnelle.[40] La notion de capacités professionnelles, dans ce contexte, permet de sélectionner les travailleurs qui peuvent avoir accès à une profession.

Depuis le traité d'Amsterdam et le conseil de Luxembourg en novembre 1997, la politique française de l'emploi s'intègre dans le processus de coordination spécifique mis en place au sein de l'Union Européenne. La stratégie européenne de l'emploi (SEE), qui repose sur la méthode ouverte de coordination, est un mécanisme qui garantit la définition d'objectifs globaux pour l'Union européenne, notamment la prévention du chômage par le soutien de l'emploi. Ces objectifs communs sont coordonnés autour de quatre piliers, parmi lesquels on retrouve le développement des compétences et des capacités d'insertion professionnelle.

La mise en œuvre de la SEE en France peut se vérifier avec l'adoption de deux mesures significatives dans la lutte contre le chômage. Ainsi la loi ayant mis en place le Plan d'Aide au Retour à l'Emploi[41] comme celle relative à la formation tout au long de la vie[42] semblent liées à la SEE. L'utilisation de la notion de capacité professionnelle dans ces deux textes vient corroborer cette analyse.

30. De plus s'il existe un certain nombre de termes juridiques destinés à recouvrir l'ensemble des qualités professionnelles d'un travailleur, aucun

[40] Art 2 de la loi n° 95–66 du 20 janvier 1995 relative à l'accès à l'activité de conducteur et à la profession d'exploitant de taxis: 'Peuvent exercer l'activité de conducteur de taxi: 1° Les titulaires d'un certificat de capacité professionnelle délivré par le préfet'.

[41] Art 14 § 2 du Règlement du 1 janvier 2001: L'entretien approfondi est l'occasion d'apprécier le degré d'autonomie du demandeur d'emploi dans sa recherche, de procéder à un examen de l'ensemble des capacités professionnelles du salarié privé d'emploi . . .

[42] Art L 930-1 C trav: L'employeur a l'obligation d'assurer l'adaptation des salariés à leur poste de travail. Il veille au maintien de leur capacité à occuper un emploi, au regard notamment de l'évolution des emplois, des technologies et des organisations. Il peut proposer des formations qui participent au développement des compétences.

de ces termes ne semble parvenir à délimiter intégralement ces qualités. Ainsi, la notion de qualification professionnelle renvoie à une délimitation des qualités professionnelles du salarié qui correspond à un niveau de formation, ou à un niveau conventionnellement établi avec l'employeur. Que la qualification professionnelle résulte d'un diplôme ou du contrat de travail, elle est un titre juridique qui garantit la compatibilité avec un travail prescrit (et non le travail réel).[43] Cette notion faille par l'aspect désincarné et intemporel qu'elle présente des qualités professionnelles.

La notion d'aptitude professionnelle semble au contraire ancrée dans l'analyse factuelle. Sa détermination résulte d'une vérification, d'une comparaison avec, non pas le travail prescrit, mais avec les tâches réellement effectuées par le salarié sur un poste de travail défini. De ce fait, l'analyse de l'aptitude professionnelle présente un caractère circonstancié peu enclin avec la mobilité professionnelle que l'on peut connaître dans les entreprises.

Enfin c'est la notion de compétence qui permettrait l'évaluation des ressources que l'individu peut mobiliser dans sa vie professionnelle.[44] Cette notion, largement présente dans les sciences de gestion, peut se définir comme une combinaison de connaissances, de savoir-faire, expériences et comportements s'exerçant dans un contexte précis. La mesure des compétences d'un travailleur se fait ainsi au regard des fonctions que celui-ci occupe dans l'entreprise. La notion de compétence permet d'établir non seulement que le salarié exécute correctement le travail que lui a confié son employeur mais qu'il l'exécute en faisant preuve d'autonomie, et qu'il se montre performant dans l'exécution de son travail du fait d'une implication personnelle importante.[45]

Ces différentes notions ne permettent toutefois d'appréhender que certains aspects des qualités professionnelles d'un travailleur. La notion de capacité professionnelle offre l'opportunité de saisir l'ensemble des ressources qu'un individu peut mobiliser pour l'exécution d'un travail puisque c'est avant tout à la personne du travailleur et à ses qualités concrètes que l'on s'attache.

Dès lors, il est possible de reconnaître un certain nombre d'effets normatifs à cette notion.

[43] P Caillaud, 'Qualification professionnelle et valeur juridique du diplôme' in *Réfléchir la compétence. Approches sociologiques, juridiques, économiques d'une pratique gestionnaire* (Octares collection colloques, 2003) 115–28; J Yung Hing, *Aspects juridiques de la qualification professionnelle* (éd CNRS, 1986).

[44] JM Joubier, 'Compétence(s), qualification(s), un enjeu de reconnaissance' (2001) 39 *Revue CFDT* 22–26; V Wauquier, 'Construction juridique et objectivation de la compétence' in *Réfléchir la compétence. Approches sociologiques, juridiques, économiques d'une pratique gestionnaire* (Octares, collection colloques, 2003) 150.

[45] Le salarié qualifié est celui qui sait faire, le salarié compétent est celui qui arrive à faire malgré les imprévus et les manques de prescriptions.

Les effets normatifs de la notion de capacité professionnelle

31. La notion de capacité professionnelle présente un certain nombre de vertus. Elle permet en premier lieu de comprendre le renforcement des obligations mises à la charge de l'employeur par le droit positif. Elle offre également l'opportunité d'adopter un nouveau modèle dans la constitution des droits du travailleur.

Sur le développement des obligations de l'employeur

32. 'La recherche de la sécurité de l'emploi se traduit par un ensemble de règles visant à stabiliser le lien contractuel'.[46] Pour que le travailleur demeure en mesure d'exécuter son contrat de travail, il ne faut pas que son intégrité physique soit altérée. C'est pourquoi certaines des mesures qui intéressent la stabilité du lien contractuel sont axées sur la protection de l'intégrité physique des salariés.

33. Ces règles juridiques permettent de renforcer la protection des capacités physiques du travailleur. Ce renforcement s'est effectué à travers un élargissement de la définition des risques professionnels.[47] Il s'est confirmé aussi par une aggravation du degré de l'obligation de sécurité mise à la charge de l'employeur.

34. Avec les transformations du travail dans notre société post-industrielle, ce sont de nouveaux risques d'accidents ou de maladies professionnelles qui sont apparues. Aux atteintes corporelles se sont ajoutées les pathologies d'ordre psychosomatique. Ce n'est plus seulement la santé physique mais c'est aussi la santé mentale des salariés qu'il faut garantir.[48] Afin de protéger l'ensemble des capacités physiologiques du travailleur, le législateur français a, dans sa loi de modernisation sociale en date du 17 janvier 2002, adopté une définition plus large de la santé au travail. Cette définition intègre la dimension psychologique du travailleur.[49] L'employeur est désormais tenu non seulement de s'assurer du respect de l'intégrité physique de ses salariés mais il doit aussi veiller à ce qu'il ne soit pas porté atteinte à leur santé mentale.

35. C'est en fait un principe de prévention qui a été mis en place à la charge de l'employeur. Si certaines mesures de prévention date de 1976,

[46] A Supiot (ed), *Le droit du travail* (2004), n° 1268, PUF, Que sais-je? 120.

[47] M Babin, 'Le risque professionnel. Etude critique', Thèse, Nantes (2003).

[48] Sur cette nouvelle définition de la santé au travail, voir: M Bonnechere, 'Santé-sécurité dans l'entreprise et dignité de la personne au travail' [2003] *Droit Ouvrier* 453; L Lerouge, *La reconnaissance de la santé mentale en droit du travail* (LGDJ, 2005) Tome 40; N Maggi-Germain, 'Travail et santé: le point de vue d'une juriste' [2002] *Droit social* 485.

[49] Maggi-Germain, *ibid.*

c'est l'intégration de la Directive-cadre du 12 juin 1989[50] qui a doté notre législation d'un véritable principe de prévention. Celui-ci constitue le noyau dur de l'obligation de sécurité, obligation qui impose à l'employeur de protéger la santé de ses travailleurs en évaluant les risques professionnels et ceci afin de prévenir et d'éviter ces risques.[51] L'importance du devoir de prévention a pris une nouvelle dimension depuis une série d'arrêts rendu par la Cour de cassation en 2002. Ces arrêts concernaient des salariés ayant travaillé au contact de l'amiante. Pour améliorer l'indemnisation de ces travailleurs, la chambre sociale a affirmé le 28 février 2002 'qu'en vertu du contrat de travail le liant à son salarié, l'employeur est tenu envers celui-ci d'une obligation de sécurité de résultat, notamment en ce qui concerne les maladies professionnelles contractées par ce salarié du fait des produits fabriqués ou utilisés par l'entreprise'.[52] Avec l'obligation de sécurité, la Cour de cassation redessine les contours du contrat de travail pour y intégrer l'obligation pour l'employeur de soutenir les capacités physiques de ses salariés.

36. Les tentatives de stabilisation de la relation de travail ont conduit à l'adoption dans notre législation de mesures destinées à combattre les effets que le temps peut avoir sur cette relation contractuelle. La durée du contrat de travail peut entraîner un décalage entre les capacités professionnelles du salarié et les besoins de l'entreprise. Pour restreindre le droit de licencier dont dispose l'employeur, le législateur a imposé le respect par celui-ci d'un certain nombre d'obligations.

37. Ainsi l'obligation de reclassement, qui se définit comme l'action positive de l'employeur visant à maintenir la situation d'emploi d'un salarié inapte ou concerné par un projet de licenciement pour motif économique, contribue à pérenniser la relation de travail.[53] L'employeur doit rechercher au sein de l'entreprise quels sont les emplois compatibles avec les capacités professionnelles dont dispose le salarié. L'exécution de l'obligation de reclassement par l'employeur est donc entièrement liée à la détermination des capacités professionnelles du salarié.[54] L'obligation

[50] Directive-cadre n° 89/391/CEE du 12 juin 1989 relative à la protection de la santé et à la sécurité des travailleurs sur leur lieu de travail, JOCE n° L 123 du 29 juin 1989, 1 s.

[51] T Aubert-Monpeyssen and PY Verkindt, 'La protection de la santé des travailleurs: approche juridique de la notion de prévention' in *La santé du salarié, Actes des journées M Despax organisées par l'Université de Toulouse 1 (mai 1999)* (edn Dalloz, collection thèmes et commentaires, sous l'égide de la Revue juridique d'Ile-de-France, 1999) 31 s.

[52] Cass soc 28 février 2002 (onze arrêts), Bull civ V, n° 81, p. 74; *Droit social* 2002, p 445, n Lyon-Caen; JCP éd G 2002, II, 10053, conclusions Benmakhlouf; D 2002, jurisp, p 2079, n Kobina Gaba; *Droit social* 2002, p 828, n Babin et Pichon.

[53] Définition proposée par F Heas, *Le reclassement en droit du travail*, préface de A Supiot (Paris, LGDJ, 2000) Tome 28, 23, § 13.

[54] Cass soc 7 juillet 2004, Bull civ V, n° 194, p 182: Les juges de la Cour de cassation, pour constater l'illicéité d'un licenciement consécutif à une mesure de reclassement, constatent 'qu'il résultait des constatations des juges du fond que les postes proposés n'étaient pas adaptés aux capacités du salarié'.

de reclassement trouve sa source dans la subsistance de capacités professionnelles du salarié et la nécessité de valoriser celles-ci en permettant la poursuite de la relation contractuelle. Le reclassement se fait ainsi par une adaptation du choix du poste de travail aux capacités professionnelles du travailleur.

38. Mais la poursuite de la relation de travail peut également se faire grâce à une adaptation des capacités professionnelles du travailleur aux besoins de l'entreprise. Cette mise en adéquation correspond alors au devoir d'adaptation qui incombe à l'employeur ou plus largement au droit à la formation reconnue au salarié.

Avec son arrêt du 25 février 1992 la chambre sociale de la Cour de cassation a créé un nouveau devoir à la charge de l'employeur.[55] L'employeur est désormais tenu d'assurer l'adaptation du salarié à l'évolution de son emploi en lui fournissant toutes les formations nécessaires à cette fin. Le devoir d'adaptation constitue un outil de gestion des capacités professionnelles du travailleur puisqu'il permet de maintenir l'adéquation entre ces capacités et l'évolution du poste de travail. Ce devoir d'adaptation, d'origine jurisprudentielle, est devenu une obligation légale depuis la loi du 19 janvier 2000. Avec l'adoption de l'article L 930-1 du Code du travail, issu de la loi du 4 mai 2004, le législateur va au-delà du maintien de l'adéquation entre les capacités professionnelles et le poste de travail du salarié.[56] Il étend l'application de ce devoir d'adaptation à l'ensemble des postes de travail que le salarié pourrait exécuter dans l'entreprise. L'objectif n'est plus d'assurer le maintien du salarié sur son poste de travail mais de lui permettre, à l'aide des formations adéquates, de trouver un emploi dans l'entreprise.[57]

La loi du 4 mai 2004 a semblé aller encore plus loin.[58] Afin d'élargir le champ de ses capacités professionnelles en dehors du plan de formation de son entreprise, le salarié dispose de certains droits qui prennent la forme d'un congé de formation (article L 931-13 et suivants du Code du travail) ou d'un droit individuel à la formation.[59]

39. Le développement de la formation tout au long de la vie, comme l'accroissement de la prévention des risques professionnels s'inscrivent

55 Cass soc 25 février 1992, arrêt Expovit, Bull civ V, n° 122, p 74; D 1992, som com, p 294, n Lyon-Caen; *Droit social* 1992, p 379.

56 Art L 930-1 C trav, ci-dessus n 42: L'employeur a l'obligation d'assurer l'adaptation des salariés à leur poste de travail. Il veille au maintien de leur capacité à occuper un emploi, au regard notamment de l'évolution des emplois, des technologies et des organisations. Il peut proposer des formations qui participent au développement des compétences.

57 MJ Gomez-Mustel, 'Les enjeux de l'obligation d'adaptation' [2004] *Droit social* n° spécial 'Le nouveau droit de la formation', 499.

58 *Ibid.*

59 Art L 933-1 C trav: Tout salarié titulaire d'un contrat de travail à durée indéterminée . . . disposant d'une ancienneté d'au moins un an dans l'entreprise qui l'emploie, bénéficie chaque année d'un droit individuel à la formation d'une durée de vingt heures . . .

dans une même politique de soutien des capacités professionnelles. Les préoccupations de la législation travailliste sont axées tout autant sur la sécurité professionnelle que sur la simple sécurité physique du travailleur. La notion de capacité professionnelle se place au cœur de ce mouvement d'extension des préoccupations de la législation travailliste.

Il est ainsi possible d'associer l'employeur au soutien des capacités professionnelles de ses salariés afin de pérenniser leur relation de travail. L'employeur est également mis à contribution dans le maintien d'un fort degré de professionnalité des travailleurs, et ceci afin de réduire les risques de chômage de ces derniers.

Le travailleur salarié peut donc s'appuyer sur son contrat de travail pour solliciter un soutien de ses capacités professionnelles par le biais du renforcement des obligations de son employeur. Mais cette politique de soutien des capacités professionnelles doit dépasser la seule relation contractuelle pour concerner l'ensemble des travailleurs, y compris ceux qui n'ont pas d'emploi salarié. C'est pourquoi la notion de capacité professionnelle peut être utilisée comme assise pour une nouvelle constitution des droits du travailleur.

Dans la constitution des droits du travailleur

40. Avant de rendre compte des opportunités offertes par la notion de capacité professionnelle dans la constitution des droits sociaux, il convient de faire un rapide état des lieux du modèle actuel de constitution des droits sociaux.

a. Le modèle actuel de constitution des droits sociaux

41. Afin de comprendre le modèle actuel de constitution des droits du travailleur, il nous faut rendre compte du contexte de son émergence, du cadre légal qu'il procure ainsi que des politiques sociales que produit ce modèle.

42. C'est dans la société industrielle du XIXème siècle que s'est développé le modèle de constitutions des droits sociaux que nous connaissons encore aujourd'hui. Le paysage industriel se caractérise par l'existence de grandes entreprises produisant en masse grâce à une organisation pyramidale du travail et une spécialisation des tâches. Dans ce contexte, le travail prend la forme d'un emploi salarié à vie et à temps plein. La relation de travail se définit essentiellement par un fort lien de subordination: l'employeur contrôle non seulement les résultats de ses salariés mais aussi les moyens que ceux-ci mettent en oeuvre. Les caractéristiques de ce modèle d'entreprise ont une influence directe sur le droit du travail.

43. Le droit du travail, dans un tel système, se fonde sur une définition étroite du travail. Celui-ci correspond à un bien marchand. Il est l'objet du contrat de travail. Le contrat de travail prend la forme d'un contrat à durée indéterminée et constitue l'accès aux droits sociaux pour le travailleur. En effet, le lien de subordination, apanage de la relation de travail, est analysé comme le fondement d'une contrepartie entre l'employeur et son salarié. Le salarié accepte de se soumettre à son employeur en échange de la sécurité que celui-ci lui assure. Tous les travailleurs obtiennent les mêmes droits sociaux. Le contrat de travail donne ainsi accès à un véritable statut professionnel.

44. Les politiques sociales qui s'inscrivent dans ce modèle font du travailleur un simple matériel humain au service du développement du marché. De ce fait, l'objectif des politiques d'employabilités est d'adapter les hommes aux besoins du marché. C'est la croissance du marché qui justifie ou limite le développement des ressources humaines dans les entreprises. Un certain nombre de conséquences politiques peuvent être déduites. En premier lieu, au nom de la flexibilité des marchés, la remise en cause du contrat de travail à durée indéterminée est inéluctable. De plus l'augmentation des profits passe par une diminution des coûts du travail. Enfin, le travailleur doit assurer lui-même sa pérennité sur le marché du travail en s'adaptant à ce marché, c'est-à-dire en assurant son employabilité.[60]

Les solutions proposées par les politiques d'employabilités pour lutter contre le chômage sont également radicales. Ces politiques laissent aux collectivités la charge de supporter le prix de l'exclusion du marché du travail.

Il est ainsi possible de conclure que l'échec de ce modèle de constitution des droits sociaux est inévitable. L'emploi continu, fondation du statut professionnel est en plein déclin. Et les méthodes de traitement du chômage n'ont généré que plus d'exclusion sociale. C'est pourquoi il semble nécessaire d'élaborer un nouveau modèle de constitution des droits sociaux.

b. Un nouveau modèle de constitution des droits sociaux

45. Face aux pressions de la concurrence des marchés, au progrès technique, à l'évolution générale des qualifications professionnelles, le

[60] B Gazier, 'L'employabilité' in J Allouche *et al* (éd), *Encyclopédie des resources humaines* (Vuibert, 2003) 418: 'Entendue comme l'aptitude à obtenir ou à conserver un emploi normal, c'est-à-dire non protégé, l'employabilité a en effet souvent focalisé l'attention de ses utilisateurs sur les aptitudes et motivations individuelles, semblant exonérer les autres acteurs du marché du travail, et en particulier les entreprises, de toute responsabilité en matière d'accès à l'emploi ou encore de qualité d'emploi'; J Igalens, 'Les transitions de carrière: de la responsabilité à l'égard de l'emploi à la responsabilité à l'égard de l'employabilité' in J Igalens (ed), *Tous responsables* (D'Organisation, 2004) 291–303.

modèle de la relation de travail a évolué.[61] Le statut professionnel offert en contrepartie de la subordination du travailleur est remis en cause avec d'une part l'autonomisation des travailleurs et d'autre part la précarisation de la relation de travail.[62] Le modèle de l'emploi salarié est en recul. Il entraîne dans sa chute la sécurité des travailleurs avec une remise en cause pour le travailleur de ses droits sociaux. Il est nécessaire d'inventer un nouveau modèle dans la constitution de ces droits.

46. La voie semble ouverte si l'on adopte une définition du travail qui ne comprend pas seulement l'emploi salarié mais toutes les formes de travail. Le travail ne se définit plus alors comme une simple marchandise mais reflète également l'expression de la personne du travailleur.[63] La constitution des droits sociaux n'est pas liée à l'existence d'une situation d'emploi mais est rattachée à la personne du travailleur.[64] A la construction des droits sociaux engendrés par une situation d'emploi, fait place la reconnaissance des droits attachés à la personne du travailleur, et plus précisément au développement de son état professionnel. Ce nouveau modèle de constitution des droits sociaux permet d'envisager une continuité dans l'existence des droits comme il existe une continuité de la vie professionnelle, en dehors de toute situation d'emploi salarié.[65] Il est également à l'origine du développement de nouveaux droits, les droits de tirages sociaux, qui autorisent l'anticipation et la mobilité professionnelle.[66] Ainsi chaque travailleur, en fonction de son parcours professionnel, constitue ses propres droits sociaux.

47. Les politiques sociales qui en résultent sont orientées vers le développement humain. Dans cette optique c'est le développement des richesses humaines qui assure le développement du marché.[67] Ces richesses humaines représentent l'ensemble des qualités humaines qu'un individu peut mobiliser dans le cadre de son activité professionnelle, c'est-à-dire ses capacités professionnelles. Dès lors, les politiques sociales contribuent à un soutien des capacités professionnelles des travailleurs.

[61] R Salais, 'Liberté du travail et capacités: une perspective pour la construction européenne?' [1999] *Droit social* 467.

[62] C Ramaux, 'L'instabilité de l'emploi est-elle une fatalité? Une lecture économique critique du rapport Boissonnat et du rapport Supiot et des travaux sur les marchés transitionnels' [2000] *Droit social* 66; G Schmid, 'Le plein emploi est-il encore possible? Les marchés du travail "transitoires" en tant que nouvelle stratégie dans les politiques d'emploi' (1995) n° 65 *Travail et Emploi* 5.

[63] A Supiot, 'Le travail, liberté partagée' [1993] *Droit social* 715; A Supiot, 'Du bon usage des lois en matière d'emploi' [1997] *Droit social* 229.

[64] R Castel, 'Droit du travail: redéploiement ou refondation?' [1999] *Droit social* 438.

[65] F Favennec-Hery, 'Travail et formation: une frontière qui s'estompe' in A Supiot (ed), *Le travail en perspectives* (Paris, LGDJ, 1998) 475–85.

[66] A Supiot, 'Transformations du droit du travail et devenir du droit du travail: une prospective européenne' (1999) 138 *Revue Internationale du Travail* 33; A Supiot, 'Droit du travail: un horizon pour l'action' (2000) n° 30 *Revue CFDT* 3.

[67] A Supiot, 'Lectures étrangères sur le devenir du droit social' [2005] *Droit social* 1003.

Ce soutien des capacités passe notamment par une formation tout au long de la vie.

De la même manière la politique de lutte contre le chômage repose sur un soutien des capacités professionnelles du demandeur d'emploi. En mettant le chômeur en position de retrouver un travail, la politique de soutien des capacités constitue une politique de lutte contre l'exclusion. Elle participe de la valorisation de chaque individu au sein de la société.

48. La notion de capacité professionnelle semble ainsi promise à un bel avenir. Elle offre une base dans l'évolution de la législation travailliste compte tenu des transformations du marché du travail à venir. Ces modifications du marché du travail en France intéressent en premier lieu les acteurs, c'est-à-dire les travailleurs. L'augmentation de la durée de cotisations va conduire à l'augmentation des salariés sexagénaires, salariés plus vulnérables physiquement.[68] Leur maintien sur le marché du travail ne peut se faire que dans le cadre d'une politique de soutien de leurs capacités professionnelles.

Les mouvements de délocalisations amorcés depuis quelques années amènent également à penser que des mutations sont à envisager concernant la nature des emplois en France. Le nombre des emplois peu qualifiés va s'amenuiser. Les emplois en France sont amenés à devenir de plus en plus techniques et le besoin de formation tout au long de la vie devrait ainsi s'amplifier.

CONCLUSION

49. Mettre en avant la notion de capacité, que ce soit dans le domaine financier ou professionnel, c'est offrir la possibilité de stigmatiser les situations de vulnérabilité du contractant, situations susceptibles de le conduire à l'exclusion sociale.

Cette révélation des différentes facettes de la vulnérabilité doit s'accompagner de la mise en place de mesures de protection du contractant en situation de faiblesse. Il est en effet possible de protéger le contractant vulnérable non pas en prononçant son incapacité, mais au contraire en soutenant sa capacité à contracter.

50. Cette démarche de soutien des capacités contractuelles du contractant vulnérable n'est pas sans conséquence sur la structure du contrat. Une telle vision dynamique de la notion de capacité contractuelle peut être

[68] C Delgoulet, M Millanvoye et S Volkoff, 'Les capacités des travailleurs vieillissants. Une approche conditionnelle' (2005) 314 *Revue Fututribles. Analyses et prospectives* 5; PY Verkindt and M Wacongne, 'Le travailleur vieillissant' [1993] *Droit social* 932.

mise en parallèle avec la théorie des capabilités d'Amartya Sen.[69] Critiquant les conséquences de politiques économiques néo-classiques ayant renforcé les inégalités, Sen appréhende la croissance du bien-être par le prisme des libertés. Dans son analyse, l'agent économique est un individu qui agit et modifie. Il s'intéresse non seulement à son avenir mais aussi à celui de ses semblables. Il est un acteur du développement de son bien-être par le renforcement de ses capacités, c'est-à-dire de ses facultés de choix.[70] Les capacités ne résident pas dans le résultat accompli mais dans les possibilités d'accomplir. Le développement humain est ainsi fondé sur la liberté de choisir.[71] Et la justice sociale ne réside pas dans l'égalité des revenus, ni dans l'égalité formelle présente dans la reconnaissance des droits, mais dans une égalité concrète fondée sur la liberté de choix offerte à chacun.[72]

51. Ces normes, qui ont pour objectif de soutenir la capacité contractuelle du contractant, peuvent être replacées dans le courant du solidarisme contractuel.[73] La loi consumériste sur le rétablissement personnel, comme la législation travailliste concernant la formation professionnelle tout au long de la vie établissent un lien de solidarité entre les contractants.[74] Le soutien des capacités du contractant vulnérable constitue un intérêt commun des parties au contrat, puisqu'il favorise la bonne exécution du contrat. Il répond également à un intérêt général puisqu'il permet de

[69] V notamment: A Sen, *Repenser les inégalités*, traduction de P Chemla (Seuil, Collection l'histoire immédiate, 2000); A Sen, *Un nouveau modèle économique. Développement, justice, liberté*, éd O Jacob, traduction de M Bessières (2000); A Sen, *L'économie est une science morale* (La Découverte/Poche, 2003).

[70] A Sen, *Repenser les inégalités* traduction de P. Chemla, (Seuil, Collection l'histoire immédiate, 2000) 81: 'Il est certain que la liberté de choisir peut revêtir une importance directe pour la qualité de vie et le bien de la personne humaine. Agir librement et être en mesure de choisir sont, de ce point de vue, des éléments directement constitutifs du bien-être'.

[71] A Bertin, 'Le liberté comme enjeu du développement, une lecture critique de Development as Freedom' [2005] *Revue Economie et société* 570: 'Focaliser notre attention sur la capabilité plutôt que sur les fonctionnements accomplis revient à se concentrer sur la liberté que possède l'individu de choisir parmi l'éventail d'options qui s'offre à lui, son processus de choix. Partant, il est nécessaire de se focaliser sur la capabilité plutôt que sur les fonctionnements pour appréhender le développement'.

[72] M Nusbaum, 'Femmes et égalité: l'approche fondée sur les capacités' (1999) 138 *Revue Internationale du Travail* 252, 263: 'La liberté ne se résume pas simplement à avoir des droits inscrits sur du papier, elle exige une situation matérielle qui permette d'exercer ces droits . . . Penser en fonction de la capacité aide à réfléchir à ce que veut réellement dire garantir un droit à quelqu'un'.

[73] Voir les trois principaux arts à l'origine de la renaissance de ce courant: C Jamin, 'Plaidoyer pour le solidarisme contractuel' in *Le contrat au début du XXIème siècle: études offertes à J Ghestin* (Paris, LGDJ, 2001) 441–72; D Mazeaud, 'Loyauté, solidarité, fraternité: la nouvelle devise contractuelle?' in *L'avenir du droit: mélanges en hommage à F Terré* (Dalloz, 1999) 603–34; C Thibierge-Guelfucci, 'Libre propos sur la transformation du droit des contrats' [1997] *RTD civ* 357.

[74] M Mignot, 'De la solidarité en général et du solidarisme contractuel en particulier ou le solidarisme contractuel a-t-il un rapport avec la solidarité ?' (2004) 4 *Revue de la Recherche Juridique, Droit prospectif* 2155: 'Etre solidaire . . . c'est centrer son attention non pas seulement sur soi, mais également sur l'autre, afin de rechercher et servir l'intérêt de ce dernier'.

neutraliser les conséquences de la vulnérabilité d'un contractant.[75] Le contractant vulnérable peut, malgré ses faiblesses, conclure des contrats, et ainsi tenir sa place dans la société.[76]

La nécessité de développer la notion de capacité est ainsi primordiale: 'La capacité à être partie à un rapport d'obligation n'est qu'un élément de la question plus vaste de la capacité de la personne à participer à la vie juridique en général et à la vie contractuelle en particulier'.[77]

Les mécanismes de soutien des capacités contribuent à une correction des inégalités entre contractants. Ils rendent le contractant moins vulnérable, plus libre dans ses choix, et donc plus responsable.[78]

75 Sur la notion d'intérêt général, voir: M Mekki, *L'intérêt général et le contrat. Contribution à une étude de la hiérarchie des intérêts en droit privé*, préface de J. Ghestin (LGDJ, 2004) Tome 411.

76 PY Verkindt, 'Le contrat de travail. Modèle ou anti-modèle du droit civil des contrats' in *La nouvelle crise du contrat, Actes du Colloque organisé par l'Université de Lille 2 le 14 mai 2001, collection thèmes et commentaires* (Dalloz, 2003) 216, § 32: 'Ce que la doctrine solidariste apporte fondamentalement à la théorie du contrat est à rechercher dans la double affirmation que la relation de travail, comme toute relation sociale n'est pas réductible au contrat et qu'il n'y a pas que du contractuel dans le contrat'.

77 J Hauser et G Wicker, 'Validité-capacité et pouvoir (article 1116 à 1120-2 du Code civil): exposé des motifs' in *Avant-projet de réforme du droit des obligations et du droit de la prescription*, présenté par P Catala le 22 septembre 2005 au Garde des Sceaux, p 23.

78 A Supiot, *Au-delà de l'emploi. Transformations du travail et devenir du droit du travail en Europe*, Rapport pour la Commission européenne, sous la direction d'A Supiot, éd (Flammarion, 1999) 85: 'Au statut de l'employé qui lie la subordination et la sécurité, devrait succéder un nouvel état professionnel des personnes, fondé sur une approche compréhensive du travail et capable de lier les impératifs de liberté, de sécurité et de responsabilité'.

6

La notion de capacité et l'évolution du droit du travail italien

AURORA VIMERCATI

OBSERVATIONS LIMINAIRES À UN DISCOURS SUR LES *CAPABILITIES*: L'ARRIÈRE-PLAN D'UN DÉBAT DIFFICILE À OUVRIR

En Italie, une réflexion autour de la notion légale de *capacité* n'est pas plus centrale dans le débat entre les civilistes qu'entre les travaillistes. Il n'existe d'ailleurs aucune politique du marché du travail, ni aucune politique sociale, ni même un modèle de développement économique, emprunté aux *capacités*.

Néanmoins, il n'est pas inutile de confronter la notion de *capacité* au droit du travail italien.

Il faut tout d'abord préciser que cette formule sera employée ici, non pas au sens propre du droit civil, mais au sens *adapté* à l'approche de Sen.[1] Le droit civil considère la capacité d'agir comme une qualité générale de l'individu. Elle pourra cependant être limitée afin de protéger la personne jeune, âgée ou infirme. Bien au contraire, dans la perspective de Sen c'est la dimension active du *développement des capacités* de la personne qu'il faut considérer.

Il est vrai que c'est surtout dans le domaine politique[2] qu'il est possible d'utiliser l'approche par les capacités pour créer ce 'processus vertueux' dans lequel les libertés réelles 'ne sont pas seulement l'objectif principal du développement, mais aussi l'un des principaux moyens de

1 A Sen, *Development as Freedom* (Oxford, Oxford University Press, 1999).

2 Sur les perspectives que l'approche par les capacités peut offrir à la politique sociale et de l'emploi en Europe, en tant qu'ensemble de principes politiques nouveaux, R Salais et R Villeneuve (dir), *Développer les capacités des hommes et des territoires en Europe* (ANACT, 2006) 10 ss; A Supiot (dir), *Au delà de l'emploi: transformations du travail et devenir du droit du travail en Europe* (Paris, Flammarion, 1999).

l'atteindre'.[3] Il appartient aux acteurs concernés, qu'ils soient publics ou privés, d'utiliser les instruments et les ressources dont ils disposent pour que ce processus soit mis en oeuvre.

L'approche par les capacités ne peut cependant ignorer la dimension juridique du problème, à savoir l'existence de droits garantissant à la personne le pouvoir d'agir. L'histoire même du droit du travail est l'histoire de l'affirmation et de la protection des valeurs de la personne dans le marché et parfois même contre le marché.[4]

Cette histoire n'est pas le fruit du hasard mais s'est développée, surtout à partir de la Constitution italienne de 1948, autour des valeurs de solidarité, d'inclusion sociale et de participation. C'est une histoire de protection et d'émancipation du travailleur, qui a conduit au développement d'un statut protecteur, devenu par la suite un véritable statut social. Elle nous a offert un modèle de protection emprunté, justement, au développement de la personne. Un modèle présentant un caractère particulier, exprimé par une formule typique en droit du travail italien: l'*inderogabilità* (*infra*). C'est à partir de ce constat élémentaire que nous estimons important d'amorcer une réflexion à propos des *capabilities* en droit du travail italien.

Ce modèle de protection est en crise, suite aux transformations structurelles du marché du travail, à la globalisation de l'économie et aux nouvelles formes d'organisation de l'entreprise. D'une part, l'existence et l'effectivité de ce modèle sont mises en cause. D'autre part, le besoin de définir les droits fondamentaux à assurer lorsqu'un individu travaille pour autrui[5] et le besoin d'élargir la protection à tout sujet en situation de

[3] A Sen, *Development as Freedom* (Oxford, Oxford University Press, 1999) 3.

[4] C'est la grande question du juste équilibre entre les dimensions économique et sociale du droit du travail qui est au centre du débat entre les économistes et les juristes. Il faut dire qu'une partie de la doctrine dénonce de plus en plus le caractère partiel et parfois manipulateur de certaines analyses économiques qui prétendent lier de façon automatique (et presque inéluctable) la libéralisation du marché du travail à l'obtention de résultats significatifs en termes d'amélioration de l'emploi. Pour une lecture attentive aux avantages de l'utilisation de l'analyse économique au sens plutôt traditionnel, en Italie, cf P Ichino, *Il lavoro e il mercato* (Milano, Mondadori, 1996); M Sacconi, P Reboani, M Tiraboschi, *La società attiva* (Venezia, Marsilio, 2004); par rapport à l'action syndicale, cf P Ichino, *A che cosa serve il sindacato?* (Milano, Mondadori, 2005). De nouvelles perspectives face au risque 'd'économiser le droit', sont offertes par P Loi, 'L'analisi economica del diritto e il diritto del lavoro' [1999] *Giornale di Diritto del Lavoro e di Relazioni Industriali* 552; R Del Punta, 'L'economia e le ragioni del diritto del lavoro' [2001] *Giornale di Diritto del Lavoro e di Relazioni Industriali*; U Carabelli, 'Organizzazione del lavoro e professionalità: una riflessione su contratto di lavoro e post-taylorismo' [2003] *Giornale di Diritto del Lavoro e di Relazioni Industriali* 1; L Zappalà, 'Tra diritto edn economia: obiettivi e tecniche della regolazione sociale dei contratti di lavoro a termine', WP CSDLE 'Massimo D'Antona' 66/2005.

[5] M Pedrazzoli, 'La parabola della subordinazione: dal contratto allo *status*. Riflessioni su Barassi e il suo dopo' [2002] *Argementi di Diritto del Lavoro* 263; E Ghera, 'Subordinazione, statuto protettivo e qualificazione del rapporto di lavoro' dans D Garofalo et M Ricci (dir), *Percorsi di diritto del lavoro* (Bari, Cacucci, 2006) 323.

faiblesse sur le marché du travail demeurent au centre du débat relatif à l'avenir du droit du travail.[6]

Dans l'exposé qui va suivre nous avons bien conscience qu'il est très difficile d'échapper à une sorte de polarisation croissante du débat italien. Certes cette polarisation ne concerne pas directement la question des capacités, mais elle procède de raisons de fond et peut donc aider à comprendre la grande difficulté qu'ont les travaillistes italiens à s'intéresser à l'approche par les capacités.[7]

Une partie de la doctrine italienne reste très attachée à la défense de la norme impérative et à la protection des droits fondamentaux qu'elle assure. D'autres juristes soulignent le besoin croissant de promouvoir la protection du travailleur *dans le marché*, en lui donnant plus d'opportunités de formation et de choix en matière d'emploi.

Nous entendons d'ailleurs insister sur l'importance centrale de la norme impérative, sur sa fonction de *protection* et celle de *promotion*. C'est justement en partant du rapport entre fonctions de protection et de promotion que nous estimons possible d'utiliser l'approche par les capacités et de faire quelques suggestions pour donner à toute personne ou collectivité la liberté effective de réaliser ses objectifs, et de lui fournir les moyens adéquats pour y parvenir.

Pour que la personne impliquée dans un contrat de travail puisse devenir acteur, utiliser ses *dotations* et assumer la responsabilité de son action, il faut la protéger et la soutenir. Or qu'il s'agisse de contrats dits atypiques ou de contrats dits précaires, on constate de plus en plus le besoin d'identifier toute personne en condition de faiblesse dans le marché afin de lui reconnaître un minimum de protection. Enfin, les droits fondamentaux deviennent la *boussole* permettant de s'orienter dans l'univers du travail *non standard* pour réviser ou renouveler la fonction de la norme indérogeable.[8]

Le fondement juridique du modèle de régulation de la *norme impérative*, directement lié à la protection et à la garantie des droits fondamentaux, se trouve dans la Constitution. Ce modèle comprend également une fonction promotionnelle (*infra*),[9] dans la mesure où son

6 De plus en plus, les travaillistes s'interrogent sur le futur du travail, et en viennent même à entamer une sorte d'*autoanalyse* du droit du travail. Cf L Mariucci, 'Il sorriso di Federico e la lampada di Aladino ' [2000] *Lavoro e Dirito* 5. Pour une approche critique des difficultés (un véritable *vice épistémologique*) des juristes à décrire les phénomènes sociaux par les notions et catégories juridiques, A Salento, *Postfordismo e ideologie giuridiche* (Milano, F Angeli, 2003) 26.

7 Exception faite de quelques auteurs comme, par exemple, B Caruso, 'Occupabilità, formazione e *capability* nei modelli giuridici di regolazione dei mercati del lavoro' [2007] *Giornale di Diritto del Lavoro e di Relazioni Industriali* 1.

8 S Sciarra, 'Norme imperative nazionali edn europee: le finalità del diritto del lavoro' [2006] *Giornale di Diritto del Lavoro e di Relazioni Industriali*; A Perulli, 'Razionalità e proporzionalità nel diritto del lavoro' [2005] *Giornale di Diritto del Lavoro e di Relazioni Industriali* 5.

9 N Bobbio, *Dalla struttura alla funzione* (Milano, Edizioni di Comunità, 1977).

but est d'encourager et de soutenir le développement de la personne, conformément aux prescriptions de la Constitution elle-même (en particulier les articles 2, 3, 4).[10] L'approche par les capacités nous permet de mettre en évidence l'importante fonction que la norme impérative est supposée jouer pour amorcer le développement de comportements *vertueux* de la part des acteurs aux différents niveaux, y compris au niveau individuel. Cette approche permettrait enfin d'aboutir au développement des libertés réelles de l'individu. Autrement dit, le *lien* entre la fonction de protection et la fonction de promotion nous révèle l'aptitude de la norme impérative à influer sur l'organisation de l'entreprise et par là même à orienter les choix de l'entreprise qui ont une répercussion en matière d'emploi et, plus généralement, à orienter les comportements des acteurs du marché du travail. Voilà le point qui risque d'être oublié dans le débat actuel. Voilà la raison pour laquelle il est important d'analyser la notion de norme impérative et indérogeable,[11] ses éléments de faiblesse, sa fonction face aux mutations récentes du travail. S'il est généralement acceptable que la loi devienne imprécise, modulable, souple quand il s'agit de promouvoir l'action et d'introduire des mesures d'incitation aux comportements vertueux, elle doit par contre rester précise, rigide, ferme quand il s'agit d'assurer les conditions de liberté réelle de l'individu face aux situations d'inégalité.

[10] Art 2: 'La République reconnaît et garantit les droits inviolables de l'homme, soit en tant qu'individu, soit dans les organisations sociales où se déroule sa personnalité, et requiert la réalisation des devoirs incontournables de solidarité politique, économique et sociale'. Art 3, I: 'Tous les citoyens disposent d'une identique dignité sociale et sont égaux devant la loi . . .', II: 'C'est un devoir de la République d'enlever les obstacles d'ordre économique et social qui, en limitant *de facto* la liberté et l'égalité des citoyens, en empêchent le plein épanouissement de la personne humaine et la participation effective de tous les travailleurs à l'organisation politique, économique et sociale du Pays'. Art 4: 'La République reconnaît à tous les citoyens le droit au travail et promeut les conditions qui rendent effectif ce droit. Chaque citoyen a le droit d'exercer, selon ses propres possibilités et son propre choix, une activité ou une fonction qui concourt au progrès matériel ou spirituel de la société'.

[11] L'explication de la notion et de la fonction de la norme impérative en droit italien est bien trop complexe pour être résumée en quelques mots. Toute norme a un caractère *impératif*. L''*inderogabilità*' du '*precetto légale*' est fortement liée à l'impérativité qui se traduit normalement par des formules telles que: 'tout pacte contraire est nul'. Si des exemples peuvent en être trouvés en droit civil, c'est le droit du travail qui est réellement 'marqué' par l'indérogeabilité. Pour de plus amples approfondissements l'œuvre qui demeure centrale en doctrine italienne: R De Luca-Tamajo, *La norma inderogabile nel diritto del lavoro* (Napoli, Giuffrè, Jovene, 1976) V. Aussi R Voza, 'Norma inderogabile e autonomia individuale assistita' [1998] *Giornale di Diritto del Lavoro e di Relazioni Industriali* 603.

L'*IMPÉRATIVITÉ DE LA NORME* EN DROIT DU TRAVAIL: DIMENSION COLLECTIVE ET DIMENSION INDIVIDUELLE DE LA PROTECTION DE LA PERSONNE

L'approche par les capacités vise à mettre le sujet—la personne—au centre du débat, première étape pour soutenir et promouvoir son pouvoir d'agir.

Grâce à la norme impérative, la personne du salarié, confrontée à l'inégalité au sein de l'entreprise, a pu atteindre une condition de liberté réelle et, par là même, sa dignité. Cependant, l'analyse n'est pas complète si l'on néglige de souligner l'apport tout à fait essentiel de l'action du syndicat.

Bien que Sen, dans ses écrits, donne souvent une version purement individualiste du développement des capacités, on peut dire que la liberté de choix effectif du salarié et, donc, son pouvoir d'agir, ne se décline qu'au collectif.

S'il est vrai que le statut protecteur fonde le pouvoir d'agir du salarié au sein du contrat de travail (dans la mesure où certaines garanties fondamentales lui sont assurées par des normes impératives), l'existence et la force même de la norme impérative découlent de la relation entre la loi et l'autonomie collective ('autonomia collettiva'); relation qui a eu lieu, jusqu'à présent, dans un milieu très favorable.

L'expérience concrète et le projet de développement social inscrit dans la Constitution présentent finalement l'organisation syndicale—et donc son action de représentation de l'intérêt collectif—comme le moteur du processus d'intégration des droits sociaux par rapport à ce que Marshall a appelé le *statut de citoyenneté*. S'il est vrai que ce sont les caractéristiques individuelles d'une personne, de la société dans laquelle elle vit et de l'environnement qui l'entoure, qui déterminent sa capacité à accéder à tout un ensemble de *fonctionnements*, les droits fondamentaux jouent eux aussi un rôle important, que ce soit en termes de droits substantiels découlant du droit positif, ou en termes de droits procéduraux.[12] Cela justifie la forme d'action tout à fait typique que le syndicat a pu avoir, grâce au soutien de la loi et conformément aux valeurs constitutionnelles mises en jeu par son action.

Cependant, cette action est en crise et cette crise va évidemment se répercuter directement sur le statut protecteur. Les raisons de cette crise ne sont pas spécifiques à l'Italie. Mais, en Italie, ce problème présente des aspects particuliers qu'il est très important d'énoncer, même brièvement.

12 V J Brown, S Deakin et F Wilkinson, 'Capacité, droits sociaux et intégration' dans Salais et Villeneuve, ci-dessus n 2, 318. Cf A Lassandari, 'La tutela collettiva nell'età della competizione economica globale', WP CSDLE 'Massimo D'Antona' INT—25/2005 (http://www.lex.unict.it/) 38, selon lequel l'approche par les *capabilities* nous rappelle (*mutatis mutandis*) la raison de l'existence même du syndicat, dans la relation avec l'entreprise.

L'action du syndicat, qui est soutenue par la loi et trouve un important fondement dans la Constitution (articles 3, 39, 40), ne fait l'objet d'aucune règle spéciale en ce qui concerne le régime juridique des conventions collectives et la très délicate question de la 'rappresentanza sindacale'. Cette situation relève du *particularisme* du système italien: la *capacité d'action collective* ne repose que sur un modèle dit 'volontariste' fondé sur le droit commun des contrats (code civile (cc), livre IV) et sur le principe de la liberté syndicale (article 39 I, Const, mais v aussi article 40 et article 3 II). Le modèle de négociation collective dit volontariste, qui a pu se développer sur le fondement de la Constitution, a joué un rôle fondamental dans la réalisation du projet de développement social envisagé par cette dernière. Ce projet reste aujourd'hui encore d'actualité. Cependant, dans le contexte économique actuel et celui de la réglementation légale du marché du travail, le syndicat est en crise et n'est plus capable de refonder son action 'en fait', comme l'a expliqué la théorie bien connue de *l'ordinamento intersindacale*.[13]

LES RÉFORMES RÉCENTES DU MARCHÉ DU TRAVAIL DANS LA PERSPECTIVE DES *CAPACITÉS*?

La notion de *norma inderogabile* nous intéresse en tant que limite aux pouvoirs privés. Il s'agit d'une technique qui ne relève pas de l'incapacité d'agir au sens traditionnel. C'est plutôt l'autonomie privée du travailleur qui est remise en question. À l'exception des cas où la loi aménage des conditions particulières lui permettant de *s'exprimer,* l'autonomie du travailleur est limitée de façon importante.

L'*inderogabilità*, de la loi comme des conventions collectives, exprime la valeur d'ordre public social d'une technique qui repose sur l'établissement d'une barrière: par l'*inderogabilità* on limite l'autonomie contractuelle (individuelle et collective) afin de protéger la *liberté réelle* de l'individu. Il s'agit d'une technique qui, en tant que mélange de protection et de liberté (réelle), est emblématique de l'*esprit* du droit du travail. Cela est si vrai que Lord Wedderburn a affirmé: '[w]e need a new word', en introduisant dans la terre d'*Albione* le mot *inderogability,* heureuse combinaison 'between rigid protections and flexibility'.[14] Cette technique reste certes essentielle face aux transformations du travail, mais c'est grâce à l'approche par les capacités qu'il peut être possible d'éviter que cette combinaison (entre protection et flexibilité) se

[13] G Giugni, *Introduzione allo studio dell'autonomia collettiva* (Milano, Giuffrè, 1960).

[14] Wedderburn, 'Inderogability, Collective Agreements and Community Law' (1992) 21 *Industrial Law Journal* 245. Pour plus d'approfondissements sur la flexibilité en droit du travail en Italie, B Caruso, 'Flexibility in Labour Law: The Italian Case' dans B Caruso et M Fuchs (dir), *Labour Law and Flexibility in Europe* (Nomos, Giuffrè, 2004) 11.

transforme, tout simplement, en obligation d'adaptation de l'individu aux transformations de l'entreprise et du marché du travail.

Le processus de réforme du marché du travail, commencé depuis quelques années, a déclenché un débat complexe et parfois même confus. Dans l'attente de connaître les effets concrets des nouveautés qui ont été introduites, il faut noter que les objectifs poursuivis sont ambitieux et correspondent, en apparence, aux stratégies européennes en matière d'emploi.

Le processus de réforme a été inspiré par le *Libro Bianco sul mercato del lavoro* d'octobre 2001. Un nouveau système de mesures sociales aurait dû venir compléter ce processus, mais il n'a jamais vu le jour. Par conséquent, la seule innovation issue du processus de réforme—initié par la loi no 30 de février 2003, suivie par le d lgs n 276 du septembre 2003[15]—demeure la flexibilisation du travail, ainsi qu'une forme d'encouragement indirect au phénomène d'externalisation et, finalement, à la déstructuration de l'entreprise (*infra*).[16]

La précarisation de l'emploi et les formes d'utilisation du travail: modifications et innovations

Les réformes sont intervenues sur les contrats de travail préexistants pour les adapter aux besoins du marché et ainsi répondre aux urgences sociales en matière d'emploi. Dans ce même objectif, de nouvelles formes d'utilisation du travail ont été introduites. Il s'agit des contrats de travail précaire, qui prétendent représenter une alternative aux rapports de travail normaux à durée indéterminée, dits *standards*. Ces contrats sont, entre autres, le contrat de *travail intermittent*, le *job sharing* (Titre V) et le *contrat à temps partiel* (article 46 du d lgs n 276/2003, qui a amendé le d lgs n 61/2000). Bien que ce dernier ne soit pas à proprement parler un contrat précaire, il est intéressant de le mentionner en raison des modifications profondes qu'il a subi, et qui ont conduit à la flexibilisation de son utilisation.[17] Ainsi, s'il n'est pas un contrat précaire dans sa structure, son

15 Il s'agit d'une loi du Parlement qui confère au Gouvernement le pouvoir d'intervenir par un *decreto legislativo* sur des domaines et dans des limites définis. Ce décret a été modifié par le d lgs 251/2004 et par la loi 80/2005. Par ailleurs, ce processus complexe a été accompagné d'une multiplicité de décrets et circulaires ministériels.

16 Plusieurs analyses ont critiqué—presque avec *indignation*—la technique grossière utilisée et les incohérences d'une loi qui n'a pas 'répondu' aux conflits sociaux actuellement les plus significatifs. Cf L Mariucci, 'Dopo la flessibilità cosa? Riflessioni sulle politiche del lavoro' dans *Studi in onore di Giorgio Ghezzi* (Padova, Cedam, 2005); F Liso, 'Analisi dei punti critici del decreto legislativo 276/2003: spunti di riflessione' dans WP CSDLE 'Massimo D'Antona' 42/2004; C Zoli, 'Contratto e rapporto tra potere e autonomia nelle recenti riforme del diritto del lavoro' [2004] *Giornale di Diritto del Lavoro e di Relazioni Industriali* 359.

17 D lgs 276/2003, Titre V. Cf R Voza, 'I contratti ad orario "ridotto, modulato o flessibile" tra lavoro e disponibilità' dans P Curzio (dir), *Lavoro e diritti* (Bari, Cacucci, 2006) 333 ss.

régime juridique peut conduire à *précariser* la situation de la personne. Une remarque analogue peut être faite au sujet de la nouvelle réglementation en matière de temps de travail, introduite par le d lgs n 66/2003 (et intégrée ensuite par le d lgs n 213/2004).[18]

Il faut en tout cas insister ici sur la flexibilisation consécutive à la réduction du rôle jusqu'alors réservé à l'autonomie collective. L'exemple peut être pris du contrat à temps partiel au sein duquel de nouveaux espaces de flexibilité viennent d'y être introduits. Pour certains, cette flexibilité permettrait non seulement au salarié de mieux concilier son temps de travail et son temps de vie, mais elle pourrait également stimuler l'activité économique et améliorer la productivité de l'entreprise.[19] Ces nouveaux espaces de flexibilité concernent principalement la modification de la durée du travail et la répartition des heures de travail, désormais aménagées par les parties sans *filtre* syndical. Ainsi, la modification de la répartition des horaires de travail ne trouve plus les garanties autrefois assurées par la nécessaire intervention de la source collective. La flexibilité est devenue, en quelque sorte, une affaire réglée par le contrat individuel. Dès lors, les choix de l'entreprise risquent d'avoir un impact disproportionné sur l'ensemble des droits du travailleur, notamment sur son droit constitutionnel à rétribution équitable (article 36 Cost).[20] Une belle occasion de mettre la *personne* au centre du discours et lui permettre ainsi d'exercer sa capacité de choix, ne serait-ce qu'en matière de temps libre. Une occasion perdue cependant: son pouvoir (illustré par la référence légale à son *consentement*) n'a que peu de chances de s'imposer face aux prérogatives managériales.

Suite à la réforme de 2001, le *contrat à durée déterminée* demeure, au contraire, tout à fait précaire.[21] Son évolution reflète l'histoire du droit du travail. À l'origine, la norme impérative excluait toute autonomie privée dans la détermination des conditions de recours à ce contrat. Pendant la

[18] Pour une lecture critique et systématique de la réglementation nouvelle, U Carabelli et V Leccese, 'Una riflessione sul sofferto rapporto tra legge e autonomia collettiva: spunti dalla nuova disciplina dell'orario di lavoro' dans *Studi in Onore di Giorgio Ghezzi*, ci-dessus n 16, 345.

[19] Au-delà des avantages offerts par les allongements d'horaires, le recours à ce contrat est également encouragé par des avantages indirects: les travailleurs *part time* ne sont comptabilisés dans les effectifs que dans une mesure 'proportionnée' au temps de travail pour l'application de certaines lois. Pour une lecture critique du *part time* en tant qu'instrument de la politique de l'emploi, A Lo Faro, 'Part Time Work in Italy' dans Caruso et Fuchs, ci-dessus n 14, 61.

[20] Comme l'avait déjà expliqué la Cour Constitutionnelle (Arrêt n 210/1992), la modification 'unilatérale' de la répartition de l'horaire de base peut empêcher le travailleur de s'engager dans d'autres formes de travail, et d'accéder ainsi à une rémunération conforme aux prescriptions de la Constitution. On aurait, alors, une violation du principe de la *rétribution équitable* (art 36). Cf E Ghera, *Il rapporto di lavoro* (Bari, Cacucci, 2006); U Carabelli, 'Part-time Work' dans B Veneziani (dir), *Collective Bargaining and Labour Flexibility in EC Countries* (Roma, ASAP-Ist Pol Stato, 1992).

[21] D lgs 368/2001 Cf L Zappalà, 'Tra diritto edn economia: obiettivi e tecniche della regolazione sociale dei contratti di lavoro a termine', WP CSDLE 'Massimo D'Antona' 66/2005.

saison du *garantismo flessibile* (*infra*), c'est le modèle de la régulation dite réflexive[22] qui a prévalu et l'utilisation de ce contrat fut alors essentiellement soumise au contrôle syndical et donc à la capacité des conventions collectives à réaliser un équilibre entre la protection des travailleurs et les pressions exercées par un système économique en transformation profonde. Suite à la réforme récente, la protection est, au contraire, adaptée aux exigences spécifiques de l'entreprise. La seule limite à ce principe réside dans l'obligation légale de respecter des critères objectifs (raisons d'ordre technique, productif, organisationnel ou substitutif).

Pour compléter la *liste* des contrats disponibles sur le 'supermarché de la flexibilité' (pour reprendre la formule très souvent utilisée par la doctrine récente), il faut mentionner les contrats à cause mixte (formation et emploi): *apprentissage* et *contrat d'insertion* (Titre VI). On a l'impression que l'*étal* va s'enrichir d'une marchandise nouvelle et appétissante. D'une part, la formation est envisagée comme une chance, opportunité pour la réalisation *de soi* (professionnelle et donc personnelle) suite à l'expérience négative des *contrats formation emploi.* D'autre part, l'*insertion* (ou réinsertion) est envisagée comme un instrument de la politique active de l'emploi, conformément à une tendance traditionnelle qui, en Italie, remonte à la loi 285/1977, révisée par la loi 863/1984.

Déjà en 1997 la loi n 197 avait essayé de rationaliser cette matière complexe dans une perspective d'intégration du système scolaire et du monde du travail, afin d'assurer aux demandeurs d'emploi (et aux jeunes surtout) l'accès à la formation et à une carrière professionnelle. En même temps, cette loi prétendait favoriser l'amélioration compétitive du système de production et donc de l'emploi.

Bien que le temps ait manqué pour aboutir à un quelconque résultat significatif, le législateur est intervenu encore une fois, en 2003, dans cet espace de proximité délicate entre le social et l'économie.[23] Une fois encore, l'occasion de développer les capacités a été perdue. À titre d'exemple: aucune obligation de formation à l'extérieur de l'entreprise n'est plus imposée dans le *contrat d'apprentissage* et la part de temps devant être consacrée à la formation n'a pas été fixée. D'ailleurs, aucune valorisation effective de la formation ne peut être assurée par une réglementation transitoire et imprécise, destinée à être intégrée par des sources réglementaires aussi hétérogènes qu'incohérentes. Plusieurs aspects cruciaux quant à l'application du contrat d'apprentissage n'ont

[22] C'est le modèle bien connu, spécialement élaboré, en droit du travail, par G Teubner et repris, en Italie, en particulier par M D'Antona, 'L'autonomia individuale e le fonti del diritto del lavoro' (1991), maintenant dans B Caruso et S Sciarra (dir), *Opere* (Milano, Giuffrè, 2000) I, 135.

[23] C'est la fameuse question des aides étatiques aux entreprises. La Commission européenne avait invité l'Italie à conformer sa réglementation en matière de contrats *formation-emploi* aux dispositions de l'article 87 du Traité de Rome (décision du 11 mai 1999).

pas encore été réglementés. Ainsi il faut encore attendre l'intervention de la législation régionale,[24] de la négociation collective (à des niveaux divers) ou du paritarisme et de la réglementation administrative. Or l'attente crée l'*incertitude*, et cette situation n'est convenable ni pour l'entreprise en particulier, ni pour le système dans son ensemble.

Des considérations similaires peuvent être faites au sujet du *contrat d'insertion ou de réinsertion* (article 54). Il s'agit d'un contrat à durée déterminée visant à encourager l'embauche de certaines catégories de personnes (comme les jeunes, les chômeurs de longue durée, les personnes âgées sans emploi, les femmes résidant dans des territoires sous-développés). L'attention du législateur se focalise alors sur le *projet* qui va être élaboré conjointement par l'employeur et le travailleur pour assurer l'adaptation des compétences professionnelles de ce dernier au travail particulier. Cela pourrait être une chance remarquable dans la perspective des capacités, s'il n'existait pas un risque d'ineffectivité d'une réglementation encore floue et dépourvue de techniques de contrôle et de gestion appropriées.[25] La *précarisation* pourrait être justifiée par une *contrepartie*: dans des conditions convenables (en termes d'avantages tant économiques[26] que normatifs),[27] l'employeur peut utiliser la prestation de travail *contre* l'obligation de formation. Mais celle-ci n'a qu'un caractère *éventuel* (article 55, c 4). Par ailleurs, l'objectif d'acquisition d'une qualification est l'enjeu d'une affaire qui n'a pas encore été réglée: la norme *légale* doit être rendue effective par la norme *conventionnelle* et cette dernière risque d'être dépassée sinon déclassée par la réglementation *administrative*. Il sera donc très difficile d'imposer aux entreprises des comportements conformes aux ambitions de la réforme en terme d'amélioration qualitative et quantitative de l'emploi. Au lieu d'encourager les comportements vertueux, le recours à ce contrat offre tout simplement à l'entreprise de nouvelles marges d'épargnes en matière de coûts de l'emploi.

La nécessité de réduire les règles et leurs rigidités l'emporte alors sur l'exigence de contrôler et de gouverner le système de production pour maintenir le meilleur degré de cohésion sociale possible. Par contre, une réalité de plus en plus complexe, souvent aux marges de la légalité, va

[24] Depuis la réforme du titre V de la Constitution, la formation professionnelle relève de la compétence régionale.

[25] La seule technique qui semble offrir quelques solutions au problème de l'efficacité de la protection de la norme légale ou conventionnelle est une garantie ancienne, empruntée au droit civil: la garantie d'une forme particulière. Cf M D'Onghia, *La forma vincolata nel diritto del lavoro* (Milano, Giuffrè, 2005).

[26] Le travailleur peut recevoir une qualification inférieure à celle requise pour le poste auquel il est affecté.

[27] À savoir que le travailleur n'est pas pris en compte dans le calcul du nombre de travailleurs employés et est ainsi exclu du champ d'application des normes de protection, comme la 'tutela reale' offerte par l'art. 18 du 'Statuto dei lavoratori' (modifié par la L 108/1991), en cas de licenciement.

être *légalisée* (et non réglementée) et ce, par un législateur incapable d'*anticiper* les effets de son intervention.

À titre d'exemple, pour compléter cet éventail des mesures de flexibilisation dite *typologique*, et avant de passer à la flexibilisation dite *organisationnelle*, il peut être mentionné la nouvelle réglementation des situations professionnelles situées dans une zone trouble entre le travail salarié et le travail non salarié (*emploi à projet* et *travail occasionnel et accessoire*, Titre VII). En raison du nombre important d'entreprises et de travailleurs impliqués, la réforme vise d'abord à lutter contre le phénomène du travail illégal et, plus généralement, contre les pratiques de détournement de la législation en matière de rapports de travail en condition de subordination. L'objet de ces contrats est l'accomplissement, dans un laps de temps déterminé, d'un projet ou d'un programme de travail, d'une phase de ce dernier (article 61),[28] voire même d'une simple tâche (article 70). De nombreux doutes vont accompagner l'interprétation des limites tant objectives (l'existence d'un projet ou d'un programme) que temporelles (le temps déterminé), qui prétendent régler le recours à ces contrats et donc leur qualification. La *coordination*, modalité d'exécution et de réalisation du travail, fait l'objet d'un *projet* défini par le commettant. Bien que la loi de 2003 vise à limiter le recours aux contrats de travail autonome dits de 'collaborazione coordinata e continuativa', elle crée en fait une occasion supplémentaire d'incertitude et de précarisation du travail.

À titre de première conclusion, on peut dire que l'entreprise ne trouve aucune *incitation* réelle à améliorer sa capacité organisationnelle et sa compétitivité—par exemple par des investissements appropriés. L'effet majeur des nouvelles mesures de flexibilité réside plutôt dans la réduction des coûts. Un tel effet a peu de chances de contribuer à la croissance du système des entreprises au niveau macroéconomique et non, seulement, au niveau microéconomique.[29]

La précarisation de l'emploi suite à son 'extériorisation'

La libéralisation du marché du travail, qui est en cours, est complétée par un ensemble de normes visant à réglementer le phénomène complexe des

[28] Il s'agit d'une sorte de nouvelle proposition en faveur de la *parasubordination*, qui n'est jamais devenue une catégorie légale en Italie, bien qu'elle soit souvent évoquée par la doctrine et la jurisprudence.

[29] À savoir: 'la compétitivité d'une entreprise réside non pas dans la réduction des coûts, mais fondamentalement dans sa capacité de travail, d'organisation et d'innovation', R Salais et R Villeneuve, 'Introduction: l'Europe et la politique des capacités' dans Salais et Villeneuve, ci-dessus n 2, 18 qui reprennent l'analyse de GB Richardson, *Information and Investment. A Study on the Working of the Competitive Economy* (Oxford, Clarendon Press, 1990). Dans le débat italien, cf MG Garofalo, 'Il diritto del lavoro e la sua funzione economico-sociale' dans Garofalo et Ricci, ci-dessus n 5, 127.

externalisations ainsi que tout processus de transformation et de désintégration de l'entreprise.

Le législateur intervient d'une part, en réformant le travail intérimaire, qualifié de 'somministrazione di lavoro' (Titre III, articles 20–28), d'autre part, en créant des règles nouvelles visant à modifier la réglementation de l''appalto' (article 29) et du 'trasferimento di ramo d'azienda' (Titre IV, article 32). Dans l'ensemble, il s'agit d'opérations d'*outsourcing* et d'*insourcing* ainsi que de *contractual integration*[30] dont la qualification légale est très large et parfois ambiguë.

Bien que le processus de séparation travail/entreprise (dissociation entre l'employeur et le bénéficiaire du travail) soit très important dans le système économique et donc dans notre discours, il faut préciser qu'en Italie le modèle traditionnel de l'entreprise dite verticale est encore une réalité considérable. Il s'agit d'un processus qui a des implications graves pour le travail et que la loi réglemente sans la moindre prétention de le maîtriser de façon sérieuse.

Pour revenir à la polarisation du débat, précédemment évoquée, une certaine partie de la doctrine prétend expliquer l'intervention du législateur à la lumière des graves problèmes du marché du travail italien. Il s'agit des nombreux phénomènes de travail irrégulier et dissimulé qui doivent *apparaître* pour obtenir un remarquable résultat: l'élévation des niveaux de protection.[31] Au lieu de régler—et, donc, de maîtriser—un phénomène crucial de notre époque—la segmentation croissante de l'entreprise—le législateur cherche à le placer sous les feux de la rampe, pour que les pratiques illégales—habituellement en vigueur dans un marché à la fois complexe et segmenté,[32] de plus en plus en souffrance face aux règles et au besoin de transparence des opérations poursuivies—gagnent le caractère de la légalité. A cette fin, la réforme a définitivement abrogé la loi n 1369 de 1960—symbole du droit du travail axé sur la norme impérative et *inderogabile*—et réglé de façon innovante plusieurs aspects du phénomène de l'externalisation.

Ce qui doit être souligné dans cet exposé, c'est le caractère non exceptionnel, et au contraire tout à fait ordinaire de la fourniture de

30 En général, P Ichino, 'Il diritto del lavoro e i confini dell'impresa' [1999] *Giornale di Diritto del Lavoro e di Relazioni Industriali* 297; R De Luca-Tamajo (ed), *I processi di esternalizzazione. Opportunità e vincoli giuridici* (Esi, Napoli, 2002); L Corazza, '*Contractual integration* e rapporti di lavoro' (Padova, Cedam, 2004); P Chieco, 'Le nuove esternalizzazioni tra fornitura di prestazioni lavorative (somministrazione e distacco) e appalti *labour intensive*' dans Curzio, ci-dessus n 17, 105; V Speziale, 'Le esternalizzazioni dei processi produttivi dopo il d lgs 276 del 2003: proposte di riforma' (ADAPT, WP CSDLE. 'Massimo D'Antona' 17/2006).

31 Cf M Tiraboschi, 'Somministrazione, appalto di servizi, distacco' dans M Tiraboschi (dir), *La riforma della legge Biagi del mercato del lavoro* (Milano, Giuffrè, 2004) 210.

32 Il suffit de souligner à cet égard les graves déséquilibres entre les différentes Régions du pays. Ainsi de profondes différences, tant du point de vue économique que social, peuvent être remarquées entre les Régions du Nord et du Sud mais également, souvent, au sein d'une même Région.

main-d'œuvre. Tellement ordinaire que l'utilisation d'un contrat de fourniture à durée indéterminée a été légalisé. Les conditions pour y recourir étant très larges, ce type de contrat va inclure presque toutes les formes de service pour l'entreprise, sans aucune limitation sérieuse ou réelle. Par ailleurs, une nouvelle définition de 'appalto' (sous-traitance) a été introduite, de sorte que les simples organisation et direction du personnel sont supposées intégrer l'objet d'un contrat de sous-traitance licite. Cela signifie, en réalité, que la limite entre les deux notions demeure si floue que le choix de la qualification est laissé au sujet effectuant l'opération d'externalisation. Un choix qui sera réalisé en fonction des coûts économiques et normatifs.

Le renoncement à un règlement du phénomène en question peut donc être critiqué car il est une occasion manquée par le législateur. En effet, ce dernier, en cherchant à lutter contre les pratiques abusives en matière de trafic de main-d'œuvre et de marché noir, obtient un effet pervers: il encourage le phénomène au lieu de le limiter.

On retrouve finalement, la même critique que celle précédemment adressée à la liste des contrats précaires ou *non standards*.

En conclusion, ce qui était hier encore fermement prohibé a été légalisé sans qu'aucun effort particulier n'ait été requis pour compenser ces légalisations. Bien au contraire, des avantages sont parfois offerts sous forme de prime. Ces avantages visent à faire émerger, sur le marché du travail, les pratiques tendanciellement et traditionnellement souterraines. Cette émersion se fait cependant en l'absence de contreparties réelles en matière d'emploi.

Il suffit ici encore de considérer la nouvelle réglementation relative à la fourniture de main-d'œuvre. La fourniture de main-d'oeuvre est définie si largement par le législateur qu'elle comprend le *staff leasing*. Par ailleurs, le contrat de formation à durée déterminée, comme le recours largement ouvert au contrat de fourniture à durée indéterminée (dès lors qu'existent des *raisons d'ordre technique, organisationnel et productif*) semblent également confirmer l'idée de fond selon laquelle il s'agit d'interventions visant à augmenter l'emploi, n'importe quelle forme d'emploi.[33]

Nous ne pouvons pas approfondir ici l'opportunité d'une telle idée et des nombreuses mesures qui accompagnent sa réalisation. Une fois encore, on assiste au recul des garanties du *droit du travail*, lequel—comme l'avait déjà montré la critique libérale—est vu comme

33 Toujours à titre d'exemple, l'art 22, point 5 du d lgs 276/03 peut être mentionné: le personnel externe qui va exécuter des services ou prestations intérieurs à l'organisation en raison d'un contrat de fourniture n'est pas pris en compte dans le calcul de l'effectif de l'utilisateur pour l'application des normes légales et conventionnelles (sauf en matière d'hygiène et de sécurité).

l'obstacle majeur au respect du *droit au travail.*[34] Nous entendons mettre en évidence quelques effets majeurs de cette évolution sur le plan des *capacités.* Le développement de n'importe quel type d'emploi est un objectif stérile qui n'offre aucune forme d'encouragement et de soutien aux comportements vertueux, ni à l'adaptation bilatérale entre l'homme et le travail. Ainsi au travailleur mis à disposition il ne reste plus qu'à compter sur lui-même, sur ses qualités déjà existantes pour évoluer de sa position mauvaise à une condition stable dans l'organisation de l'entreprise qui utilise sa prestation.

Parallèlement à la fourniture de main-d'œuvre, des résultats similaires et des avantages supplémentaires peuvent être obtenus par le contrat de sous-traitance (article 29, d lgs 276/2003). Ce contrat semble d'ailleurs jouir d'un étrange traitement par la loi. L'obligation d'égalité de traitement imposée par l'article 23.2 aux cas de fourniture de main-d'œuvre ne se retrouve pas dans la réglementation relative à la sous-traitance d'œuvre ou de service. C'est pourquoi, le risque d'une compétition aux effets pervers entre les institutions normatives a été dénoncé.[35]

Considérer la réforme dans son ensemble permet donc de découvrir la faiblesse et le manque de cohérence du projet qui l'inspire. Par ailleurs l' 'extériorisation de l'emploi'[36] reste une opération convenable parce que désormais licite, mais aussi parce qu'elle permet une réduction des coûts directs et indirects de main-d'œuvre. C'est une opération stérile s'il s'agit de développer les capacités et la construction d'un cadre de sécurité active pour faire face aux transformations du travail et à l'incertitude économique.

Cette 'renonciation' à contrôler les processus de segmentation de l'entreprise est également présente dans la nouvelle réglementation en matière de transfert d'entreprise (article 32, d lgs 276/2003). Elle semble déclencher une sorte de 'synergie négative'[37] entre le contrat de sous-traitance et le transfert d'une partie de l'entreprise. Cela se déduit déjà de l'extrême liberté laissée pour identifier la 'partie' de l'entreprise qui va être concernée par la modification de la situation juridique de l'employeur.[38]

[34] C'est la célèbre formule de G Lyon-Caen, 'Le droit au travail' in *Le sans emploi et la loi* (Calligrammes, 1988) 203.

[35] L Corazza, *'Contractual integration' e rapporti di lavoro* (Padova, Cedam, 2004) 251; V Speziale, 'Le esternalizzazioni dei processi produttivi dopo il d lgs 276 del 2003: proposte di riforma' (ADAPT, WP 17/2006) 8.

[36] C'est la formule permettant d'inclure—selon une large partie de la doctrine—tant la fourniture de main d'œuvre que les autres contrats par lesquels une personne (voire entreprise) s'engage à fournir une prestation à une autre personne (voire entreprise), même s'il s'agit de la simple organisation et direction du travail (c'est-à-dire la fourniture d'une activité *labour intensive*). Cf Chieco, ci-dessus n 30, 191 ss.

[37] Cf V Speziale, cité, 9.

[38] La notion actuelle de 'transfert d'une partie de l'entreprise' est en fait si floue que sa *qualification* risque d'être laissée aux soins des sujets concernés dans l'opération d'externalisation.

En dernier lieu, il faut rappeler que le capitalisme managérial actionnaire italien est si faible et si dépourvu de toute instrumentation efficace qu'il est très difficile pour lui d'assurer un contrôle convenable de ces phénomènes complexes et de maîtriser ses dérives majeures, en particulier en matière d'emploi.

LA CRISE DE LA NOTION DE *NORMA INDEROGABILE* ET LA CRISE DE L'ACTION SYNDICALE

La crise de la notion de 'norma inderogabile' est parallèle à celle de l'action syndicale. Cette dernière est généralement décrite comme le résultat de la désyndicalisation et du recul du militantisme, phénomène caractéristique de la transformation de la *civilisation du travail* telle qu'on la connaissait avant la *fin du travail*.[39]

Cette question, par ailleurs très bien connue et largement étudiée surtout dans les analyses des sociologues et des économistes, ne peut être approfondie ici. Il est cependant important de mettre en évidence le fait que plusieurs dispositions de loi renvoient à l'intervention du syndicat—à différents niveaux—aussi bien dans l'intégration de la réglementation du rapport du travail que dans la régulation du marché du travail. Cette fonction va se répercuter sur les questions cruciales qui concernent les *sujets* et la *structure* de la négociation collective. Au lieu d'introduire, dans le respect du principe constitutionnel de la liberté d'organisation et de l'action syndicale, des règles claires et cohérentes là où le système le requiert, le d lgs 276 donne l'impression d'intervenir—de façon aussi peu claire qu'incohérente[40]—sur les règles existantes, qui sont le produit remarquable du système—autonome et volontariste—des relations professionnelles.

Quelques exemples peuvent être donnés pour illustrer le prétendu nouveau modèle de rapport entre la loi et les conventions collectives tel qu'il est envisagé par les réformes récentes. Ces illustrations permettront d'expliquer la *souffrance*[41] croissante du modèle. Plusieurs dispositions de loi donnent, en fait, aux conventions collectives la tâche d'intégrer la loi et de la rendre effective. À première vue rien de nouveau à ce sujet,[42] mais

39 Il s'agit de phénomènes bien connus, qui ont été analysés dans une littérature très vaste, et à laquelle on ne peut que renvoyer en termes très généraux. Cf U Beck, *Il lavoro nell'epoca della fine del lavoro* (Einaudi, 2000).

40 Cf L Bellardi, 'Concertazione, dialogo sociale, contrattazione e rapporto tra legge e autonomia collettiva' dans Garofalo et Ricci, ci-dessus n 5, 180 s.

41 C'est l'expression utilisée dans un essai axé cependant surtout sur la nouvelle intervention législative en matière d'aménagement du temps de travail: Carabelli et Leccese, ci-dussus n 18, v I.

42 C'est le modèle de la législation réflexive, dont il a été questionné précédemment.

en réalité certains changements minimes ont parfois des effets importants.

Lors des réformes des années 80–90, de considérables espaces de flexibilité avaient été introduits sous le contrôle de la négociation collective. Ce phénomène a été décrit comme le passage d'un système fondé sur le *garantismo individuale* à un système fondé sur le *garantismo collettivo*. Autrement dit, le passage d'un système de protection des travailleurs assurée par l' *inderogabilità* des modèles contractuels et des règles prévues par la loi et la négociation collective, à un système dans lequel cette protection est, au contraire, assurée par l'attribution aux syndicats du pouvoir de *disposer* des ressources de flexibilité, et même de certains droits des travailleurs, en fonction d'un intérêt collectif (surtout l'intérêt à l'emploi).[43]

Par cette voie, et dans le respect du projet constitutionnel axé sur le 'travail' (valeur fondamentale du système républicain), on a cherché le juste équilibre entre les droits et les intérêts individuels et collectifs, en attribuant de préférence aux forces sociales organisées la fonction de promouvoir le chemin vers l'égalité substantielle entre tous les citoyens (cf spec article 3 Cost, II). Le *garantismo collettivo* (surtout dans le cadre des politiques dites de concertation) était conçu comme la solution italienne classique pour assurer d'une part, une flexibilisation et une modernisation des règles du marché du travail, (non pas 'sauvages', mais au contraire équilibrées et contrôlées), et d'autre part, la sauvegarde des droits fondamentaux des travailleurs et la poursuite du projet émancipateur de la Constitution.

Quel est alors l'état actuel du processus d'adaptation aux nouvelles dynamiques sociales et économiques, caractérisées par l'affirmation de l'entreprise *post-industrielle*, c'est-à-dire flexible et légère?

Le législateur a été parfois audacieux, s'éloignant des parcours déjà éprouvés par le passé.

En premier lieu, une nouvelle méthode gagne l'intérêt du législateur. Hommage stérile au modèle dit européen du dialogue social et véritable dépassement de la concertation sociale qui avait accompagné et soutenu le processus d'adaptation des politiques législatives aux grandes mutations de la société et de l'économie jusqu'à la fin du siècle. L'un des résultats remarquables de ce changement d'orientation est l'épuisement de la négociation législative.[44] Un autre effet crucial résulte des nombreuses dispositions qui portent atteinte, plus ou moins directement,

[43] Pour une vision d'ensemble, U Carabelli, 'Informe italiano' dans A Marzal (dir), *Dialectica empleo-desempleo y derecho social* (Esade, 1999) 23; Caruso, ci-dessus n 14.

[44] Une technique de régulation qui est capable, finalement, de conjuguer l'autonomie de *l'ordinamento intersindacale* et l'origine consensuelle de l'intervention publique. V U Romagnoli, *Il lavoro in Italia. Un giurista racconta* (Bologna, Il Mulino, 1995) 172 ss; M Rusciano, *Contratto collettivo e autonomia sindacale* (Torino, Utet, 2003) 163 ss; G Giugni, *Diritto sindacale* (Bari, Cacucci 2006) 199 s.

à la technique dite de la flexibilité négociée et au système de relations industrielles introduit et soutenu par le Protocole du 23 de Juillet 1993.[45] Trop souvent la loi renvoie à la source collective, mais il s'agit souvent de renvois purement formels et superflus. Dans la plupart des cas, la convention collective est invoquée pour réglementer des domaines qui relèvent normalement de l'autonomie privée.

Plus généralement, on assiste à la fragmentation de la fonction normative des conventions collectives. La liste comportant les sujets syndicaux, auxquels la loi attribue la charge de négocier les conventions collectives, risque d'aboutir à la conclusion d'un accord ou d'une convention en dépit du désaccord de certaines organisations syndicales, même si elles sont fortement représentatives. C'est donc cette nouvelle forme d'abstentionnisme législatif qui suscite la plupart des critiques, dans la mesure où des règles éparses vont introduire un principe étranger au système syndical: le principe majoritaire fondé sur le nombre des sujets souscrivant l'accord (trilatéral ou bilatéral) plutôt que sur leur représentativité.

Par ailleurs, une importante partie de la doctrine italienne a émis des doutes quant à l'opportunité et à la légitimité de ces clauses de renvoi.[46] Bien que la plupart des affaires soumises à la source collective n'aient qu'un caractère marginal, il existe souvent une sorte de menace d'intervention réglementaire ministérielle pour les cas où l'intervention des sources collectives s'avèrerait infructueuse.

Cependant, c'est surtout la valorisation de l'autonomie contractuelle individuelle au détriment de l'autonomie collective qui caractérise la législation récente. Souvent, de nouveaux espaces de liberté (voir de flexibilité) sont offerts en l'absence de garanties réelles. Seul le consentement du travailleur est alors requis en présence de raisons à caractère technique ou de raisons liées à la production ou à l'organisation du travail. Finalement, il s'agit d'un hommage à la liberté qui a peu de chances de s'exprimer. Le pouvoir collectif vient d'être affaibli dans sa capacité de contrôle, et est parfois même supplanté par le consentement individuel, nouvelle forme de valorisation de la personne. Quelques exemples notables résident dans la nouvelle réglementation du contrat à durée déterminée (d lgs 368/2001), en matière d'aménagement du temps de travail (d lgs 66/2003, amendé par le d lgs 213/2004), du travail à temps partiel (article 46 d lgs 276/2003) et de la fourniture de main-d'oeuvre (Titre III, d lgs 276/2003). Bien que ces exemples

[45] Il s'agit d'un pacte de concertation tripartite, ensuite institutionnalisée par le Pacte de 1998. Selon certains auteurs, le *Protocollo* représente une véritable Charte constitutionnelle pour les relations syndicales.

[46] Cf L Bellardi, 'Concertazione, dialogo sociale, contrattazione e rapporto tra legge e autonomia collettiva' dans Garofalo et Ricci, ci-dessus n 5, 171.

mériteraient d'être approfondis et mieux illustrés, il n'est pas possible de le faire ici.[47]

LE DROIT *AU* TRAVAIL ET *POUR* LE TRAVAIL: LA *FORMATION* COMME *OPPORTUNITÉ* POUR LE DÉVELOPPEMENT DES *CAPACITÉS* DANS LE CONTRAT DE TRAVAIL

Les transformations brièvement décrites donnent l'impression que l'individu, de plus en plus *seul* sur le marché et dans le contrat de travail, est convaincu que sa *solitude* est en fait sa *liberté réelle*, parce que c'est à lui de choisir *ce* qu'il veut faire et *comment*. L'*employabilité*, au sens d'*adaptation*, serait donc un moyen qui lui est offert pour résister aux transformations du travail.

Les questions de l'emploi sont importantes dans un discours sur les capacités. L'usage de l'emploi, sa quantité ainsi que sa qualité, dépendent de plusieurs facteurs, et la politique publique de l'emploi est supposée envisager les stratégies et les mesures propres à inciter et à soutenir les investissements dans la recherche, le développement, l'éducation et la formation, c'est-à-dire les antidotes[48] à la flexibilité et véritables conditions préalables au développement des capacités.

Dans notre discours il a fallu faire l'impasse sur la formation en tant que prétendu effet légal naturel du contrat de travail subordonné. Jamais cette thèse n'a pu se fonder sur le droit positif, bien qu'une tendance, remontant à l'introduction des contrats *formation-emploi* et, plus récemment, aux règles relatives aux congés de formation (L 53/2000), présente le droit à la formation continue comme l'instrument permettant la redéfinition de l'équilibre entre les intérêts en présence et donc la promotion de sa fonction dans la société. Le fondement d'une telle lecture serait l'article 35, I, de la Constitution (la République 'veille à la formation et au perfectionnement professionnel des travailleurs') et son objectif serait l'expansion du droit *du* travail vers le droit *pour* le travail.

De plus, une certaine doctrine essaie de valoriser le lien entre la formation et la sauvegarde des compétences professionnelles, au sens dynamique du terme. Elle va jusqu'à affirmer que la formation pénètre la *cause* du contrat, et que l'employeur est obligé d'assurer le maintien des compétences par rapport au contexte organisationnel.[49] Finalement,

[47] V, respectivement L Zappalà, 'Tra diritto edn economia: obiettivi e tecniche della regolazione sociale dei contratti di lavoro a termine' (WP CSDLE 'Massimo D'Antona' 66/2005); Carabelli et Leccese, ci-dussus n 18, v I; Voza, ci-dessus n 17; Chieco, ci-dessus n 30, 105 ss.

[48] Cf B Veneziani, 'La flessibilità del lavoro edn i suoi antidoti. Un'analisi comparata' [1993] *Giornale di Diritto del Lavoro e di Relazioni Industriali* 235.

[49] Il faut prendre garde à l'ambivalence de l'obligation de formation. C'est une obligation qui peut aboutir à l'extension de l'obligation du travailleur en l'absence de véritables

l'existence d'un droit à la formation serait le nouvel essor du droit à la citoyenneté, à opposer soit à l'employeur, soit au système public (tout en gardant à l'esprit les insuffisances du système public en matière de formation professionnelle).[50]

Au-delà de ces suggestions, envisager la formation comme l'objet d'un droit du travailleur ne correspond à l'intervention directe d'aucune norme légale. Les seules bases juridiques qui permettent d'ouvrir des perspectives nouvelles quant à la valorisation de la formation, seraient offertes en guise de protection, tant des compétences professionnelles (article 2103 cc) que de la personnalité (article 2087 cc).[51]

1. En premier lieu, les limites de la pertinence concrète de cette protection viennent de la notion, large, de compétences professionnelles (*professionnalità*). D'un côté, la formation peut être conçue comme l'intérêt du travailleur à progresser dans sa carrière. Intention à faire valoir, bien entendu, dans le marché et non dans le contrat. D'un autre côté, au sein du contrat, il existe une protection uniquement *contre* un certain exercice du pouvoir organisationnel de l'employeur (*jus variandi*). Il s'agit, enfin, d'une protection offerte par une norme impérative et *inderogabile* contre le risque de la déqualification professionnelle. Il s'agit néanmoins d'une protection contre un comportement et aucune obligation de soutenir ou de promouvoir la progression par la formation ne peut être fondée en droit positif, du moins dans le cas du fonctionnement physiologique de l'entreprise ou de toute autre forme organisationnelle. Au contraire, c'est dans les cas pathologiques qu'il est admis, parfois, d'imposer à l'employeur une obligation d'activation. Cette obligation sera consécutive à l'urgence sociale qui accompagne par exemple sa décision de procéder à un licenciement collectif. Ce n'est que dans le cas du licenciement économique (pour *giustificato motivo oggettivo*) que la jurisprudence permet d'envisager une telle solution, et ce uniquement sous une forme minimale: le repêchage (le licenciement n'est alors légitime que comme *extrema ratio*). C'est d'ailleurs au sens *statique* qu'il faut l'entendre comme expression de l'obligation créancière de coopération. Aucune obligation de modifier l'organisation ne peut être imposée à l'employeur, qui n'est pas même obligé d'assurer la formation du travailleur pour préserver le rapport. Il s'agit, finalement, de

contreparties et d'instrumentation appropriée au contrôle et à la gestion du processus de formation et d'adaptation. Cf U Carabelli, 'Organizzazione del lavoro e professionalità: una riflessione su contratto di lavoro e post-taylorismo' [2003] *Giornale di Diritto del Lavoro e di Relazioni Industriali* 1.

50 Cette dernière proposition ressortirait de la réglementation en matière de congé-formation: M Magnani, 'Organizzazione del lavoro e professionalità tra rapporti e mercato del lavoro' [2003] *Giornale di Diritto del Lavoro e di Relazioni Industriali* 19.

51 Pour une lecture générale, cf C Alessi, *Professionalità e contratto di lavoro* (Giuffré, 2004).

l'irresponsabilité totale de l'entreprise par rapport à toute forme d'entretien du personnel.[52] Ceci est tellement vrai que, dans le cas du licenciement collectif, la seule possibilité offerte pour maintenir l'emploi est l'adoption de mesures alternatives devant être négociées avec les syndicats. Plutôt que de fonder une obligation de requalification, la loi n 223/1991 a suivi la voie de la *déqualification*: à l'occasion de la négociation collective, les parties peuvent décider de *déroger* aux limites imposées par l'article 2103 cc: l'employé doit être assigné aux *mansioni*, ou tâches (c'est à dire le poste et toutes les activités qui correspondent à ce poste), pour lesquelles il a été recruté, ou aux tâches relatives aux catégories supérieures successivement atteintes, ou aux dernières tâches effectivement exercées, sans la moindre diminution de son salaire.

2. En second lieu, l'obligation à la formation pourrait trouver sa base juridique dans le droit plus général à la personnalité prévu à l'article 2087 cc (protection des conditions de travail), et elle serait comprise dans les obligations de l'employeur en matière de sécurité. Il s'agit, finalement, d'une obligation primaire, similaire à l'obligation d'assurer l'intégrité physique du travailleur[53] et est donc autonome par rapport au principe général de bonne foi dans l'exécution des contrats, suite auquel les parties sont tenues au respect de la personne (et non du seul patrimoine) de l'autre contractant (c'est la catégorie des obligations secondaires).

Qu'elle se fonde sur l'article 2103 ou sur l'article 2087 et même si la doctrine et la jurisprudence en matière de préjudice biologique et de *mobbing* offrent déjà quelques développements à ce sujet, la principale limite de toute prétention à affirmer l'existence d'une obligation de formation réside, en l'état actuel, dans sa protection, qui intervient uniquement *a posteriori* avec l'indemnisation du préjudice.

L'absence d'une véritable obligation de formation dans le contrat de travail est d'ailleurs confirmée par les choix en matière de politique de l'emploi et de politique industrielle précédemment décrits: la formation sert souvent de justification aux bénéfices tant économiques que normatifs offerts aux entreprises qui utilisent certains emplois précaires ou non standards.

C'est donc vers les contrats dits atypiques, *non-standards* ou précaires (principalement le contrat d'apprentissage et le contrat d'insertion ou de réinsertion) que le législateur se tourne pour encourager et soutenir la formation et donc l'employabilité. C'est sans doute l'intérêt pour les aides

[52] Cf M Magnani, 'Organizzazione del lavoro e professionalità tra rapporti e mercato del lavoro' [2003] *Giornale di Diritto del Lavoro e di Relazioni Industriali* 19.

[53] Art 2087, intégré par l'art 9 du Statuto dei lavoratori et par le d lgs n 626/1994 (modifié en 1996) transposant la Directive cadre n 91/383 en matière de sécurité au travail.

à la formation (économiques et normatives) qui l'emporte sur l'intérêt à la formation. Pourquoi l'employeur devrait-il s'impliquer dans la formation d'un travailleur dont le contrat va cesser et qui va être remplacé par un autre travailleur temporaire ou intérimaire? Pourquoi devrait-il investir dans la formation quand l'entreprise elle-même va se transformer dans sa structure, suite aux processus d'extériorisation et de désintégration verticale? Pourquoi le travailleur aurait-il intérêt à se former et à s'*adapter* à l'entreprise qui utilise sa prestation dans le cadre, par exemple, d'un contrat de fourniture?

Pour conclure, il semble que la formation n'a que peu de chances de constituer un antidote à la flexibilité (en tant que précarité), à moins que le juge d'une part et la négociation collective d'autre part, soient capables de compenser les limites d'un cadre législatif favorisant une idée de la flexibilité de l'emploi très proche de la précarité. Une précarité qui pourrait aussi se traduire par la précarisation tendancielle de l'entreprise, du système productif et de la société.

LE DÉVELOPPEMENT DES *CAPACITÉS* ET LA POLITIQUE ACTIVE DE L'EMPLOI

On revient alors à la question du pouvoir de l'individu d'agir et de choisir la vie qu'il préfère quand il se trouve (*tout) seul* (sans emploi ou avec un emploi précaire) sur le marché du travail.

En attendant les réformes en matière d'amortisseurs sociaux, les essors de la jurisprudence et de l'autonomie collective, ainsi que toute nouvelle intervention du législateur suite au récent retournement du scénario politique, il est important de tourner, une fois encore, notre attention vers la Constitution. Il faut, en particulier, regarder ces normes et ces principes du droit du travail, hier encore dans la pénombre, et qu'il faudrait plutôt éclairer sur la rampe des transformations demandées au travail dit post-industriel, dans son acception large de l'article 35[54] et dans sa fonction sociale (article 4[55]). Le droit *au* travail (article 4 I)—à *toutes formes* de travail (article 35 I)—est la garantie première de la réalisation du principe d'égalité substantielle (article 3 II)[56] et un moyen

[54] Art 35: 'I. La République protège le travail sous toutes ses formes et dans toutes ses applications'.

[55] Art 4: 'I. La République reconnaît à tous les citoyens le droit au travail et crée les conditions qui rendent ce droit effectif. II. Tout citoyen a le devoir d'exercer, selon ses possibilités personnelles et son choix, une activité ou une fonction contribuant au progrès matériel ou spirituel de la société'.

[56] Art 3: 'I. Tous les citoyens ont une même dignité sociale et sont égaux devant la loi, sans distinction de sexe, de race, de langue, de religion, d'opinions politiques, de conditions personnelles et sociales. II. Il appartient à la République d'écarter les obstacles d'ordre économique et social qui, en limitant dans les faits la liberté et l'égalité des citoyens,

nécessaire pour l'affirmation de la personne et la réalisation de ses exigences spirituelles (articles 1 et 2).[57]

Sur la base de ces articles et, en particulier, de l'article 4, II, aucun véritable droit *au* travail ne peut occulter l'importance de l'*activation*, non seulement de l'employeur, mais également du travailleur (ou du demandeur d'emploi). Dans cette perspective, la *formation* est supposée représenter une ressource importante bien qu'*ambivalente*: elle relève de l'action publique ainsi que de l'autonomie privée et, en tout cas, elle est supposée garantir la stabilité du marché du travail. Un exemple récent en est donné par le travail dans le secteur public, où le législateur a prévu le droit / devoir à la formation professionnelle comme *moyen* de remplir les objectifs de fond des administrations publiques (cf. article 7 IV, TU n 165/2001).

Plus généralement, la dimension active de la personne révèle une tendance à l'abandon de la traditionnelle approche 'curative' du chômage au profit d'une plus large intervention sur l'organisation juridique du marché du travail. Cette intervention a pour ambition, à la fois, de réaliser un 'système efficace et cohérent' de moyens visant à 'garantir la transparence et l'efficience du marché du travail' et à améliorer les 'capacités d'insertion professionnelle des demandeurs d'emploi' (article 3 I, d lgs 276/2003).

C'est pourquoi les réformes récentes prétendent poursuivre la *décentralisation* (conformément à la réforme constitutionnelle de 2001 en matière de répartition des compétences entre l'Etat et les Régions), l'*intégration* avec le système de la formation (dans une acception très vaste) afin de raccorder ce dernier aux exigences du marché, et la *concurrence* entre les institutions publiques et les services privés. Il est en effet affirmé qu'une telle compétition public/privé serait la meilleure garantie du bon fonctionnement des services pour l'emploi.[58]

Plusieurs mesures ont été mises en place afin de soutenir le passage d'un système de placement, axé sur la *mise en relation* à un système axé

s'opposent au plein épanouissement de la personne humaine et à la participation effective de tous les travailleurs à l'organisation politique, économique et sociale du Pays'.

[57] Art 1er: 'I. L'Italie est une République démocratique, fondée sur le travail'. Art 2: 'La République reconnaît et garantit les droits inviolables de l'homme, aussi bien en tant qu'individu que dans les formations sociales où se développe sa personnalité, et exige l'accomplissement des devoirs imprescriptibles de solidarité politique, économique et sociale.'

[58] Le mauvais fonctionnement du système public de placement avait d'ailleurs fait l'objet de l'intervention de la Cour de justice (décision C–55/1996), qui avait relevé son inadéquation avec les prescriptions de l'art 86 (TCE). Ce fut l'impulsion pour la mise en oeuvre d'un processus de transformation qui a finalement abouti à l'abandon du système public de placement, dont l'institution remontait à la loi no 264/1949. Les institutions publiques intervenants sur le marché du travail—dans le cadre de la législation régionale—perdent donc toute fonction d'entremise entre l'offre et le demande d'emploi et se transforment en services pour l'emploi (d lgs 181/2001, ensuite modifié et intégré par le d lgs 297/2002).

plutôt sur l'information[59] et, plus généralement, afin de moderniser le système des services pour l'emploi dans une perspective de modernisation du marché du travail.

La principale nouveauté de cette transformation, dans la perspective qui nous intéresse, réside dans la nouvelle relation entre les services pour l'emploi et les usagers. Les deux parties de cette relation ont un rôle à la fois actif et passif et le chômage est considéré comme une condition dont il faut sortir au plus tôt par une 'attitude laborieuse'. Le chômeur actif doit donc s'engager dans une relation fondée sur la triade: information—orientation—formation.[60] Un passage qui révèle, d'ailleurs, l'abandon de l'approche curative au profit d'une approche peut-être répressive, dans la mesure où la formation *pour* le marché va devenir l'objet d'une *obligation* de la personne qui prétend entrer ou rester dans le marché du travail plutôt que l'occasion de développer ses capacités en tant que liberté de choix et d'action pour réaliser son propre projet de vie.[61]

La participation à toutes les initiatives d'orientation, d'insertion dans le marché du travail, de formation et de requalification professionnelle serait finalement la condition pour garder le statut de chômeur. Cette participation ferait, de plus, l'objet d'une *relation* entre l'usager et le service pour l'emploi, dont la nature juridique est ambiguë. Quelle que soit la nature juridique de cette 'relation pour la promotion de l'emploi', l'*activation* de la personne en condition de faiblesse dans le marché du travail est soumise, encore une fois, à un instrument ressemblant au contrat. Un 'contrat' qui est cependant dépourvu de véritable garantie au profit de la partie la plus faible: l'usager est obligé de consacrer toute sa disponibilité à s'activer sans la moindre contrepartie réelle. Comme le démontre l'approche par les capacités, en l'absence de tout 'cercle vertueux' garantissant l'exercice responsable de sa liberté, il sera alors difficile pour la personne de convertir ses potentialités en réalités.

LA *PRÉCARITÉ* DE L'EMPLOI ET LE RISQUE DE *PRÉCARISATION* DU SYSTÈME ÉCONOMIQUE ET PRODUCTIF: L'ÉCHEC DU DÉVELOPPEMENT DES CAPACITÉS

L'approche par les capacités nous permet, en conclusion, de mettre *en perspective* le débat autour des mesures visant à la flexibilisation du

59 Cf D Garofalo, *Formazione e lavoro tra diritto e contratto* (Bari, Cacucci, 2004) 261; F Liso, 'Articolo 3. Finalità' dans M Pedrazzoli (dir), *Il nuovo mercato del lavoro. D lgs 10 settembre 2003, n 276* (Bologna, Zanichelli, 2004) 43 ss.

60 Garofalo, *ibid*, 271.

61 Cf B Caruso, 'Occupabilità, formazione e *capability* nei modelli giuridici di regolazione dei mercati del lavoro' [2007] *Giornale di Diritto del Lavoro e di Relazioni Industriali* 1.

travail et à la réduction de son coût, conséquence presque automatique de la précarisation de l'emploi et des processus d'externalisation. Comment peut-on concevoir un modèle de compétition axé entièrement sur la réduction des coûts (ce qui risque d'ailleurs de retarder de façon sérieuse le processus de requalification managériale et technologique du système industriel italien)? Cela est d'autant plus grave si l'on considère la présence croissante sur le plan mondial des économies nouvelles. Il s'agit de ces pays d'Asie ou d'Europe de l'Est contre lesquels il sera difficile de *résister* si la compétition se limite à la question des coûts de production.

L'approche par les capacités nous permet, enfin, d'attirer l'attention sur le besoin de contrer la tendance à la rupture avec la *civilisation du travail* et de retrouver la véritable fonction de la norme impérative, condition préalable pour (re)découvrir et, donc, développer, sa *fonction promotionnelle*.

Par cette approche, on constate alors le besoin de retrouver ou de renouveler les liens institutionnels qui peuvent assurer le fonctionnement du système social dans son ensemble. Ces liens nous rappellent le rôle important de l'autonomie collective pour assurer un certain équilibre entre les exigences de justice et de cohésion sociale, d'une part, et les contraintes économiques de l'autre. Si l'on considère les nombreuses insuffisances—presque endémiques—de l'organisation étatique italienne et ses répercussions en matière d'organisation, gestion et contrôle du marché du travail, on comprend bien l'importance de l'action syndicale. La saison du *garantismo collettivo* a été l'exemple parfait de l'inaptitude de l'administration publique du travail à offrir les services adéquats aux besoins du marché, et de l'imbrication croissante entre les dimensions publique et privée dans l'organisation juridique du marché du travail, empruntée au *polycentrisme*.[62] Pour revenir à l'actualité, l'autonomie collective est victime en quelque sorte de l'excès de son rôle dans la régulation du marché du travail et par rapport au contrat de travail. Les pouvoirs publics, quant à eux, vont remplir une fonction importante dans ces deux domaines. Ils sont de plus en plus supposés accompagner, stimuler, et même assister[63] l'action des acteurs privés. Ils doivent également contrôler[64] de façon plus efficace et plus sérieuse le respect des protections du travail, afin de répondre aux graves problèmes de l'illégalité et du marché noir.

62 D'Antona, ci-dessus n 22, 53 s.

63 On peut mentionner, à ce propos, l'introduction de la certification (arts 75-84, d lgs 276/2003). Il s'agit d'une activité administrative supposée assister les parties privées dans l'exercice de leur autonomie afin de réduire le contentieux judiciaire et donc (essayer de) rendre les relations contractuelles certaines. Il s'agit d'une opinion technique sur la qualification du contrat, qui vise tout simplement à influencer le juge lors de son intervention. Cf MG Garofalo, 'Contratti di lavoro e certificazione' dans Curzio, ci-dessus n 17, 581.

64 V. La réforme en matière des pouvoirs et des compétences des Inspecteurs du travail (d lgs no 124 de 2004).

Cependant, le problème de l'ineffectivité des règles juridiques et des institutions demeure l'un des défis majeurs du *droit du travail* qui prétend devenir le *droit pour le travail*. On assiste par ailleurs à l'effet paradoxal de la récente profusion législative: les entreprises ont elles-mêmes du mal à se servir des nouveaux avantages en matière de flexibilité! *Much ado about nothing* pourrait-on dire, mais l'ambition 'rationalisatrice'[65] du droit et la vocation de redistribution du droit du travail, pour prévenir et compenser les échecs du marché, risque de s'épuiser.

Annotation (septembre 2008)

Cet exposé a été terminé en décembre 2006. Dans ces deux dernières années le cadre politique et législatif italien a beaucoup changé. Cependant, l'on peut dire que rien n'a véritablement changé. Il faut surtout remarquer que le gouvernement de centre-gauche dirigé par M. Prodi (mai 2006—mai 2008) n'a pu réaliser le projet de réforme qu'il avait annoncé et le retour au gouvernement de M. Berlusconi (le 8 de mai 2008) semble de plus en plus confirmer la ligne politique qu'on a décrite précédemment. On assiste au désengagement progressif de l'Etat régulateur ainsi qu'au malaise croissant des organisations intermédiaires pour compenser ce désengagement qui, comme nous l'avons souligné, est la conséquence (et en même temps la cause) de la liberté toujours plus grandes reconnue aux instances privées dans le marché.

Encore une fois on peut donner seulement quelques exemples.

Il faut d'abord mentionner la méthode d'intervention du législateur et donc la reprise de la concertation sociale par le gouvernement de M. Prodi, ceci dans un contexte difficile à cause de la complexité des matières traitées ainsi que des divergences au sein de la majorité; donc, cette expérience est en réalité profondément différente si on la compare à celle de 1993, institutionnalisée par la suite en 1998.[66] A la suite de la concertation, le 23 juillet 2007 était conclu le 'Protocole social sur la prévoyance sociale, le travail et la compétitivité, pour l'équité et la croissance durable', qui incluait la réforme des retraites et du marché du travail. Ce Protocole a été transposé (avec quelques modifications) dans la loi no 247 du 24 décembre 2007.

Pour ce qui concerne ses contenus, la loi no 247/2007 est intervenue, par exemple, en matière de contrat à durée déterminé, ainsi qu'en matière de contrat temporaire (dit de 'somministrazione') ou d'emploi à temps partiel. Il s'agit d'interventions qui ont pour but de limiter le recours

65 Cf A Perulli, 'Razionalità e proporzionalità nel diritto del lavoro' [2005] *Giornale di Diritto del Lavoro e di Relazioni Industriali* 1.

66 Cf L Bellardi, 'Sul metodo e sui contenuti del negoziato per la revisione della struttura contrattuale', WP CSDLE 'Massimo D'Antona' no 74/2008.

abusif à ces formes d'emploi. Sans entrer dans le mérite de l'efficacité de ces interventions, notons qu'à la suite du changement du contexte politique, le décret no 112 du 2008 (loi de conversion no 133 du 6 août 2008) a déjà introduit des nouveautés et pourrait, vraisemblablement, en introduire d'autres, c'est-à-dire plus de déréglementation et de fragmentation au prétexte d'un plus grand développement économique et d'une majeure compétitivité. Comme l'a bien explique le Ministère du travail, il faut 'libérer le travail' (document du 19 juin 2008), ce qui est tout à fait différent de la libération du travailleur comme *processus d'expansion des libertés*. Ce n'est pas une idée de 'développement comme liberté', où la liberté est à la fois l'identité et le moyen de réalisation du développement, mais c'est plutôt un développement libre, c'est-à-dire sans un véritable objectif, sans une réelle gouvernance à long terme. Encore une fois il faut se demander s'il s'agit d'un projet de réforme compatible avec l'idée de développement reconnue par notre Constitution et qui est axée sur la valeur de la personne qui travaille.[67]

[67] Pour une interprétation (plus) systématique des principes de la Constitution en ce qui concerne la structure de rapports de production qui représente encore de nos jours un des obstacles majeurs qui s'opposent au plein épanouissement de la personne humaine et à la participation effective de tous les citoyens à l'organisation politique, économique et sociale du Pays (art 3, II, de la Constitution), cf MG Garofalo, 'Unità e pluralità del lavoro nel sistema costituzionale' [2008] *Giornale di Diritto del Lavoro e di Relazioni Industriali* 1.

7

La recherche d'un concept de capacitas *en droit du licenciement allemand*

WIEBKE BROSE

INTRODUCTION

Le but de cette contribution est de démontrer les contextes divers dans lesquels on retrouve l'idée de la capacité et la façon de laquelle elle est traitée par le législateur ainsi que les effets qu'il confère à la présence et respectivement à l'absence de la capacité au sein du droit du licenciement allemand. Cette approche sert à rechercher un concept, car de prime abord le droit du licenciement allemand ne semble traiter la question de capacité que de manière sporadique, sans système visible. Ainsi, le point de départ de l'établissement de ce bilan est une compréhension très ouverte de la notion de *capacitas*. Pour des raisons de clarté et par souci de laisser la catégorie la plus souple possible, la notion de capacité sera utilisée de façon générale sans faire de nuances par rapport à la terminologie.

La notion même de capacité—*Fähigkeit*—n'est pas perçu en droit du licenciement allemand comme une notion ayant un champ d'application bien circonscrit et elle n'est que rarement expressément utilisée par le législateur. Mais cela ne signifie pas que l'idée de capacité y est inexistante. Au contraire, la capacité et encore plus souvent son absence est en grande partie à la base du droit du licenciement et par conséquent elle y est finalement omniprésente. Ainsi, l'incapacité des parties du contrat de travail de remplir leurs obligations contractuelles peut permettre à l'employeur de rompre le contrat de travail par voie de licenciement. C'est donc la raison d'existence même du droit du licenciement.

Mais il y a aussi des tendances récentes qui montrent la notion de capacité sous un autre angle. Le législateur allemand a d'un côté infligé des obligations à l'employeur ayant pour but de rétablir la capacité de travail du salarié et même de prévenir une incapacité ayant des répercussions sur l'emploi. En même temps, on trouve aussi la tendance inverse qui a pour effet de protéger les salariés spécialement performants contre le licenciement.

Dans la suite, il y aura d'abord une présentation de l'émergence 'classique' de la capacité en tant que cause du licenciement pour ensuite examiner les nouvelles tendances dans ce domaine et en tirer des conclusions à la fin.

Mais avant de commencer par l'examen de la notion de capacité, il faut encore faire quelques brèves remarques par rapport à la structure du droit du licenciement allemand pour pouvoir mieux placer les résultats dans le contexte global du droit du licenciement. La spécificité la plus importante du droit du licenciement allemand se trouve du côté des effets juridiques d'un licenciement irrégulier. Le droit du licenciement allemand est basé sur l'idée du maintien de l'emploi (*Bestandsschutz*).[1] Il s'ensuit qu'un licenciement irrégulier est nul et que le contrat de travail continue d'exister.[2] La nullité du licenciement est donc la sanction normale, il ne s'agit pas d'une sanction spécialement sévère. En conséquence, il n'existe pas de système d'indemnisation, l'idée de payer une indemnité en cas de licenciement régulier ou irrégulier y est en principe absente.[3] La deuxième remarque concerne le champ d'application de la loi de protection contre le licenciement (Kündigungsschutzgesetz = KSchG) qui prévoit entre autres des règles relatives à la capacité du salarié et qui servira de base de l'examen suivant. Cette loi n'est applicable que dans les entreprises occupant plus que dix salariés et le salarié concerné doit avoir une ancienneté de plus de six mois (§§ 1, 23 KSchG).[4] Pour savoir si un licenciement est valable,

[1] Gemeinschaftskommentar Kündigungsrecht/*Griebeling*, 8e édition 2007, § 1 KSchG n° 29.

[2] Cependant dans la pratique, l'employeur et le salarié se mettent souvent d'accord à la fin d'un procès sur le paiement d'une indemnité au lieu de réintégrer le salarié dans l'entreprise.

[3] Avec la loi relative aux réformes du marché de travail (*Gesetz zu Reformen auf dem Arbeitsmarkt*) du 24.12.2003, le législateur a fait un premier pas vers une indemnisation du salarié en insérant le § 1a dans la loi relative à la protection contre le licenciement (*KSchG*). Cette norme vise uniquement le licenciement pour motif économique et donne au salarié le droit à une indemnisation (0.5 de la rémunération mensuelle par an d'ancienneté) à condition qu'il n'intente pas une action en protection contre le licenciement dans les trois semaines qui suivent le licenciement (ce qui est le délai légal pour intenter une action) et que l'employeur ait indiqué cette possibilité au moment du licenciement. Même si cette nouvelle règle a été établie dans le souci de rendre compte de la pratique répandue de payer des indemnisations au lieu de réintégrer le salarié en cas de licenciement irrégulier, elle n'englobe que quelques cas très précis et dépend du choix du salarié. Elle ne mène pas à un changement du concept légal du maintien de l'emploi.

[4] Le droit du licenciement allemand est divisé en deux régimes différents donnant un degré de protection plus ou moins fort aux salariés. Pour une catégorie de salariés c'est la loi de protection contre le licenciement (*Kündigungsschutzgesetz = KSchG*) qui est applicable, pour une deuxième catégorie le contrôle des licenciements se fait uniquement par le biais du droit commun (§ 242 BGB) et les droits fondamentaux (Art. 12 al 1 GG). Le droit de licenciement prévu par la loi de protection contre le licenciement (*Kündigungsschutzgesetz*) prévoit un

cette loi ordonne d'examiner si le licenciement est justifié socialement. Il faut donc tenir compte du fait que les normes de cette loi présentées comme suit ne sont pas applicables à tous les salariés licenciés.

LE DOMAINE D'APPLICATION CLASSIQUE DE LA NOTION: L'INCAPACITÉ EN TANT QUE CAUSE DE LA RUPTURE DU CONTRAT DE TRAVAIL

En droit du licenciement allemand, il existe trois motifs de licenciement qui servent de justification sociale au sens de la loi de protection contre les licenciements (v § 1 al 2 KSchG): le motif personnel (= motif inhérent à la personne du salarié), le comportement (en règle générale fautif) et le motif résultant des besoins urgents de l'entreprise, donc le motif économique. Dans la suite, l'exposé de trois cas spécifiques de licenciement permettra—à titre exemplaire—d'examiner l'effet de l'absence de capacité sous des angles différents: le licenciement en cas de maladie, le licenciement pour manque d'efficacité et le licenciement pour fermeture de l'entreprise.

Le licenciement en cas de maladie

Le licenciement en raison d'absence au poste de travail pour maladie est le cas d'application le plus important du licenciement pour motif personnel[5] et en même temps le cas où l'existence de l'incapacité est le plus évident. L'aspect de la capacité concerné est l'état physique du salarié qui fait qu'il n'est pas capable de remplir son obligation contractuelle. Il faut distinguer la maladie de courte durée qui revient de manière répétée et la maladie de longue durée.

La maladie répétée de courte durée

Pour l'examen de la justification d'un licenciement pour une maladie de courte durée, la jurisprudence a établi un examen en trois étapes.[6] D'abord, elle vérifie si au moment de la notification du licenciement il y a des faits objectifs justifiant la possibilité que dans le futur le salarié sera

contrôle plus sévère de la légitimité du licenciement (c'est pour cela qu'on l'appelle des fois aussi le droit du licenciement de '1ère classe') et c'est à cette loi qu'on se réfère tout d'abord quand on parle du droit du licenciement allemand.

5 Ascheid/Preis/Schmidt/*Dörner*, Kündigungsrecht, 3e édition 2007, § 1 KSchG n° 134.

6 BAG 5.7.1990 AP § 1 KSchG 1969 Krankheit Nr 27; BAG 29.4.1999 EzA § 1 KSchG 1969 Krankheit Nr 46; Gemeinschaftskommentar Kündigungsrecht/*Griebeling*, 8e édition 2007, § 1 KSchG n° 323.

aussi souvent malade que dans le passé. C'est ce qu'on appelle le 'pronostic de santé négatif' (*negative Gesundheitsprognose*).[7] Il s'agit finalement d'une appréciation de la capacité physique du salarié qui est dirigée vers le futur et qui vise le manque de capacité.

Deuxièmement, ces absences pronostiquées doivent conduire à une perturbation importante des intérêts de l'entreprise. Cette perturbation peut selon la jurisprudence entre autres être justifiée par les frais qui sont causés par l'obligation de continuer de payer le salaire convenu en cas de maladie. D'après la conception légale, l'obligation de continuer de payer le salaire convenu n'excède pas la durée de six semaines (§ 3 al 1 EFZG). Mais cette règle ne concerne que le cas où le salarié est malade de manière continue. En cas de maladie répétée, cette obligation peut naître à plusieurs reprises et durer en tout plus que six semaines. Dans ce cas de figure, la Cour fédérale du travail (Bundesarbeitsgericht = BAG) considère que l'obligation de l'employeur de continuer de payer le salaire peut conduire à une perturbation importante des intérêts de l'entreprise.[8] Ceci conduit à une situation paradoxale: le législateur voulait protéger le salarié malade, donc incapable, en lui donnant un droit au paiement de salaire et c'est justement cette protection qui peut justifier un licenciement parce que ce système de protection peut coûter trop cher à l'employeur—et engendrer le cas échéant son 'incapacité financière'.[9] Mais la période de six semaines n'est qu'une première valeur indicative. La question, si la maladie cause des frais trop élevés pour l'employeur, se décide encore en fonction d'autres facteurs, comme par example des absences des autres salariés.[10] L'impact de l'incapacité du salarié s'apprécie donc aussi par rapport à la capacité des autres salariés.

Finalement, il faut procéder à une pondération des intérêts respectifs de l'employeur et du salarié. Dans ce cadre, il faut rechercher, s'il y a des mesures tolérables que l'employeur peut prendre pour surmonter les périodes d'absence du salarié dans l'entreprise, comme par example l'embauche de personnel auxiliaire.[11] Ainsi, le salarié a le droit d'être incapable jusqu'à un certain point, jusqu'où c'est à l'employeur de tolérer l'incapacité et de prendre des mesures pour la compenser.

[7] BAG 7.11.2002 AP § 1 KSchG 1969 Krankheit Nr 40; BAG 29.4.1999 AP § 1 KSchG 1969 Krankheit Nr 36; BAG 14.1.1993, NZA 1994, 309.

[8] BAG 29.7.1993 AP § 1 KSchG 1969 Krankheit Nr 27; BAG 5.7.1990 AP § 1 KSchG 1969 Krankheit Nr 26; BAG 20.1.2000 EzA § 1 KSchG Krankheit Nr 47.

[9] Cette jurisprudence a suscité beaucoup de critique dans la doctrine, *v* p ex Münchener Kommentar/*Schwerdtner*, 4e édition 2005, § 622 Anh n° 276 s; *von Hoyningen-Huene/Linck*, Kündigungsschutzgesetz, 13e édition 2002, § 1 n° 233 et s; *Preis*, Arbeitsrecht, p 743.

[10] D'autres facteurs peuvent être p ex l'ancienneté du salarié concerné ou son âge ; *v* pour les critères p ex Stahlhacke/Preis/*Preis*, Kündigung und Kündigungsschutz im Arbeitsverhältnis, 9e édition 2005, p 501 n° 1234.

[11] BAG 14.1.1993, NZA 1994, 309; BAG 12.12.1996 EzA § 1 KSchG Krankheit Nr 41; Ascheid/Preis/Schmidt/*Dörner*, Kündigungsrecht, 3e édition 2007, § 1 KSchG n° 155, n° 173.

Le licenciement pour maladie répétée traduit l'idée d'une incapacité temporaire. En tout, on ne peut donner de formule exacte, à partir de quand des absences répétées en raison d'une maladie peuvent justifier un licenciement, car il y a toujours les spécificités de l'entreprise autant que des critères tenant à la personne du salarié qui doivent être prises en considération. Ceci mène à une première conclusion que dans ce contexte: l'incapacité qui engendre des conséquences est une notion relative. Le même taux d'absences en raison de maladies répétées peut justifier un licenciement dans une entreprise tout comme il peut être à tolérer par l'employeur dans une autre entreprise.

La maladie de longue durée

En cas de maladie de longue durée, il faut procéder au même examen en trois étapes qu'en cas de maladies répétées. On peut qualifier cette forme d'incapacité comme une incapacité 'probablement durable'. Il n'y a pas non plus de limite précise concernant les absences du salarié à partir desquelles un licenciement est justifié. D'après la jurisprudence, il s'agit d'une maladie de longue durée qui peut justifier un licenciement, si le salarié est malade depuis huit mois, mais il faut toujours procéder à un pronostic par rapport au rétablissement de la capacité de travail.[12] La Cour a donné dans ce cas comme échelle de pronostic une période de 24 mois, mais il suffit que ce rétablissement est incertain pour que le licenciement soit justifié.[13] La certitude que le salarié ne retrouvera pas son entière capacité n'est pas nécessaire. En principe, on peut transférer les réflexions faites à propos de la maladie répétée. Mais on peut observer que l'évaluation des intérêts respectifs change quand il s'agit d'une maladie de longue durée. Car en ce cas, les effets de la maladie sur la marche de l'entreprise sont plus prévisibles qu'en cas de maladie répétée et l'employeur peut plus facilement trouver des solutions pour réagir aux absences du salarié. En même temps, l'état physique du salarié demande un degré de protection plus élevé.[14] Ainsi, l'appréciation de l'incapacité et ses effets diffère encore en fonction de l'entreprise et la capacité de l'entreprise de vivre avec l'incapacité du salarié.

La maladie durable

Le troisième cas de figure constitue l'incapacité de travail durable en

[12] BAG 21.5.1992 EzA § 1 KSchG Krankheit Nr 38; BAG 29.4.1999, NZA 1999, 978; le fait de se référer à une certaine période pour apprécier la justification sociale en raison d'une maladie est pourtant critiqué par la doctrine, *v* p ex Stahlhacke/Preis/*Preis*, Kündigung und Kündigungsschutz, 9e édition 2005, p 506 n° 1241.

[13] BAG 29.4.1999 AP § 1 KSchG 1969 Krankheit Nr 36.

[14] Kittner/Däubler/Zwanziger/*Kittner/Deinert*, Kündigungsrecht, 7e édition 2008, § 1 KSchG n° 101.

raison d'une maladie. Il s'agit d'une incapacité durable. Dans le cas où le salarié est malade depuis 18 mois et la fin de la maladie n'est pas prévisible, la jurisprudence l'assimile à une maladie durable. La maladie durable—et ainsi l'incapacité physique durable—donne à l'employeur le droit de licencier le salarié. Une maladie est considérée comme durable si on ne peut plus s'attendre à une amélioration de l'état physique du salarié dans les 24 mois à venir.[15] Dans ce cas, une pondération des intérêts respectifs explicite n'est plus nécessaire. Le fait que le salarié se trouve dans l'impossibilité durable de remplir son obligation de travail justifie le licenciement.[16] Les exigences établies par la Cour fédérale du travail en cas de maladie pour arriver au stade où l'appréciation de l'incapacité ne se fait plus par rapport à l'entreprise (et sa capacité de compenser les effets) sont donc très hautes. Une maladie, qui dure un an par example, ne peut pas encore justifier en elle-même un licenciement, un pronostic négatif, une appréciation de l'impact sur l'entreprise ainsi qu'une pondération des intérêts respectifs restent toujours nécessaires.

Le licenciement pour manque d'efficacité

Le licenciement peut également être justifié par un manque d'efficacité. Il est bien établi dans la jurisprudence que ce manque peut constituer une violation des obligations contractuelles en raison d'un comportement fautif du salarié dans le cas où il n'exploite pas suffisamment sa capacité de travail.[17] Finalement, ceci revient à l'établissement d'une obligation du salarié de faire son travail en utilisant sa capacité entière. Si la quantité et la qualité de l'obligation due par le salarié n'est pas concrétisée dans le contrat de travail, ce qui est le cas normal, cette concrétisation se fait par rapport au pouvoir de direction de l'employeur et par rapport à l'efficacité du salarié. Dans ce cadre, c'est l'efficacité, donc la capacité personnelle et subjective[18] du salarié qui est déterminante.[19] Ainsi, on utilise la capacité du salarié en tant que moyen pour déterminer les obligations contractuelles.

Dernièrement, un autre aspect du manque d'efficacité a été examiné. La Cour fédérale du travail a rendu un arrêt selon lequel un licenciement

[15] BAG 12.4.2002, NZA 2002, 1081; Kittner/Däubler/Zwanziger/*Kittner/Deinert*, Kündigungsrecht, 7e édition 2008, § 1 KSchG n° 102.

[16] BAG 28.2.1990 AP § 1 KSchG 1969 Krankheit Nr 25; BAG 3.12.1998, DB 1999, 589; BAG 19.4.2007, BB 2007, 1904.

[17] BAG 26.6.1997 RzK I 5i Nr 126; BAG 21.5.1992 AP § 1 KSchG 1969 Verhaltensbedingte Kündigung Nr 38; BAG 22.7.1982 DB 1983, 180; BAG 11.12.2003 AP § 1 KSchG 1969 Verhaltensbedingte Kündigung Nr 48.

[18] En allemand, le terme de *subjektives Leistungsvermögen* est devenu une expression établie dans ce contexte.

[19] BAG 17.1.2008, DB 2008, 1274.

peut également être justifié en raison d'un manque d'aptitude personnelle qui se manifeste dans un manque d'efficacité. En visant l'aptitude personnelle, la Cour a qualifié le manque d'efficacité de motif personnel. Ce motif personnel peut justifier le licenciement, si le salarié rend un travail d'une qualité largement en dessous de la moyenne pendant une période suffisamment longue.[20] Il n'y a pas eu de précisions relatives au degré d'insuffisance—à part une vague référence à un arrêt où l'efficacité d'un salarié handicapé était un tiers en dessous de la moyenne de l'entreprise—ou à la durée de la période. Mais cette jurisprudence montre un aspect nouveau, celui de la prise en compte d'une incapacité partielle justifiant un licenciement. Cependant, il s'agit d'une jurisprudence très jeune qu'on ne peut pas encore considérer comme établie.

Le licenciement pour motif économique

Ce n'est pas seulement du côté du salarié qu'une incapacité de remplir l'obligation contractuelle peut justifier un licenciement. On peut aussi trouver un raisonnement partant du point de vue de l'employeur. Sans pouvoir entrer dans les détails, on peut donner comme l'exemple le plus parlant la fermeture de l'entreprise. Une des obligations primaires de l'employeur est de fournir du travail au salarié. En cas de fermeture de l'entreprise, il devient incapable de remplir cette obligation. Une fermeture définitive justifie régulièrement un licenciement pour motif économique.[21] On pourrait qualifier cette incapacité d'incapacité économique.

Dans ce cadre, il faut de plus tenir compte du fait que le régime du licenciement pour motif économique est marqué par le principe de la libre décision de l'employeur (*freie Unternehmerentscheidung*) qui est à la base du licenciement économique. C'est une décision qui consiste à façonner et à modifier la structure de l'entreprise selon les conceptions de l'employeur. Par rapport à cette décision, le contrôle du juge est restreint, il ne peut rechercher que s'il s'agit d'une décision arbitraire ou qui est de tout évidence déraisonnable.[22] L'employeur peut donc volontairement provoquer son incapacité économique d'employer le salarié en prenant une telle décision. Il s'ensuit qu'il peut y avoir une incapacité

[20] BAG 11.12.2003 AP § 1 KSchG 1969 Verhaltensbedingte Kündigung Nr 48.

[21] BAG 18.1.2001, NZA 2001, 719; BAG 3.9.1998, NZA 1999, 147; BAG 27.2.1987 EzA § 1 KSchG Betriebsbedingte Kündigung Nr 46; Stahlhacke/Preis/*Preis*, Kündigung und Kündigungsschutz im Arbeitsverhältnis, 9e édition 2005, p 358 n° 971.

[22] BAG 30.4.1987 AP § 1 KSchG 1969 Betriebsbedingte Kündigung Nr 42; BAG 9.5.1996 AP § 1 KSchG 1969 Betriebsbedingte Kündigung Nr 79.

économique 'volontaire' ainsi qu'une incapacité 'involontaire' de l'employeur, les deux pouvant le cas échéant justifier un licenciement.

UNE NOUVELLE TENDANCE: LES OBLIGATIONS DE L'EMPLOYEUR VISANT À RÉTABLIR LA CAPACITÉ

Parmi les obligations incombant à l'employeur qui visent à rétablir la capacité du salarié en vue d'éviter un licenciement, on peut discerner deux catégories englobant deux aspects différents de la capacité. Le premier aspect peut être qualifié comme une incapacité due à un manque de qualification. Le deuxième aspect concerne l'incapacité physique de travailler.

§ 1 al 2 KSchG: Le droit à une formation continue ou une reconversion professionnelle

La teneur et l'objectif du § 1 al 2 KSchG

Selon le § 1 al 2 KSchG, le licenciement n'est pas socialement justifié et en conséquence nul, si l'employeur prononce le licenciement malgré le fait que le maintien de l'emploi est possible après avoir procédé à des mesures de formation continue ou de reconversion professionnelle tolérables (*zumutbar*) pour l'employeur. Mais cette obligation n'existe qu'à condition que le conseil d'entreprise (*Betriebsrat*) se soit opposé au licenciement et que le salarié ait donné son accord par rapport aux mesures proposées. La jurisprudence a rajouté à ces conditions qu'il doit être sûr ou au moins suffisamment prévisible qu'à la fin de ces mesures, le salarié peut être employé dans l'entreprise. Il faut qu'il y ait un poste de travail libre,[23] ce qui s'apprécie au niveau de l'entreprise et non seulement au niveau de l'entité économique concerné.[24]

Si ces conditions sont remplies, l'obligation de l'employeur confère en même temps au salarié le droit à la mise en œuvre des mesures visées par le § 1 al 2 KSchG. Mais ce droit ne sert qu'à garder un emploi qui correspond à celui que le salarié a occupé jusque-là, il ne s'agit pas de donner au salarié la possibilité d'accéder à une promotion.[25] Avec cette règle, le

[23] BAG 7.2.1991 AP § 1 KSchG 1969 Umschulung Nr 1; Gemeinschaftskommentar Kündigungsrecht/*Griebeling*, 8e édition 2007, § 1 KSchG n° 231.

[24] Gemeinschaftskommentar Kündigungsrecht/*Griebeling*, 8e édition 2007, § 1 KSchG n° 722.

[25] BAG 29.3.1990 AP § 1 KSchG 1969 Betriebsbedingte Kündigung Nr 50; Gemeinschaftskommentar Kündigungsrecht/*Griebeling*, 8e édition 2007, § 1 KSchG n° 724; il faut déroger à ce principe dans le cas où l'employeur a revalorisé l'emploi et le salarié peut suffire aux nouvelles exigences après avoir participé à des mesures de formation ou de

législateur a tenu compte de l'aspect de la qualification dans le monde du travail, en essayant de compenser une incapacité due à un manque de qualification. Ainsi, il est tenu compte des changements rapides dans le monde du travail moderne par rapport au profil et aux exigences de l'emploi.

Le contenu exacte des mesures visées par le § 1 al 2 KSchG n'est pas défini par la loi. On ne peut recourir sans réserve aux définitions données par la loi relative à la formation (§§ 1, 46, 47 BBiG).[26] Le but de la loi de protection contre le licenciement est un autre que celui de la loi relative à la formation.[27] Les mesures au sens du § 1 al 2 KSchG servent à maintenir le salarié dans l'entreprise, ce n'est pas sa formation qui est au premier plan.[28] L'objectif est de rétablir la performance que le salarié a perdu en raison d'un manque de qualification. Il faut donc interpréter ces notions de manière plus large que dans le cadre de la loi relative à la formation, ces définitions pouvant seulement servir à trouver des critères de distinction entre les deux mesures.[29] La notion de reconversion professionnelle ainsi que celle de formation continue englobent *toute mesure* qui peut permettre d'occuper le salarié dans l'entreprise. La reconversion professionnelle regroupe les mesures servant à donner des connaissances et du savoir-faire nécessaire à l'exercice d'un autre métier que celui qui a été exercé par le salarié concerné jusque-là. La conséquence d'une reconversion professionnelle ayant eu du succès, mène en règle générale à un changement du contrat de travail.[30] La formation continue sert en revanche à rendre le salarié capable de remplir les exigences augmentées de son métier.[31] Ces mesures restent donc dans le cadre des obligations émanant du contrat de travail du salarié, après la formation continue celui-ci remplira les mêmes fonctions qu'avant.[32]

L'exigence que la mesure envisagée doit être acceptable (*zumutbar*) n'existe que par rapport à l'employeur. Il faut prendre en compte les intérêts respectifs de l'employeur et du salarié.[33] La question qui est sous-jacent à cet examen est de savoir, jusqu'où va l'obligation de l'employeur de rétablir la capacité du salarié pour qu'il puisse suffire aux obligations contractuelles. Il n'existe pratiquement pas de jurisprudence

reconversion au sens du § 1 KSchG, Ascheid/Preis/Schmidt/*Kiel*, Kündigungsrecht, 3e édition 2007, § 1 KSchG n° 618.

26 Gemeinschaftskommentar Kündigungsrecht/*Griebeling*, 8e édition 2007, § 1 KSchG n° 723.

27 BAG 7.2.1991 AP § 1 KSchG 1969 Umschulung Nr 1.

28 Erfurter Kommentar zum Arbeitsrecht/*Oetker*, 8e édition 2008, § 1 KSchG n° 390.

29 Ascheid/Preis/Schmidt/*Kiel*, Kündigungsrecht, 3e édition 2007, § 1 KSchG n° 617.

30 *Ibid*.

31 Gemeinschaftskommentar Kündigungsrecht/*Griebeling*, 8e édition 2007, § 1 KSchG n° 723.

32 Ascheid/Preis/Schmidt /*Kiel*, 3e édition 2007, § 1 KSchG n° 617.

33 Ascheid/Preis/Schmidt/*Kiel*, 3e édition 2007, § 1 KSchG n° 619.

concrétisant la notion d'acceptabilité, dans la suite ce sont les développements faits par la doctrine qui seront présentés.[34] On peut constater globalement que plus les mesures ont une influence négative sur les besoins économiques de l'entreprise, plus elles doivent augmenter les chances de sauvegarder le maintien du salarié.[35] Au fil du temps, beaucoup de critères ont été développés dont par example l'ancienneté du salarié dans l'entreprise, son âge, son aptitude personnelle et professionnelle, le fait que le salarié peut continuer de remplir une partie de ses obligations contractuelles pendant la période de formation, les frais et la durée de la mesure envisagée.[36] En même temps, il faut tenir compte du déroulement antérieur de la relation de travail et du motif de licenciement. Ainsi, les exigences vis-à-vis l'employeur sont plus élevées quand il s'agit d'un licenciement pour motif économique ou d'une inaptitude due à un accident de travail que dans le cas d'un licenciement pour un comportement fautif.[37]

La restriction de l'obligation de l'employeur aux mesures acceptables démontre qu'il ne s'agit pas d'une obligation 'absolue' mais plutôt variable. Ceci démontre également une certaine insécurité par rapport à l'existence de cette obligation, mais cette insécurité juridique est tolérée pour garantir des solutions plus adaptées au cas particulier. Si on transfère ces constats à la capacité et plus précisément son aspect de la qualification professionnelle—qui est finalement à la base de cette obligation—cela mène à en déduire que les exigences varient en fonction de l'entreprise et en fonction de la personne du salarié.

L'influence sur le contrôle du motif de licenciement

Dans le cas où l'employeur ne remplit pas l'obligation prévue par le § 1 al 2 KSchG, il s'agit de ce qu'on appelle une cause d'injustification sociale absolue (*absolute Sozialwidrigkeit*) et le licenciement est nul.[38] Ceci a une grande influence sur le contrôle du motif du licenciement. En principe, il faut procéder à une prise en compte des intérêts respectifs par rapport au licenciement (*Interessenabwägung*). Les intérêts de l'employeur et du salarié, dans le cadre du contrôle du motif de licenciement. Cet examen ne doit pas être fait s'il existe une cause absolue d'injustification sociale.[39] Le licenciement est donc nul dès que l'employeur ne suffit pas aux exigences du § 1 al 2 KSchG.

[34] *Ibid*, § 1 KSchG n° 616.
[35] Erfurter Kommentar zum Arbeitsrecht/*Oetker*, 8e édition 2008, § 1 KSchG n° 390 et s.
[36] Ascheid/Preis/Schmidt/*Kiel*, 3e édition 2007, § 1 KSchG n° 620.
[37] *Ibid*, § 1 KSchG n° 621.
[38] Kittner/Däubler/Zwanziger/*Kittner/Deinert*, Kündigungsschutzrecht, 7e édition 2008, § 1 KSchG n° 354.
[39] *Ibid*.

L'extension de l'obligation du § 1 al 2 KSchG

La jurisprudence a étendu l'obligation de procéder à des mesures de formation continue ou de reconversion professionnelle au cas où le conseil d'entreprise ne s'est pas opposé au licenciement si les autres conditions sont remplies.[40] Mais contrairement à l'obligation rentrant dans le champ d'application du § 1 al 2 KSchG, le manquement à cette obligation créée par les juges n'engendre pas une injustification sociale absolue. Il faut toujours peser les intérêts respectifs de l'employeur et du salarié. C'est dans le cadre de l'examen de la prédominance des intérêts qu'on doit tenir compte de la possibilité de prendre des mesures de formation continue ou de reconversion professionnelle.[41]

Même si le non-respect de cette obligation n'a pas les mêmes conséquences que celui dans le cadre du § 1 al 2 KSchG, cette jurisprudence montre qu'elle confère une grande importance au problème de l'absence d'une qualification suffisante en tant qu'aspect de la capacité.

§ 84 al 2 SGB IX: Le rétablissement de l'état de santé

Le législateur allemand a récemment tenu compte de l'aspect physique de la capacité du salarié par la loi relative à la promotion de la formation et de l'emploi des personnes handicapées du 23 avril 2004.[42] Cette loi inflige à l'employeur l'obligation d'aider à rétablir la capacité de travail du salarié en cas de maladie. Le § 84 al 2 SBG IX (*Sozialgesetzbuch IX*) qui prévoit cette obligation est aussi une des rares dispositions employant la notion de capacité.

Les conditions d'application et la teneur du § 84 al 2 SGB IX

Selon le § 84 al 2 SGB IX, l'employeur doit rechercher en collaboration avec les représentants des salariés et les représentants des handicapés comment la capacité de travail (*Arbeitsfähigkeit*) peut être rétablie et maintenue, si un salarié se trouve dans l'incapacité de travailler pendant une période supérieure à six semaines au cours d'une année. Le salarié concerné doit être impliqué dans le processus et donner son accord.[43] La notion d''incapacité de travailler' (*Arbeitsunfähigkeit*) signifie en droit du

[40] BAG 13.9.1973 EzA § 102 BetrVG Nr 7; BAG 17.5.1984 EzA § 1 KSchG Betriebsbedingte Kündigung Nr 32; Kittner/Däubler/Zwanziger/*Kittner/Deinert*, Kündigungsschutzrecht, 7e édition 2008, § 1 KSchG n° 357; Gemeinschaftskommentar Kündigungsrecht/*Griebeling*, 8e édition 2007, § 1 KSchG n° 708.

[41] Kittner/Däubler/Zwanziger/*Kittner/Deinert*, Kündigungsschutzrecht, 7e édition 2008, § 1 KSchG n° 357.

[42] BGBl I S 606.

[43] *Feldes*, Soziale Sicherheit 2004, 270, 276.

travail et droit social allemand qu'un salarié est empêché de travailler en raison d'une maladie.[44] C'est donc l'aspect physique de la capacité du salarié qui est visé par cette disposition. Le but de cette nouvelle règle est de renforcer la prévention dans les entreprises pour éviter les licenciements pour maladie.[45]

Le champ d'application de cette norme a été très discuté. Dans la doctrine s'opposaient les auteurs qui veulent appliquer cette règle à tous les salariés[46] et ceux qui veulent restreindre son champ d'application aux handicapés graves.[47] Selon un arrêt récent de la Cour fédérale du travail, la norme s'applique à tous les salariés ce qui augmente considérablement son importance pratique.[48]

De même, la loi n'est pas très claire par rapport au contenu exacte de l'obligation. Selon le § 84 al 2 SGB IX, l'employeur et les représentants des salariés et des handicapés recherchent des 'possibilités' pour surmonter l'incapacité de travailler et des 'prestations' et des 'aides' pour prévenir une nouvelle incapacité de travailler. Les notions de 'possibilités', de 'prestations' et d''aides' sont très larges. Cela traduit la volonté du législateur de donner le plus de liberté possible aux destinataires de la norme en évitant des restrictions produites par la formulation. On peut citer à titre exemplaire des changements du lieu de travail pour l'adapter aux problèmes de santé du salarié ou un traitement par le médecin d'entreprise qui accompagne le travail.

L'influence sur la validité du licenciement pour maladie

La nouveauté et l'obscurité du texte conduit encore à des insécurités en ce qui concerne la question de l'influence du non-respect du § 84 al 2 SGB IX sur la validité du licenciement. D'après le premier arrêt de la Cour fédérale rendu sur cette question, il s'agit d'une concrétisation du principe de l'ultime remède (*Ultima-Ratio-Grundsatz*), un des grands principes régissant le droit du licenciement allemand. Selon ce principe, le licenciement doit être la dernière mesure envisagée, sinon il est nul; avant la notification du licenciement l'employeur doit donc recourir à des mesures ayant des conséquences moins graves pour le salarié pour éviter un licenciement. La Cour formule prudemment que si une telle mesure aurait pu être trouvée au cours de la procédure prévue par le § 84 al 2 SGB IX mais l'employeur ne l'a pas suivie, le licenciement peut être nul.[49]

44 *Feldes*, Soziale Sicherheit 2004, 270, 275.
45 BT-Drs 15/1783, p 1, 15 et s.
46 *Eldes*, Soziale Sicherheit 2004, 270, 275; *Rehwald/Kossack*, AiB 2004, 604, 608; *Gaul/Süßbrich*, ArbRB 2004, 308.
47 *Balders/Lepping*, NZA 2005, 854; *Brose*, DB 2005, 390 et s; *Namendorf/Natzel*, DB 2005, 1794.
48 BAG 12.7.2007, NZA 2008, 173.
49 *Ibid*.

La nullité n'est donc pas la conséquence automatique d'un manquement à la procédure.

Avec la nouvelle règle, le législateur a étendu l'obligation de l'employeur de tenir compte de l'état physique du salarié. En même temps, il a donné au conseil d'entreprise et aux représentants des handicapés graves le droit de demander de l'employeur l'exécution de la procédure du § 84 al 2 SGB IX. Une telle implication des institutions collectives en cas de maladie du salarié est nouveau et souligne l'importance accordée par la législateur à la prise en charge au moins partielle du maintien de la capacité par l'entreprise.

LA TENDANCE CONTRAIRE: LA PROTECTION DES SALARIÉS SPÉCIALEMENT PERFORMANTS

On retrouve un autre aspect de la capacité dans le cadre de ce qu'on appelle le choix social (*Sozialauswahl*) prévu par la loi de protection contre le licenciement. Le choix social doit être fait avant de prononcer un licenciement pour motif économique si plusieurs salariés peuvent entrer en ligne de compte. Il faut que ces salariés soient comparables et qu'ils travaillent dans la même entité économique.[50] En ce cas, le choix du salarié à licencier doit être fait selon des critères sociaux cités par la loi, § 1 al 3 KSchG (l'ancienneté, l'âge, l'handicap grave et les obligations alimentaires). L'idée de cette loi est que l'employeur doit licencier le salarié le moins défavorisé d'un point de vue social. Sinon, le licenciement n'est pas justifié socialement et par conséquent nul.

Mais la loi de protection contre le licenciement prévoit aussi des exceptions à ce principe. Selon le § 1 al 3 phrase 2 KSchG, l'employeur peut exclure de ce choix les salariés qui sont le plus performants ce qui signifie en fin de compte que ces salariés ne seront pas licenciés, indépendamment du fait que la personne licenciée peut être socialement plus défavorisée.

Conditions d'application du § 1 al 3 phrase 2 KSchG (*Leistungsträgerklausel*)

Selon le § 1 al 3 KSchG, les salariés dont le maintien est d'un intérêt justifié pour l'entreprise en raison notamment de leur connaissance, leurs capacités et leur rendement, peuvent ne pas être pris en compte dans le cadre du choix social. Il s'agit d'une option de l'employeur, il peut

[50] BAG 22.5.1986 § 1 KSchG 1969 Konzern Nr 4; BAG 2.6.2005—2 AZR 158/04—; Erfurter Kommentar zum Arbeitsrecht/*Oetker*, 8e édition 2008, § 1 KSchG n° 318.

invoquer les qualités d'un salarié s'il l'estime nécessaire, mais il n'y est pas obligé.[51] En revanche, le salarié lui-même ne peut pas invoquer sa connaissance, ses capacités ou son rendement dans un procès quand il a été licencié pour invoquer qu'il aurait dû rester en dehors du choix social.[52]

Il faut d'abord un intérêt justifié de l'entreprise (*berechtigtes betriebliches Interesse*) qui se réfère au maintien d'un certain salarié dans l'entreprise. Pour savoir si l'intérêt est réellement justifié, la jurisprudence—très critiquée d'une partie de la doctrine[53]—compare ces intérêts avec les besoins sociaux du salarié qui est concerné par le licenciement, si le salarié plus performant n'entre pas dans le choix social.[54] Plus ce salarié est socialement faible, plus les intérêts de l'entreprise doivent être importants.

La loi donne quatre exemples qui peuvent constituer des intérêts de l'entreprise. Ce sont la connaissance, les capacités et le rendement du salarié d'un côté et le maintien de la structure du personnel de l'autre. Ce sont les trois premiers cas qui rentrent dans le sujet de cette contribution.

Il s'agit d'une des rares fois où la notion de capacité est utilisée par le législateur en droit du licenciement allemand. Mais aussi les deux autres notions peuvent toucher à des aspects de la capacité. La notion de connaissance (*Kenntnisse*) se réfère à des faits que le salarié a connu au cours d'une formation continue ou de l'exercice de son travail ou bien en raison d'autres expériences.[55] Les capacités (*Fähigkeiten*) citées par le § 1 al 3 KSchG se réfèrent à l'aptitude du salarié à remplir les tâches prévues par le contrat de travail.[56] La notion de capacité est comprise d'une manière très large dans ce contexte. Elle n'est pas restreinte à un certain aspect. Il peut s'agir d'une capacité dans le domaine de la qualification professionnelle mais aussi dans le domaine sociale ou physique.[57] Des exemples souvent cités sont par example la capacité de résoudre des conflits entre les collègues, la capacité de diriger un groupe de salariés ou encore la capacité de faire des travaux qui demandent des qualifications très spécifiques.[58] C'est également dans ce cadre qu'il faut poser la question si le fait qu'un salarié moins fragile de santé et par conséquent

[51] *Schiefer/Worzalla*, NZA 2004, 345, 347.

[52] Gemeinschaftskommentar Kündigungsrecht/*Griebeling*, 8e édition 2007, § 1 KSchG n° 632; *Schiefer/Worzalla*, NZA 2004, 345, 347.

[53] *Bauer*, NZA 2004, 38, 41; Gemeinschaftskommentar Kündigungsrecht/*Griebeling*, 8e édition 2007, § 1 KSchG n° 627.

[54] BAG 12.4.2002 AP § 1 KSchG 1969 Soziale Auswahl Nr 56 = NZA 2003, 42.

[55] Une connaissance au sens de cette règle est p ex le fait de maîtriser une langue étrangère. Gemeinschaftskommentar Kündigungsrecht/*Griebeling*, 8e édition 2007, § 1 KSchG n° 635a.

[56] Gemeinschaftskommentar Kündigungsrecht/*Griebeling*, 8e édition 2007, § 1 KSchG n° 635a.

[57] Ascheid/Preis/Schmidt/*Kiel*, Kündigungsrecht, 3e édition 2007, § 1 KSchG n° 755k.

[58] Gemeinschaftskommentar Kündigungsrecht/*Griebeling*, 8e édition 2007, § 1 KSchG n° 635a.

moins souvent malade qu'un salarié qui est en principe plus faible d'un point de vue social peut être mis en dehors du choix social en raison de sa meilleure constitution physique. Cette question est très controversée. Il existe de la jurisprudence à propos de la règle prédécesseur qui prévoit que ce fait ne peut être pris en compte que si le salarié socialement plus faible se trouve dans un état de santé qui peut aussi justifier un licenciement pour motif inhérent à la personne.[59] Mais par le nouveau § 1 al 3 KSchG, les intérêts de l'entreprise ont été renforcés. Un premier arrêt de la Cour fédérale dans ce domaine constate qu'en principe le seul fait qu'un salarié a moins d'heures d'absence ne peut pas justifier de l'exclure du choix social. Mais en même temps, la Cour laisse la porte ouverte pour deux exceptions: quand il s'agit d'un travail qui ne peut pas être repris à court terme par un autre salarié et le cas où après le choix social il ne resteraient essentiellement que de salariés dans l'entreprise qui ont beaucoup d'heures d'absence.[60] Dans l'attente d'une jurisprudence confirmée, il reste à constater que depuis, le courant qui admet la prise en compte des heures d'absence dues à une maladie sans qu'elles doivent en même temps pouvoir justifier un licenciement, devient de plus en plus important.[61] Le troisième exemple donné par la loi est le rendement (*Leistung*) du salarié. La notion de rendement se réfère à la qualité et au volume du travail fait par le salarié.[62]

Ces trois notions ne sont pas strictement détachées l'une de l'autre. Il y a souvent des chevauchements et ainsi c'est aussi la vue globale de ces trois aspects qui peut justifier l'exclusion d'un salarié du choix social.[63]

L'évolution du § 1 al 3 KSchG et l'objectif de la nouvelle règle

La version présentée du § 1 al 3 KSchG a été créée par la loi relative aux réformes du marché de l'emploi (*Gesetz zu Reformen am Arbeitsmarkt*) entrée en vigueur le 1er janvier 2004. Ce n'est pas la première fois qu'une telle règle existe. La législation a été hésitante par rapport à ce concept. La règle a déjà été insérée dans la loi de protection contre le licenciement sous le gouvernement des chrétiens-démocrates dans la période de 1996 à 1999. Avec le changement gouvernemental, la loi a également été changée et la possibilité de l'employeur d'exclure des salariés spécialement

[59] BAG 24.3.1983 AP § 1 KSchG 1969 Betriebsbedingte Kündigung Nr 12; BAG 20.10.1983 AP § 1 KSchG 1969 Betriebsbedingte Kündigung Nr 13.

[60] BAG 31.5.2007, NZA 2007, 1362.

[61] V. dans ce sens Gemeinschaftskommentar Kündigungsrecht/*Griebeling*, 8e édition 2007, § 1 KSchG n° 637; v *Hoyningen-Huene/Linck*, Kündigungsschutzgesetz, 13e édition 2002, § 1 KSchG n° 479a; *Bauer*, NZA 2004, 38, 41 ; *Schiefer/Worzalla*, NZA 2004, 345, 348.

[62] Gemeinschaftskommentar Kündigungsrecht/*Griebeling*, 8e édition 2007, § 1 KSchG n° 638.

[63] Ascheid/Preis/Schmidt/*Kiel*, Kündigungsrecht, 3e édition 2007, § 1 KSchG n° 755 et s.

importants pour l'entreprise du choix social a été restreint considérablement. Mais le même gouvernement est revenu en 2004 sur ce changement et a quasiment repris la règle du gouvernement de Kohl qui existait de 1996 à 1999. Un changement législatif qui est dû à la situation économique et plus spécialement au taux de chômage élevé qui n'a pas cessé d'augmenter. Le but est de renforcer les intérêts économiques et d'éviter de restreindre la productivité de l'entreprise.[64] Le législateur a utilisé dans ses travaux préparatoires une expression allemande (*Leistungsfähigkeit*) dont la traduction littérale est la 'capacité de rendement'. Cette règle, qui est aussi des fois appelées le 'paragraphe olympique' (*Olympiaparagraph*) en raison de son caractère 'élitaire', reflète un revirement dans la perception de la notion de capacité en droit du licenciement. Et ceci d'autant plus que et le gouvernement conservateur et le gouvernement social-démocrate ont finalement opté pour cette règle. Pour la 1re fois, la présence d'une certaine forme de capacité est utilisée expressément pour garantir le maintien de l'emploi et cela dans l'unique intérêt de l'entreprise. Il s'agit d'un traitement nouveau de la question de capacité qui est dû à l'évolution du marché du travail et à la situation économique d'un pays.

CONCLUSIONS

Caractéristiques de la capacité en droit du licenciement allemand

Il n'existe pas de définition de la notion de capacité en droit du licenciement allemand. Quand on recherche les caractéristiques de cette notion, il faut constater que la capacité ou l'incapacité apparaît sous des angles très diversifiés. Mais le point commun est le point de référence qui est toujours l'obligation contractuelle. Il y a incapacité dès qu'une des parties du contrat de travail ne peut plus remplir ses obligations émanant de ce contrat. De plus, la capacité ou le manque de capacité ayant des conséquences pour la relation de travail, varie régulièrement en fonction des parties au contrat et leurs conditions.

Les formes sous lesquelles la notion de capacité apparaît en droit du licenciement allemand

Le manque de capacité ayant des conséquences peut avoir des degrés différents en droit du licenciement allemand. Dans le cas du licenciement

[64] BT-Drs 15/1204, p 11.

pour maladie, il peut y avoir une incapacité temporaire, probablement durable et durable qui peut justifier un licenciement et qui peut donc entraîner des effets juridiques. Il y a aussi l'incapacité partielle qui vient de faire son entrée en droit du licenciement allemand par le biais du licenciement pour manque d'efficacité.

En droit du licenciement, la capacité devient important sous des aspects différents. Ainsi, on peut distinguer l'incapacité physique en cas de maladie, l'incapacité due à un manque de qualification, l'incapacité économique, la capacité au sens de la performance d'un salarié et aussi la capacité de rendement par rapport à l'entreprise.

Les tendances existant par rapport au traitement de la capacité en droit du licenciement allemand

Le champ d'application 'classique' de la capacité est l'absence de capacité en tant que cause du licenciement. En fait, il s'agit d'une prémisse du droit du licenciement. Une incapacité peut justifier un licenciement.

Mais il y a aussi une autre utilisation de la capacité. Dans certains cas, la loi inflige à l'employeur l'obligation de prendre des mesures pour rétablir la capacité du salarié avant de pouvoir procéder au licenciement. On trouve cette obligation par rapport à l'aspect physique tout comme par rapport au manque de qualification. Même s'il ne s'agit que d'une obligation de moyens, cette obligation peut paraître contraire aux principes du droit du licenciement. Car cela signifie en fait que l'employeur doit éliminer la cause du licenciement qui lui donne en principe justement le droit de licencier. Le but est de protéger le salarié et d'éviter des licenciements de manière préventive.

Une troisième tendance paraît encore contraire à celle présentée avant. Le législateur à également pris comme point de départ une capacité spécialement développée chez certains salariés qui sont par conséquent plus performants que les autres. Cette fois-ci, l'objectif n'est pas la protection du salarié, mais la protection des intérêts de l'entreprise. Dans ce raisonnement, on trouve un aspect tout à fait nouveau que le législateur a invoqué dans les travaux parlementaires, celui de la capacité de rendement de l'entreprise. Il ne s'agit donc plus de la capacité d'une personne physique.

L'existence d'un concept cohérent?

Après avoir élaboré ces tendances contradictoires, il se pose la question s'il existe un concept cohérent de capacité en droit du licenciement allemand. Une question à laquelle il faut donner une réponse négative.

Mais ceci s'explique par les particularités de la matière. Le droit du licenciement est tout d'abord la traduction de ce qu'on appelle en allemand '*Arbeitnehmerschutzrecht*', le droit de protection des salariés. Cependant, cette matière doit aussi tenir compte du droit de l'employeur de rompre le contrat, le cas échéant même dans le but de sauver l'entreprise. Ce sont donc deux intérêts contraires qui doivent être harmonisés et pour lesquels il faut trouver un compromis vivable pour les deux côtés. C'est pour cela qu'on ne peut éviter que la notion de capacité est traitée sous des angles différents.

La deuxième raison pour l'absence d'homogénéité dans ce cadre est l'influence des données économiques et politiques sur le droit du licenciement. Un exemple parlant est l'exclusion des salariés performants du choix social. Ceci est un facteur qui peut engendrer des changements imprévisibles à long-terme et qui rend la création d'un concept cohérent de capacité encore plus difficile.

8

'Capacitas' and Capabilities in International Labour Law

RENÉE-CLAUDE DROUIN

INTRODUCTION

Is there a legal concept of *capacitas* emerging in the field of international labour law? At first glance, the concept of capacity in modern law, referring to the ability of individuals and legal persons to consent to legally binding obligations,[1] seems, to some extent, removed from the preoccupations underlying the development of international labour regulation. Traditionally, while private law has focused on the protection of incapable persons and the validity or invalidity of contracts, labour law's interventions, including those with an international character, have concentrated on the protection of workers and the rectification of the inequality of power between employers and employees inherent in the contract of employment.[2] Accordingly, for most of its existence, the International Labour Organisation (ILO) has encouraged the adoption by its Member States of a set of labour standards and social policies of the kind associated with the welfare state. In recent decades, however, the regulatory criticisms that have called into question the efficiency of labour regulation and brought the Keynesian model into disrepute have not spared the Organisation. The ILO could not avoid the generalised economic discourse that called for the adaptation of labour policies in the light of industrial and technological changes associated with the new economy and the process of globalisation. Still, the need to balance economic development with the

[1] See the contributions by Simon Deakin and Martijn Hesselink in this volume for more precise definitions of the concept of capacity in civil and common law systems.

[2] P Davis and M Freedland, *Kahn-Freund's Labour and the Law* (London, Stevens, 3rd edn, 1983) 18. For an analysis of the rationales underlying labour law at the international level, see J Murray, *Transnational Labour Regulation: The ILO and EC Compared* (The Hague, Kluwer Law International, 2001).

protection of workers' rights was not solely envisaged by the Organisation as a question of finding the most effective trade-off between these two objectives. Instead, the new orientations taken by the ILO to respond to the challenges of globalisation, namely, the promotion of fundamental labour rights and the advancement of its decent work agenda, clearly articulate the conviction that economic and social policies are interdependent factors and that both have a role to play in the pursuit of sustainable development.

From this perspective, fundamental labour rights are seen as enabling rights that allow individuals to improve their ability to obtain productive work performed in a decent working environment and gain a fair share in the economic benefits they have helped to generate.[3] In turn, these rights have been said to be 'preconditions to real market participation'.[4] This article suggests that we can perceive in the decent work agenda of the ILO the outlines of a legal concept of *capacitas*, reminiscent of the one that existed in Roman law, which transcends the strict notion of today's private law and purports to truly act as 'a gateway to involvement in the operations of a market economy'.[5] This concept of *capacitas* is embodied in the fundamental principles and rights at work proclaimed in the 1998 ILO Declaration, and is informed by Amartya Sen's work on capabilities. It is the aim of this chapter to analyse how fundamental labour rights can form the basis for a revised concept of *capacitas* in international labour law. The first section of the chapter examines, from a historical and evolutionary perspective, the relationship between market concerns and the protection of social rights in the development of standard-setting within the ILO. The second section considers the enabling role of fundamental labour rights within the ILO decent work agenda.

THE INTERPLAY BETWEEN MARKET CONCERNS AND THE PROTECTION OF SOCIAL RIGHTS WITHIN THE ILO

The ILO was founded in the aftermath of the First World War as an autonomous organisation associated with the League of Nations and invested with the authority to establish international labour rules.[6] From

[3] International Labour Organisation, *Declaration on Fundamental Principles and Rights at Work and its Follow-up* (ILO, 1998) Preamble, para.

[4] BA Langille, 'Core Labour Rights—The True Story (Reply to Alston)' (2005) 16 *European Journal of International Law* 409, 430.

[5] See the contribution by Simon Deakin in this volume.

[6] International labour standards are established by the International Labour Conference, the 'legislative' body of the ILO, through the adoption of Conventions and Recommendations. Member States have the duty to submit to their competent authorities, for the enactment of legislation or other action, a Convention or Recommendation adopted by a positive majority vote of two-thirds of the delegates present at the Conference. The binding

its inception, defining the social realm and its interplay with the economy has always been one of its central preoccupations.[7] The positions adopted at various times by the Organisation to address the apparent tensions between the economic and the social were influenced by the profound practical and ideological changes that affected the market economy during the twentieth century.[8] It is not surprising, therefore, that the evolution of international labour regulation within the realm of the ILO followed a trajectory similar to the one that stems from the history of social rights in industrialised states during the same period.[9] Four different phases that can generally be associated with corresponding market and social ideologies were especially important in this evolution: the era of the liberal state and industrialisation, during which the first employment and labour laws were adopted; the era of the welfare state, characterised by legislative interventions in the labour market; the rise of neo-liberal orthodoxies accompanied by the crisis of the socio-economic model of governance; and the response to the deregulation discourse based on social rights and deliberative processes.[10] Throughout these stages, the perception of the interplay between the economic and the social at any given point in time was reflected in the constitutive instruments of the Organisation: the 1919 ILO Constitution, the 1944 Declaration of Philadelphia concerning the Aims and Purposes of the International Labour Organisation,[11] and the 1998 ILO Declaration on Fundamental Principles and Rights at Work.

While the recent decent work agenda of the ILO clearly establishes a positive correlation between economic development and fundamental labour rights, social rights have long been perceived as conflicting with

effect of a Convention is not automatic, but conditional upon its being ratified by the government of each State. Recommendations, for their part, are non-binding instruments. The ILO's labour standards are therefore voluntary obligations in the sense that the Organisation does not hold the power to force ratification or implementation of a ratified Convention upon a Member State.

7 I Duplessis, 'Le recours à la constitution de l'OIT dans l'acquisition de son autonomie institutionnelle' (2004) *Revue Belge de droit international* 37, 39.

8 For instance, while trade in goods and services essentially occurred between states at the time the ILO was founded, it is now dominated by the powerful global players that transnational corporations have become.

9 Naturally, the development of labour law within different countries has followed distinct evolutionary paths. The different stages identified here are those that certainly had the most important resonance worldwide.

10 See notably S Deakin, *Renewing Labour Market Institutions* (Geneva, ILO Social Policy Lectures, International Institute for Labour Studies, 2004) and S Deakin, 'Social Rights in a Globalized Economy' in P Alston (ed), *Labour Rights as Human Rights* (Oxford, Oxford University Press, 2005). Bob Hepple identifies these four stages as 'historical and comparative models of rights at work': B Hepple, 'Rights at Work' in D Ghai (ed), *Decent Work: Objectives and Strategies* (Geneva, International Labour Office, International Institute for Labour Studies, 2006) 33 (first published as a discussion paper by the International Institute for Labour Studies: DP/147/2003, Geneva, International Institute for Labour Studies, 2003).

11 This Declaration was incorporated into the text of the ILO Constitution in 1946.

market value. During the industrialisation period in the nineteenth century, western states initially objected to the adoption of protective labour laws on the grounds that these measures would affect their competitiveness and reduce their comparative advantage with regard to goods produced in foreign countries that did not respect the same standards.[12] It was mainly because international competition could act as a hindrance to the development of national labour laws that proponents of social reforms began advocating international labour regulation as a solution for overcoming the then industrialising countries' resistance to the adoption of minimum working conditions.[13] However, despite this early international outlook based largely on market considerations,[14] labour laws, before the First World War, paradoxically developed essentially at the national level,[15] where several governments enacted diverse measures that were protective of workers, notably maximum working hours for children and women.[16]

Thus, one might have expected the adoption of national labour laws to have tempered the significance of the comparative advantage argument by the time of the ILO's creation in 1919. However, the Preamble to the Organisation's Constitution implicitly refers to the need for collective action on labour standards in order to regulate competition. One of the fundamental ideas expressed in the text is that:

> the failure of any nation to adopt human conditions of labour is an obstacle in the way of other nations which desire to improve the conditions in their own countries.

The modern concern over a race to the bottom in labour rights was therefore already anticipated in the ILO's founding instrument.[17] Still, the

[12] A Alcock, *History of the International Labour Organisation* (London, Macmillan Press, 1971) 5; VY Ghebali, *The International Labour Organisation, A Case Study on the Evolution of UN Specialised Agencies* (Dordrecht, Martinus Nijhoff Publishers, 1989) 3.

[13] In a review of the origins of the ILO, Bob Hepple mentions that the idea that social problems require international solutions is generally attributed to Jacques Necker, a Swiss banker, while Daniel Legrand, an Alsatian manufacturer, was the first reformer to argue that international labour law was needed to overcome the international competition argument: B Hepple, *Labour Laws and Global Trade* (Oxford, Hart Publishing, 2005) 26.

[14] Legrand also argued that improving workers' labour conditions would prevent social unrest and promote peace: Ghebali, above n 12, 2–3.

[15] There were only two international conventions adopted before the First World War, one prohibiting the use of white phosphorous in the manufacture of matches (accepted by 14 nations) and one prohibiting the employment of women for night work in industry (accepted by seven nations): Hepple, above n 13, 28; see also JM Servais, *Normes internationales du travail* (Paris, LGDJ, 2004) 6.

[16] These measures varied from one country to another according to social, economic and political factors: see Hepple, above n 13, 26–7.

[17] RJ Flanagan, 'Labour Standards and International Competitive Advantage', paper presented at the International Labor Standards Conference, Stanford University, 20 May 2002, quoted in BA Langille, 'Re-reading the Preamble to the 1919 ILO Constitution in the Light of Recent Data on FDI and Worker Rights' (2003) 42 *Columbia Journal of Transnational Law* 87, 91.

economic argument was only enunciated in the third paragraph of the Preamble, while the opening statement asserted as a principle that 'universal and lasting peace can only be established if it is based upon social justice', and this statement was followed by a claim that there were unjust conditions of labour that imperilled the harmony of the world and necessitated urgent action.[18] This certainly showed the lesser prominence of the economic rationale at a time when the sufferings endured during the war were still very much felt.[19] Yet, as regards their interplay with the economy, international labour rights were envisioned largely as a means of redressing the negative impact of trade and market competition on social conditions.

During the inter-war period, the standard-setting activities of the ILO mostly reflected the subjects of 'special and urgent importance' identified in the Organisation's Constitution,[20] as conventions were adopted concerning working hours, minimum age, employment of women, and safety and health. These instruments tackled labour matters that were often already addressed in Member States' legislation,[21] but little attention was paid to human rights issues.[22] Interestingly, the protection granted, in a number of international labour conventions, to certain categories of individuals, such as women and children, implicitly reflected private law concerns regarding the capacity of parties to a contractual exchange to validly enter into an agreement.[23]

The Declaration of Philadelphia, adopted in 1944, shortly before the end of the Second World War, marked the beginning of a new stage in the development of standard-setting activities within the ILO. This second 'constitutional moment'[24] was an opportunity for the Organisation to

18 Preamble to the 1919 ILO Constitution. Paul O'Higgins identifies two additional reasons for international labour standards: social injustice, hardship and deprivation undermine good order; humanity and decency require the adoption of minimum labour standards everywhere: P O'Higgins, 'The Interaction of the ILO, the Council of Europe and European Union Labour Standards' in B Hepple (ed), *Social and Labour Rights in a Global Context. International and Comparative Perspectives* (Cambridge, Cambridge University Press, 2002) 55, 56.

19 This was later reflected in the actual activities of the ILO, since the idea of international labour law as a means of regulating competition received only slight consideration for some years: Hepple, above n 13, 33.

20 These subjects were first mentioned in Art 41 of the original ILO Constitution and are now reflected in para 3 of the Preamble to the Constitution: B Creighton, 'The Future of Labour Law: Is There a Role for International Labour Standards?' in C Barnard *et al* (eds), *The Future of Labour Law. Liber Amicorum Sir Bob Hepple QC* (Oxford, Hart Publishing, 2004) 254.

21 Hepple, above n 13, 31.

22 Creighton, above n 20, 254. There were only two exceptions to this state of affairs: Convention 11 concerning the Rights of Association and Combination of Agricultural Workers (1921) and Convention 29 concerning Forced or Compulsory Labour (1930).

23 Hepple, above n 10, 45.

24 BA Langille, 'The ILO and the New Economy: Recent Developments' (1999) 15 *International Journal of Comparative Labour Law and Industrial Relations* 229; I Duplessis, 'La déclaration de l'OIT relative aux droits fondamentaux au travail. Une nouvelle forme de régulation efficace?' (2004) 59 *Relations industrielles/Industrial Relations* 52.

reassert the relevance of its original mandate after the disbanding of the League of Nations and the subsequent years of conflict. The Declaration reaffirmed the fundamental principles on which the ILO had been founded, more specifically that labour is not a commodity; freedom of expression and of association are essential to sustained progress; poverty anywhere constitutes a danger to prosperity everywhere; and the war against want needs to be carried out with unrelenting vigour. There is in the text of the Declaration a slight departure from earlier beliefs about the impact of labour standards on international competition. The affirmation in the 1919 Constitution regarding the need for collective action to counter possible regulatory competition was not repeated in the 1944 instrument. The Declaration also put new emphasis on the role of economic and labour policies in the attainment of social justice. This is especially noticeable in the second paragraph of the document, which points out that

> all human beings, irrespective of race, creed or sex, have the right to pursue both their material well-being and their spiritual development in conditions of freedom and dignity, of economic security and equal opportunity.

This makes this right the principal goal of national and international policy. The connection between the social and the economic is further emphasised by the affirmation that

> all national and international policies and measures, in particular those of an economic and financial character, should be judged in this light and accepted only in so far as they may be held to promote and not to hinder the achievement of this fundamental objective.

This leads to the conclusion that 'social and human objectives were seen to be paramount aims of economic development'.[25] Thus, the economic was meant to serve the social, with pre-eminence being given to the latter sphere.

Policies and measures promoted by the ILO in the years following the Declaration of Philadelphia were deeply influenced by the economic context of mass production, characterised, in Cooney's words, by

> rising unionism, standardized employment relations, direct state involvement in a wide range of economic activities, and various forms of societal corporatism.[26]

[25] Hepple, above n 13, 33.

[26] S Cooney, 'Testing Times for the ILO: Institutional Reform for the New International Political Economy' (1999) 20 *Comparative Labor Law and Policy Journal* 365, 369.

For instance, international labour standards adopted during this period included the two fundamental conventions on freedom of association and the right to collective bargaining[27]; the equal remuneration convention and the discrimination convention[28]; the social security (minimum standards) convention[29]; and the abolition of forced labour conventions.[30] Standard-setting activities reflected and supported the welfare state model that provided citizens with a large range of social and economic rights. As Hepple notes, '[t] hese rights were seen as being collective and substantive, not merely individual or procedural'.[31] In this era, labour legislation and institutions were seen as means by which to establish a balance between employers and workers. Worker subordination in the employment relationship was compensated by the assurance of job security and workplace participation.[32]

From the beginning of the 1980s, the ascendancy of the neo-liberal discourse and its impact on national regulatory policies, especially the pressures for labour market deregulation, had a certain influence within the ILO. Some Member States that embraced the new economic orthodoxy, which rejects any government intervention in the functioning of the labour market,[33] became reluctant to adopt new standards and critical of existing ones.[34] This led to 'a transnational adaptation of the neo-liberal argument about labour regulation' whereby 'international rules should be made which would aid the process of deregulation in the national sphere'.[35] Even the ILO Director General acknowledged these pressures in his 1988 report, stating that

> existing ILO standards are being questioned as imposing too rigid a framework and as standing in the way of new practices.[36]

This had at least a relative impact on standard-setting activities since it is

27 Convention 87 concerning freedom of association and protection of the right to organise and Convention 98 concerning the application of the principles of the right to organise and to bargain collectively.

28 Convention 100 concerning equal remuneration for men and women workers for work of equal value and Convention 111 concerning discrimination in respect of employment and occupation.

29 Convention 102 concerning minimum standards of social security.

30 Convention 105 concerning the abolition of forced labour.

31 Hepple, above n 13, 33.

32 Hepple, above n 10, 47.

33 Essentially, with regard to labour law, neo-liberal doctrine is highly sceptical about the necessity of setting aside the private law principles of contract in the context of the employment relationship. Hepple, above n 10, 52.

34 Creighton, above n 20, 265.

35 J Murray, 'The Sound of One Hand Clapping? The "Ratcheting Labour Standards" Proposal and International Labour Law' (2001) 15 *Australian Journal of Labour Law* 306.

36 ILO, "Human Rights—A Common Responsibility", Report of the Director General to the International Labour Conference, ILO, Geneva, 1988, 46.

generally perceived that some standards adopted during this period were designed to increase labour market flexibility.[37]

While the relevance of international labour standards was being questioned, one of the ILO's major preoccupations was to adapt its traditional means of action to the new global reality: the end of the bipolar world and the consequent triumph of the market economy, the withdrawal of the state from the economic sector, and the erosion of the welfare state along with the concomitant rise in the importance of private enterprise. The urgency for the ILO to reaffirm the significance of its mission was apparent in the Director General's 1994 annual report to the International Labour Conference, which stressed the need to reconsider the ILO's activities in light of a process of economic globalisation that was engendering deep inequalities. Expressing mounting scepticism about the ability of market forces, left alone, to ensure the social well-being of every citizen in the world, the report triggered a long reflection on the appropriate means by which to increase the pertinence and effectiveness of labour standards in order to promote the constitutional objective of social justice in a globalised, free trade environment. A first response to these global challenges came in 1998 with the adoption of the Declaration on Fundamental Principles and Rights at Work. This was reinforced one year later, on the eve of the new millennium, with the presentation of an elaborate action plan, namely the decent work agenda.

The shift to the promotion of fundamental labours rights[38] as a means of institutional renewal for the ILO was in large part influenced by a number of events which were external to the Organisation.[39] The 1995 Copenhagen World Summit for Social Development first focused attention on fundamental labour rights by concluding that every state should respect a set of four core workers' rights—now contained in the 1998 ILO Declaration.[40] The emphasis on these core standards was further strengthened by an OECD report published in 1996, which concluded that respect for non-discrimination standards and the elimination of forced and child labour could improve economic efficiency.[41] In

[37] For instance, Convention 171 on night work (1990); Convention 175 on part-time work (1994); and Convention 181 on private employment agencies (1997). See Creighton, above n 20, 265; Murray, above n 35; L Vosko, 'Legitimizing the Triangular Employment Relationship: Emerging International Labour Standards from a Comparative Perspective' (1997) 19 *Comparative Labor Law and Policy Journal* 43.

[38] What Bob Hepple has termed 'retreat to core labour rights': B Hepple, 'New Approaches to International Labour Organization' (1997) 26 *Industrial Law Journal* 353, 358.

[39] Langille, above n 24; Duplessis, above n 24.

[40] V Leary, '"Form Follows Function": Formulations of International Labor Standards—Treaties, Codes, Soft Law, Trade Agreements' in RJ Flanagan and WB Gould IV (eds), *International Labor Standards. Globalization, Trade and Public Policy* (Stanford, Stanford University Press, 2003) 179, 189.

[41] Organisation for Economic Cooperation and Development, *Trade, Employment and Labour Standards: A Study of Core Workers' Rights and International Trade* (Paris, OECD, 2006).

the same breath, based on empirical evidence, this report dismissed common fears that fundamental rights such as freedom of association and collective bargaining could have a negative impact on economic development and trading positions. The refusal by the newly founded World Trade Organisation (WTO) to consider the adoption of a social clause[42] as well as the adoption of the 1996 Singapore Ministerial Declaration, which renewed the commitment of the WTO's Members States to observe internationally recognised core labour standards while affirming that '[t]he International Labour Organisation (ILO) is the competent body to set and deal with these standards',[43] also had an impact on the ILO's subsequent course of action.

At the time of its adoption in 1998, the Declaration on fundamental principles and rights at work was considered within the ILO to be an absolute priority in order to prevent the institution becoming marginalised in the prevailing context of economic integration and to offer an appropriate response to the statement by the WTO's Member States enclosed in the Singapore Ministerial Declaration.[44] The central piece of the Declaration is the affirmation of the fundamental principles and rights at work, the 'core' labour standards that have gained general acceptance over the last decade, namely: freedom of association and the effective recognition of the right to collective bargaining; the elimination of all forms of forced or compulsory labour; the effective abolition of child labour; and the elimination of discrimination with respect to employment and occupation. Its provisions declare that all Member States have an intrinsic obligation to respect these principles and rights, which are recognised as being fundamental both inside and outside the Organisation, regardless of whether or not the Member States have ratified the specific conventions concerning the four fundamental rights.[45] This obligation comes from the States' membership in the

42 A social clause can be simply described as 'a clause in a trade agreement by which economic advantages are deprived from a country wishing to participate in international trade if social dumping is found by referring to a set of standards usually known as fair labour standards': SI Ago, 'A Crossroad in International Protection of Human Rights and International Trade: Is the Social Clause a Relevant Concept?' in *Mélanges en l'honneur de Nicolas Valticos* (Paris, Éditions A Pedone, 1999) 539. Consequently, it 'makes it possible to restrict or halt the importation or preferential importation of products originating in countries, industries or firms where labour conditions are inferior to certain minimum standards': G Van Liemt, 'Minimum Labour Standards and International Trade: Would a Social Clause Work?' (1989) 128 *International Labour Review* 433.

43 World Trade Organisation, Singapore Ministerial Declaration, para 4, WT/MIN(96)/DEC/W, 13 December 1996. This Declaration was reaffirmed in the closing Declaration of the Doha Ministerial Conference in November 2001 Doha World Trade Organisation Ministerial Declaration 2001, WT/MIN(01)/DEC/1, adopted on 14 November 2001, para 8.

44 See Langille, above n 24, 242.

45 The core labour conventions are: Convention 29 concerning forced or compulsory labour, Convention 87 concerning freedom of association and protection of the right to organise,

Organisation and their endorsement of the principles and rights set out in the ILO Constitution and in the Declaration of Philadelphia. This fact confers a unique legal character on the Declaration.[46]

While the 1998 Declaration embodies a new approach to the promotion of international labour standards, it is firmly grounded in the historical and constitutional legacy of the ILO. Some of the premises of the 1998 Declaration bring to mind those of the Declaration of Philadelphia. For instance, the 1998 Declaration is based on the precept that 'economic growth is essential but not sufficient to ensure equity, social progress and the eradication of poverty'.[47] It encompasses the economic perspective that social and economic policies are interdependent and that both have a role to play in the pursuit of sustainable development. Workers' entitlement to fundamental labour rights is considered to be essential in 'seeking to maintain the link between social progress and economic growth'. There is also an acknowledgement that different levels of development imply different social policies. In this regard, the Declaration points out that countries

> have undertaken to work towards attaining the overall objective of the Organisation to the best of their resources and fully in line with their specific circumstances.[48]

The preoccupation of Member States concerning the preservation of their comparative advantage in trade is expressed, however, in very different terms from those used in the 1919 Constitution. In this regard, the ILO 1998 Declaration echoes the debate over the inclusion of a social clause in trade agreements and condemns the use of labour standards for protectionist trade purposes.[49] It expressly states that the 'comparative

Convention 98 concerning the application of the principles of the right to organise and to bargain collectively, Convention 100 concerning equal remuneration for men and women workers for work of equal value, Convention 105 concerning the abolition of forced labour, Convention 111 concerning discrimination in respect of employment and occupation, Convention 138 concerning minimum age for admission to employment and Convention 182 concerning the prohibition and immediate action for the elimination of the worst forms of child labour.

[46] Hepple, above n 13, 59.

[47] 1998 ILO Declaration, para 2 of the Preamble.

[48] 1998 ILO Declaration, Art 1(a).

[49] One of the arguments against the use of social clauses in trade agreements is that the imposition of international labour standards on developing countries constitutes a disguised protectionist measure coming from industrialised countries. The proponents of this position contend that competition arising from the production of goods in developing countries at a lower cost has put enormous pressures on a number of competing industries in developed countries and has provoked unemployment in certain industrial sectors. In this context, some perceive that the imposition of minimal labour standards on developing countries is shifting the burden of structural adjustments from developed countries to developing countries. See J Bhagwati, 'Trade Liberalisation and "Fair Trade" Demands: Addressing the Environmental and Labour Standards Issues' (1995) 18 *World Economy* 745, 756; TN Srinivasan, 'International

advantage of any country should in no way be called into question by this Declaration and its follow-up'.[50] However, unlike the original constitution, it fails to acknowledge that the comparative advantage argument can also have a negative impact on the protection of fundamental labour rights if it is used unduly by governments to justify their inaction on the social front or the actual violation of the core standards.[51]

The identification of a subset of rights to which pre-eminence must be given has raised questions about the rationales underlying this choice. The most compelling justification for the selection of the four core labour rights is that they are process-oriented rather than result-oriented rights.[52] Another way to express this rationale is to say that these rights are enabling rights on which the enjoyment of all other labour rights depends.[53] As the preamble to the Declaration asserts,

> the guarantee of fundamental principles and rights at work is of special significance in that it enables the persons concerned to claim freely and on the basis of equality of opportunity their fare share of the wealth they have helped to generate, and to achieve fully their human potential.[54]

What is interesting is that we can discern in these passages of the Declaration a profound preoccupation on the part of the ILO concerning the ability of individuals to fully participate in the economic life of society. Fundamental labour rights are meant to allow people to actively take part in the labour market in conditions of freedom and equality. The concept of *capacitas* in its original Roman form is therefore embedded in this most recent 'constitutional moment' of the international labour regime.

There has been a clear evolution over the years in the perception of the interplay between economic imperatives and social concerns inside the ILO. Social and economic objectives are no longer envisaged, as they initially were, as antagonistic aspirations, but rather as deeply intertwined factors. Fundamental labour rights are now presented by the ILO as enabling rights, a concept that brings to mind the primary meaning of

Trade and Labour Standards from an Economic Perspective' in P van Dijck and G Faber (eds), *Challenges to the New World Trade Organization* (The Hague, Kluwer Law International, 1996) 219, 222.

50 1998 ILO Declaration, art 5.

51 Langille, above n 24, 249–50.

52 C McCrudden and A Davies, 'A Perspective on Trade and Labor Rights' (2000) 3 *Journal of International Economic Law* 43, 51. SH Cleveland, 'Why International Labor Standards?' in Flanagan and Gould, above n 40, 129, 153.

53 F Maupain, 'Revitalization Not Retreat: The Real Potential of the 1998 ILO Declaration for the Universal Protection of Workers' Rights' (2005) 16 *European Journal of International Law* 439, 448.

54 1998 ILO Declaration, para 5 of the Preamble.

capacitas. The implications of this new approach can only be grasped if we envisage the promotion of the rights enclosed in the 1998 ILO Declaration in connection with the Organisation's decent work agenda.

THE PROMOTION OF FUNDAMENTAL LABOUR RIGHTS AND THE DECENT WORK AGENDA

As part of its policy response to the need to humanise economic globalisation, the ILO has refocused its activities, since 1999, around a unifying concept—decent work—that is presented as the Organisation's main objective:

> The primary goal of the ILO today is to promote opportunities for women and men to obtain decent and productive work, in conditions of freedom, equity, security and human dignity.[55]

The significant importance of work in people's lives means that different personal goals and desires can be attained through decent work, as underlined by the ILO Director General in his 2001 report:

> The goal of decent work is best expressed through the eyes of people. It is about your job and future prospects; about your working conditions; about balancing work and family life, putting your kids through school and getting them out of child labour. It is about gender equality, equal recognition, and enabling women to make choices and take control of their lives. It is about your personal abilities to compete in the market-place . . . about receiving a fair share of the wealth that you have helped to create and not being discriminated against; it is about having a voice in your workplace and your community.[56]

The ILO decent work agenda puts forward four strategic objectives in view of attaining this goal: the promotion of rights at work, employment, social protection and social dialogue. These elements represent the integrated vision of decent work. The fundamental labour rights proclaimed in the 1998 Declaration are at the centre of the legal component of the decent work agenda: the promotion of rights at work.

Decent work is presented by the ILO as 'a way of expressing the goals of development in human terms.'[57] This vision of decent work is based on

[55] International Labour Organisation, 'Decent Work', Report of the Director-General to the International Labour Conference, International Labour Conference, 87th Session (Geneva, International Labour Office, 1999).

[56] *Ibid*, 7–8.

[57] International Labour Organisation, 'Reducing the Decent Work Deficit: A Global Challenge', Report of the Director General to the International Labour Conference, International Labour Conference, 89th Session (Geneva, International Labour Office, 2001) 26.

the work of Nobel Prize winner Amartya Sen, in particular, his expression of development goals as an expansion of the capabilities and freedoms of human beings.[58] Sen's approach changes the traditional views on development according to which economic development is a precondition to social development, and envisages these two goals as being intrinsically enmeshed. From his perspective, development is not strictly the measurement of income growth, but the expansion of individual freedoms. The concept of capability is described in Sen's writings on economics and development as an alternative approach to the evaluation of a person's well-being, that is, 'in terms of a person's ability to do valuable acts or reach valuable states of being'.[59] One of the ideas underpinning this approach is the notion of 'functionings' : 'a combination of various things a person may value doing or being'. The functionings valued by an individual may vary considerably from basic issues, such as being well fed, to more complex activities, such as taking part in societal life.[60] Capabilities are

> the various alternative combinations of functionings, any one of which the person can choose to have. In this sense, the capability of a person corresponds to the freedom that a person has to lead one kind of life or another.[61]

It is in light of Sen's perspective on development that fundamental principles and rights at work are perceived within the decent work agenda. For the ILO Director General,

> Achieving fundamental rights is not only a goal in itself; it is also a critical determinant of the capabilities of people to realise their aspirations. So, fundamental principles and rights at work are the essential foundation, the floor of decent work.[62]

While it is clear from the ILO's policies that the promotion of core labour rights is self-evident as a matter of human rights and does not need any further justification, the Organisation argues that there is an economic dividend with respect to fundamental labour rights. Implicitly, the ILO embraces, at least partly, a rights-based regulation approach which envisages certain social rights as entitlements or resources that must be provided to individuals in order for the labour market to function properly.[63] In short, the whole society—and the market system—suffers a

[58] A Sen, *Development as Freedom* (Oxford, Oxford University Press, 1999).
[59] A Sen, 'Capability and Well-being' in M Nussbaum and A Sen (eds), *The Quality of Life* (Oxford, Clarendon Press, 1993) 30.
[60] M Nussbaum and A Sen, 'Introduction' in Nussbaum and Sen, *ibid*, 1, 3.
[61] *Ibid*.
[62] International Labour Organisation, above n 57, 27.
[63] Hepple, above n 10, 53.

loss when deep inequalities affect a person's ability to participate in the operations of the market economy.[64] Simon Deakin has argued that one possible implication of the 'capability approach' developed by Sen is a market-creating role for social rights. As he explains:

> If capabilities are a consequence not simply of the endowments and motivations of individuals but also of the access they have to the processes of socialisation, education, and training that enable them to exploit their resource endowments, then by providing the conditions under which access to these processes is made generally available, mechanisms of redistribution may be not just compatible with, but become a precondition to, the operation of the labour market. In this way, social rights may play a pivotal role in providing an institutional foundation for individual capabilities.[65]

In the context of the ILO's decent work agenda, respect for fundamental labour rights ensures that every person can enter the labour market on terms of freedom and equality.

How exactly do core labour rights enhance individuals' capabilities and enable them to more fully participate in the activities of the economy and society in general? As is well known, freedom of association and the correlative right to collective bargaining usually improve the fairness and equity of the contractual exchange between workers and their employer. By joining forces, workers are in a better position to make gains during negotiations with employers and therefore secure decent working conditions that protect their health and safety and include a remuneration that represents 'a fair share in economic benefits'.[66] By giving individuals an opportunity to express their needs and play a part in the creation of labour regulation, the right to freedom of association and collective bargaining is also conducive to democratic participation in the workplace.[67] This form of citizenship entails that participants are not only beneficiaries of rights but also the subjects of a law-making process.[68] The benefits obtained from the effective application of freedom of association and collective bargaining extend beyond the workplace since the outcomes resulting from the exercise of this right affect peoples' overall ability to meet their needs. Moreover, it is considered that freedom of association and collective bargaining have positive societal side effects,

[64] As Simon Deakin puts it: 'Extremes of inequality have the effect of excluding certain groups from the market altogether. The result is not just that these individuals no longer have access to the goods that the market can supply; the rest of society also suffers a loss from their inability to take part in the system of exchange. Resources that could have been mobilised for the benefit of society as a whole will, instead, remain unutilised.' Deakin, above n 10, 55.

[65] *Ibid*, 57.

[66] International Labour Organisation, above n 57, 28.

[67] A Blackett and C Sheppard, 'Collective Bargaining and Equality: Making Connections' (2003) 142 *International Labour Review* 419, 428.

[68] Langille, above n 4, 430.

notably because they foster cooperation between different social groups.[69] Finally, the right to organise and bargain collectively can advance the effective implementation of the three remaining fundamental labour rights proclaimed by the 1998 ILO Declaration.[70]

There can be no real possibility for the fulfilment of human aspirations and, in fact, no real labour market participation for those who are forced to work. People who are deprived of the most basic right to choose whether or not to work cannot truly decide the kind of life they want to live. It is therefore obvious that the elimination of all forms of forced or compulsory labour enhances peoples' capabilities by removing a major obstacle to the exercise of freedoms and rights. In other respects, the interdiction of child labour is necessary to ensure that all members of society are given a genuine opportunity to develop their capabilities.[71] There is, embedded in this prohibition, the idea of protecting the disadvantaged party to an exchange which is also an integral part of the private law of contract and which is expressed by the very concepts of capacity and incapacity. Children are particularly vulnerable to all forms of exploitation that can occur in the labour market. Preventing their employment under a minimum age and in dangerous conditions is a way of making sure they are not taken advantage of. It further promotes education, an essential component of social and economic development, by releasing children from the obligation of performing other tasks.

Also crucial for individuals' possibilities to benefit from the same opportunities to obtain decent work and take part in economic and social activities is freedom from discrimination.[72] Abolition of discrimination in terms of employment prevents the exclusion of people from the labour market based on personal characteristics, such as sex, race, age and sexual orientation, without regard to their actual working skills. It can potentially foster a rise in labour market participation that has overall positive effects for society.[73] On a micro-level, some studies have suggested that enterprises that respect equal opportunity programmes

[69] A study conducted for the World Bank and published in 2002 highlighted the positive economic effects of unions and collective bargaining in a global environment and underlined the potential of sound industrial relations in establishing a stable economy and promoting better investment climates: T Aidt and Z Tzannatos, *Unions and Collective Bargaining. Economic Effects in a Global Environment* (Washington, World Bank, 2002). See also: BA Langille, 'Seeking Post-Seattle Clarity—and Inspiration' in J Conaghan, RM Fischl and K Klare (eds), *Labour Law in an Era of Globalization* (Oxford, Oxford University Press, 2002) 137, 155.

[70] Langille, *ibid*, 154.

[71] International Labour Organisation, above n 57, 28.

[72] *Ibid*, 28.

[73] This point is illustrated with the example of laws against discrimination by Deakin, above n 10, 57. See also J Brown, S Deakin and F Wilkinson, 'Capabilities, Social Rights and European Market Integration' in R Salais and R Villeneuve (eds), *Towards a European Politics of Capabilities* (Cambridge, Cambridge University Press, 2004).

are likely to be more productive.[74] Aside from these economic considerations, freedom from discrimination, like all core labour rights, is undoubtedly an essential component of human dignity. Each of the four core labour rights therefore holds a certain potential to foster peoples' capabilities. But it is their combination and the interaction between them, as well as their mutually reinforcing effect, that give fundamental labour rights their profound value as enabling rights.

One of the most welcome aspects of the decent work agenda is its universality of coverage, in that it includes all workers, irrespective of their form of employment, as well as the unemployed.[75] The conception of workers' rights conveyed by the ILO transcends the classic model of the employment relationship and does not restrict itself to the traditional categories of labour law: the subordinate employee, the employer and the contract of employment. As underlined by the ILO Director General, this is necessary considering the vast number of people working in the informal economy worldwide:

> The majority of the working-age population in many countries is in the informal economy. This is the main reason why the ILO does not simply concentrate on rights at work; it would otherwise be missing out on the majority of workers in the world who are unemployed and/or who are active in the informal economy but not included in the statistics.[76]

While respect for fundamental labour rights is relevant in both the formal and the informal economy, the way people exercise core labour rights in these different contexts can vary significantly.[77] For example, the process of organisation through the agency of trade unions, which is the usual route for the exercise of freedom of association in industrialised countries, might not be adequate in the informal sector of developing countries.[78] Other vehicles and actors, such as women's groups and small contractors' organisations, might play a role in ensuring that people involved in the informal economy can enjoy the benefits provided by the exercise of the right to freedom of association.[79]

If the promotion of fundamental labour rights can be seen as a way of enabling people to fully develop their capabilities, the adoption of the 1998 Declaration and the implications of the ILO's focus on a small

[74] V Perotin and A Robinson, 'Employee Participation and Equal Opportunity Practices: Productivity Effects and Potential Complementarity' (2000) 38 *British Journal of Industrial Relations* 557 cited International Labour Organisation, above n 57, 20.

[75] A Sen, 'Work and Rights' (2000) 139 *International Labour Review* 119, 120.

[76] J Somavia, 'The ILO Decent Work Agenda as the Aspiration of People: The Insertion of Values and Ethics in the Global Economy' in D Peccoud (ed), *Philosophical and Spiritual Perspectives on Decent Work* (Geneva, International Labour Office, 2004) 3, 7.

[77] International Labour Organisation, above n 57, 29.

[78] Blackett and Sheppard, above n 67, 429.

[79] International Labour Organisation, above n 57, 30.

number of labour rights have not been without criticism. For instance, some authors have wondered why the protection of health and safety rights is not included within the core rights since 'working conditions free of grave risk of injury or illness seems as fundamental a right as working without discrimination'.[80] Others see the use of the term 'principle' with regard to these standards as a downgrading of their status due to the use of 'regressive terminology'.[81] It has also been argued that the concept of core rights 'constitutes a very significant departure from the insistence within the international human rights regime on the equal importance of all human rights'[82] and has the unintended consequence of 'shrinking the international labour code'.[83] For Member States, the four core labour standards represent, in a certain sense, 'the lowest common denominator of worker protection' and the Declaration allows for great flexibility in their implementation, in accordance with the national development level.[84] As a number of authors have pointed out, the fundamental labour rights are expressed in the form of somewhat vague principles and the Declaration avoids specific commitments.[85] This has been criticised as leaving the rights open to interpretation.[86]

In other respects, critics have argued that the weakness of the monitoring process comprised in the Follow-up to the 1998 Declaration has encouraged the 'privatization of enforcement'[87] and resulted in 'an unstructured and unaccountable decentralization of responsibility'.[88] By reason of their procedural orientation, it has also been said that the four core labour rights are amenable to neo-liberal philosophy and in harmony with free trade principles.[89] While there is certainly some worth

80 P Macklem, 'Labour Law Beyond Borders' (2002) 5 *Journal of International Economic Law* 605, 620, quoting L Compa, 'Promise and Peril: Core Labor Rights in Global Trade and Investment' in G Andreopoulos (ed), *International Human Rights: A Half Century after the Universal Declaration* (New York, Peter Lang Publishing, 2002).

81 P Alston, '"Core Labour Standards" and the Transformation of the International Labour Rights Regime' (2004) 15 *European Journal of International Law* 457, 483.

82 *Idem* 459.

83 P Alston and J Heenan, 'Shrinking the International Labor Code: An Unintended Consequence of the 1998 ILO Declaration on Fundamental Principles and Rights at Work?' (2004) 36 *International Law and Politics* 101. These authors further argue that '[t]he Core approach risks undermining the indivisibility of the overall corpus of the International Labor Code' (p 132).

84 Macklem, above n 80, 619.

85 Hepple, above n 13, 62; Maupain, above n 53, 453. This implicitly indicates that respect for core labour rights does not necessarily require the full observance of the more detailed provisions of the eight core conventions: Hepple, *idem*, 65; Langille, above n 4, 424.

86 P Alston, 'Facing Up to the Complexities of the ILO's Core Labour Standards Agenda' (2005) 16 *European Journal of International Law* 467, 477.

87 This term is borrowed from B Hepple, 'Enforcement: The Law and Politics of Co-operation and Compliance' in B Hepple (ed), *Social and Labour Rights in a Global Context* (Cambridge, Cambridge University Press, 2002) 238, 246.

88 Alston, above n 81.

89 McCrudden and Davies, above n 52, 51–2.

to these critical appraisals of the new orientations taken by the ILO with the adoption of the 1998 Declaration and the decent work agenda, one must recall that this approach is not, in fact, at odds with the traditional objectives and means put forward by the Organisation. For one thing, some labour standards considered as human rights, such as the right to freedom of association and collective bargaining, have long held a privileged place within the international labour code.[90] For its part, the process of decentralisation in terms of setting labour standards began to emerge some years before the adoption of the 1998 Declaration, at the beginning of the 1990s. The elaboration of transnational labour standards by non-state actors obviously raises important questions about the definition of standards. The 1998 ILO Declaration holds the potential to address some of the problems attached to the phenomenon of decentralisation by serving as a benchmark and guide for the conduct of non-state actors.[91]

The assessment of the ILO's strategic orientations also depends on how the realisation of fundamental labour rights and the role of the ILO in promoting respect for these rights are envisaged. In the past, the existence of mechanisms that guarantee the possibility for collective action has proven to be essential in order for the exercise of individual labour rights to be meaningful.[92] The fulfilment of core labour standards in the context of economic globalisation also calls for collective institutions. This is rightly acknowledged by the ILO, since the Organisation's favoured approach to the advancement of labour rights is grounded on advocacy, voice and partnership.[93] Within the decent work agenda, social dialogue is considered as both a strategic objective in itself and a means by which to promote fundamental labour rights, employment and social security, the three other strategic orientations. The essential elements of

[90] The importance of the right to freedom of association and collective bargaining is expressly recognised in the 1944 Declaration of Philadelphia. As Brian Langille notes, '[t]he ILO has long recognized that there is a hierarchy of conventions with those dealing with basic human rights at the top.' Langille, above n 4, 424.

[91] Janelle Diller has highlighted the role the ILO can play in this regard: 'The core labour standards of the Declaration serve increasingly as minimum points of reference for the conduct of labour, capital and public authority. The Declaration's four categories provide a normative framework for a variety of initiatives in the context of international co-operation, foreign direct investment, global production networks, local entrepreneurial development and even informal economic institutions.' J Diller, 'Globalization, Values and International Law in the World of Work' in JC Javillier and B Gernigon (eds), *Les normes internationales du travail: un patrimoine pour l'avenir. Mélanges en l'honneur de Nicolas Valticos* (Geneva, International Labour Office, 2004) 645, 647. As Jean-Michel Servais also rightly stressed, 'the ILO Declaration is the one (instrument) with the greatest potential for transcending the strucktly (sic) inter-governmental framework, even though it is primarily directed at ILO Member States'. JM Servais, 'Globalization and Decent Work Policy: Reflections upon a New Legal Approach' (2004) 143 *International Labour Review* 185, 192.

[92] A Supiot, 'The Labyrinth of Human Rights: Credo or Common Resource?' (2003) 21 *New Left Review* 118, 135; Deakin, 'Social Rights in a Globalized Economy', above n 10, 59–60.

[93] International Labour Organisation, above n 57, 54.

social dialogue, participation and freedom of association are, for the ILO, among the foundations of a democratic development path.[94] This strongly emphasises the special significance of the right to freedom of association and collective bargaining as an empowering tool for people.

With regard to the implementation process, the ILO is relying on its traditional means of action—regulatory conversations with its Member States and the use of cooperation, technical assistance and shame—as primary tools with which to induce respect for core labour rights in national legislations and practices since it does not hold coercive powers to impose the enforcement of international labour standards on governments.[95] To ensure follow-up to the promotion of the fundamental labour rights entrenched in the 1998 Declaration, the ILO has, more precisely, banked principally on a review mechanism provided for in its constitution: periodic Member States' reports concerning unratified fundamental conventions.[96] The role of the ILO with regard to core labour rights which represent, in international labour law, a new version of the concept of *capacitas* is therefore to provide technical assistance to Member States, educate governments on existing best practices and offer some guidance to ensure national public policy choices that are consistent with the obligations stemming from the 1998 ILO Declaration. While the role of the ILO in this regard is invaluable, core labour rights can only truly play their enabling function once they are integrated into national labour legislation and enforced by national bodies. These are the well-known traditional limits to the application of international labour law.

CONCLUSION

There has, over the years, been a remarkable evolution in the positions

[94] *Ibid*; International Labour Organisation, Report of the Director-General, 'Organizing for Social Justice', Global Report under the Follow-up to the ILO Declaration on Fundamental Principles and Rights at Work, International Labour Conference, 92nd Session, Report I(B) (Geneva, International Labour Office, 2004) para 73.

[95] The term 'regulatory conversation' is borrowed from Julia Black and has been used by Jill Murray to describe the dynamic of the relationship between the ILO and its Member States: J Black 'Regulatory Conversations' (2002) 29 *Journal of Law and Society* 163; J Murray, 'Relabelling the International Labour Problem: Globalization and Ideology' in C Dauvergne (ed), *Jurisprudence for an Interconnected Globe* (Aldershot, Ashgate, 2003) 129. Edward Weisband uses the expression 'discursive multilateralism' to describe the same dynamic: E Weisband, 'Discursive Multilateralism: Global Benchmarks, Shame, and Learning in the ILO Labor Standards Monitoring Regime' (2000) 44 *International Studies Quarterly* 643.

[96] This is provided in Section II Annual Follow-up Concerning Non-Ratified Fundamental Conventions of the Follow-up to the 1998 Declaration. These reports are requested from Members under Art 19, para 5(e) of the ILO Constitution. The follow-up to the 1998 Declaration also comprises a global annual report on each one of the four categories of fundamental rights in turn.

adopted by the ILO concerning the interplay between market concerns and the protection of labour rights. If social rights were long envisaged as means by which to protect individuals against the negative consequences engendered by the free reign of market forces, they are now perceived as foundational components of a dynamic labour market. Within the decent work agenda, the fundamental labour rights entrenched in the 1998 ILO Declaration constitute the 'floor of rights', a minimum which is essential in order for all other rights to be fulfilled, and represent the basic conditions for meaningful participation in the social and economic life of society. As such, the enabling rights of the 1998 ILO Declaration can be envisaged in the field of international labour law as a revisited concept of *capacitas*. Considering the inherent limits of international labour law, the effectiveness of fundamental labour rights in enhancing individuals' capabilities will depend upon the willingness and ability of ILO Member States to fully respect their obligations in accordance with the terms of the 1998 ILO Declaration.

9

En guise de conclusion: la capacité, une notion à haut potentiel

ALAIN SUPIOT

Un honnête homme n'est pas un pot
Entretiens de Confucius[1]

Au terme de cette réflexion collective, on est tenté d'appliquer à la capacité juridique un qualificatif très en vogue en matière d'exploitation des ressources humaines, et de dire qu'il s'agit d'une notion 'à haut potentiel'. Le rapprochement n'a rien d'innocent compte tenu de la tendance eurocratique à réduire l'homme à l'état d'un ustensile dont il faut assurer l'employabilité et l'adaptabilité aux besoins du marché. Or si le sens premier de la capacité est bien celui de la contenance d'un récipient, son sens juridique désigne l'aptitude d'une personne à souscrire des obligations. Autrement dit la capacité présente dans l'univers juridique cette particularité de relever à la fois de l'état des personnes et du droit des contrats. L'exigence de capacité interdit de considérer le contrat comme une pure mécanique qui pourrait faire abstraction de l'identité et des aptitudes des contractants. Elle rencontre donc les préoccupations de ceux qui pensent que le maintien de cet interdit est une condition de viabilité de l'économie de marché à l'échelle internationale.

Exposée par Simon Deakin dans son introduction, l'hypothèse dont procédait ce livre était que la notion de capacité pouvait constituer à l'échelle européenne une référence normative commune, qui soit cohérente avec les évolutions du droit positif et qui puisse guider les

[1] 'Junzi bu qi', traduction Pierre Ryckmans (Paris, Gallimard, 1987). Sur les problèmes de traduction de cet aphorisme, v Pierre Lévy, 'À propos de quatre mots des Entretiens de Confucius et de ses disciples' (1994) XIII(1–2) *Études chinoises* 285, qui observe que le mot *qi* (récipient d'une certaine capacité) prend au sens verbal celui de 'tenir compte de/évaluer la capacité' et propose la traduction suivante 'L'homme de qualité ne traite personne en ustensile'.

efforts de redéfinition de la citoyenneté sociale dans un contexte de délitement des protections et des solidarités issues de l'âge industriel. Nous venant du droit romain, la capacité a l'avantage de participer du patrimoine juridique commun des pays européens. Elle fait donc sens aussi bien en terre de *Common law* qu'en Europe continentale, ce qui n'est pas le cas des notions de 'capability' ou d' 'état professionnel des personnes', qui demeurent marquées par leur ancrage dans l'une ou l'autre de ces deux cultures juridiques. De cette origine romaine, il faut également retenir la distinction entre les incapacités de droit et les incapacités de fait: les premières procédaient du statut de la personne (qui devait être un homme libre, citoyen romain et père de famille), et les secondes de leur inaptitude concrète à s'engager librement (à raison de l'âge, du sexe, de la maladie mentale ou de la prodigalité).[2] Cette distinction a été supplantée dans les législations modernes par celle des incapacités d'exercice et des incapacités de jouissance, mais elle pourrait reprendre du service dès lors que, vidée de son contenu romain, la notion de 'capacité de fait' servirait à donner consistance juridique à la notion économique de 'capability' et à débarrasser au passage celle-ci de son ambiguïté.

Les chapitres de ce livre consacrés à l'évolution du droit positif dans différents pays européens confirment cette hypothèse de départ. Ils montrent tout d'abord que sur ses terres juridiques d'origine, celles du droit civil, la notion de capacité connaît un essor tout à fait spectaculaire et prend le pas sur son inverse longtemps dominant: l'incapacité des personnes. Ce retournement est parfaitement mis en lumière par Jean Hauser, qui montre comment le droit contemporain évolue d'une logique de qualification des incapables vers une logique de soutien des capacités. Soutenir dans la mesure du possible les capacités des personnes n'ayant pas le plein usage de leurs facultés fait naître une zone grise entre capacités et incapacité. Cette zone grise s'étend tout d'abord sous la forme d'une casuistique des degrés de la capacité, destinée à adapter les mesures de soutien aux aptitudes et aux besoins concrets des personnes. Cette zone grise s'étend aussi dans le temps, avec la mise en œuvre d'une gestion prévisionnelle des incapacités, qui permet de devancer les évènements susceptibles d'affecter le libre gouvernement de soi-même. Il n'en reste pas moins, qu'aussi dosées soient-elles, les mesures affectant la capacité civile réduisent la liberté individuelle et qu'il y aurait danger à leur donner une extension inconsidérée. Ainsi que le relève Jean Hauser, l'abus de la notion de prodigalité n'apparaît de ce point de vue que comme un mauvais remède à des problèmes qui relèvent plutôt du droit de la consommation.

[2] Cf F Girard, *Manuel élémentaire de droit romain* (Paris, Rousseau, 4ème éd, 1911) spéc 31 et suiv et 463 et suiv.

Cela pourrait justifier, ainsi que le soutient Sandrine Godelain, de recourir en ce domaine à une notion autonome de capacité financière. La proposition pourra choquer les gardiens du temple civiliste. Déjà enclins à voir dans le droit de la consommation une fâcheuse excroissance, ils s'inquièteront de ce qu'ils pourront considérer comme un dévoiement de la vieille notion de capacité civile. Force est pourtant de reconnaître que l'intelligibilité du droit positif suppose de prendre en considération . . . tout le droit positif, aussi désordonné qu'il advienne, si l'on veut y mettre de l'ordre et de la cohérence. De ce point de vue, la notion de capacité financière, qui émerge dans certains textes[3] ainsi qu'en jurisprudence, apparaît pertinente pour au moins trois raisons. La première est que le recours au concept juridique de capacité marque clairement les risques d'atteinte aux libertés que recèlent les techniques de contrôle (*credit scoring*), voire de sanction (interdiction bancaire) des personnes, techniques qui sont aujourd'hui pour l'essentiel aux mains des établissements de crédit. La seconde est que la notion de capacité financière permet de rendre compte de dispositions qui limitent la liberté de prendre certains engagements précisément déterminés, sans affecter la capacité civile au sens propre du terme. La troisième est que l'une des particularités de la protection de la partie vulnérable en matière de consommation est d'obliger la partie forte à veiller aux intérêts de son contractant, comme le montre le devoir de conseil qui pèse sur les professionnels dans leurs relations avec les consommateurs. Or cette obligation est caractéristique du régime des capacités de fait, telle qu'il émerge sans discussion possible en droit social.

De fait, c'est en droit du travail que les nouveaux usages de la notion de capacité sont le plus manifestes, comme le montrent notamment les contributions de Wiebke Brose et Sandrine Godelain dans les ordres juridiques internes et celle de Renée-Claude Drouin dans l'ordre international. Le rapprochement de ces études de cas met en lumière les trois facettes de la capacité en droit du travail.

La première est la *capacité physique*. Commune à toute espèce de contrat de travail, elle est justement appelée droit allemand *Arbeitsfähigkeit*: capacité de travailler.[4] C'est l'exemple topique d'une capacité de fait, à défaut de laquelle le contrat ne saurait être conclu, exécuté ou maintenu. Le contrat de travail engage la personne physique du travailleur et c'est

[3] V C trav art L 951-4 relatif à l'agrément des organismes paritaires de formation professionnelle: 'L'agrément . . . est accordé en fonction de la capacité financière des organismes paritaires, de leur organisation territoriale, professionnelle ou interprofessionnelle, et de leur aptitude à assurer leur mission compte tenu de leurs moyens'.

[4] Le droit français se réfère fréquemment à la *capacité de travail* ou la *capacité de gain* pour arrêter la situation juridique des handicapés (cf C trav art L 323-3, *C sec soc* art L 341-1 et suiv, L 815-24).

pourquoi le droit du travail a été le premier à devoir faire place à l'éventualité d'une incapacité physique ignorée du droit commun des contrats. Le régime juridique de cette incapacité de fait ne pouvait évidemment se couler dans celui des incapacités civiles, qui concernent le consentement plutôt que l'objet du contrat. D'où l'élaboration en droit du travail de techniques particulières, visant à contrôler, protéger, et restaurer la capacité de travailler: la suspension du contrat, la réparation des accidents du travail, l'assurance maladie et l'assurance vieillesse, la médecine du travail, les règles de santé et de sécurité au travail, sont autant de dispositifs indexés sur la capacité de travail entendue au sens individuel mais aussi au sens collectif de la capacité physique de travail d'une nation.

La capacité de travailler relève de l'exécution du contrat, là où les incapacités civiles concernent plutôt la validité de l'acte. D'où la différence des régimes juridiques de ces deux types d'incapacité: un contrat conclu par un incapable de droit encourt la nullité, tandis que le constat d'une incapacité physique du travailleur doit conduire à la suspension, la modification ou la rupture de son contrat. Un travailleur dont la capacité est réduite par la maladie ou l'accident peut librement conclure un contrat de travail à la mesure de ses forces, alors qu'un majeur protégé ou un mineur ne peut en principe s'engager sans être assisté ou représenté par un tiers. Enfin le partenaire contractuel d'un incapable de droit (dûment assisté ou représenté) n'a pas de devoir particulier à son égard une fois le contrat valablement conclu, tandis que l'employeur d'un salarié en bonne santé a l'obligation contractuelle de ne pas mettre sa santé en péril et d'adapter son emploi à ses capacités physiques si celles-ci sont affectées par la maladie ou l'accident.

Seconde facette de la notion de capacité qui émerge en droit du travail: la *capacité professionnelle*. Jusqu'à il y a peu, on ne la rencontrait guère qu'en matière de professions indépendantes, sous la forme d'une condition légale d'exercice d'un métier déterminé. Ce sens n'est pas inconnu en droit du travail, car certaines de ces professions peuvent faire l'objet d'un exercice salarié. Plus généralement, la capacité professionnelle fait partie des critères d'identification des emplois qu'est susceptible d'occuper un chômeur. Mais c'est aussi sous un jour beaucoup plus novateur que la capacité professionnelle émerge en droit du travail: non plus seulement comme condition d'exercice d'une activité déterminée, mais comme objet d'une obligation contractuelle.

Ainsi, aux termes de la loi française,

> L'employeur a l'obligation d'assurer l'adaptation des salariés à leur poste de travail. Il veille au maintien de leur capacité à occuper un emploi, au regard notamment de l'évolution des emplois, des technologies et des organisations.

Il peut proposer des formations qui participent au développement des compétences.[5]

La gradation opérée ici entre l'*adaptation* au poste de travail, la *capacité* à occuper un emploi et le développement des *compétences* va de pair avec un dégradé des devoirs de l'employeur: à mi-chemin entre l'*obligation* d'assurer l'adaptation du salarié et la simple *possibilité* de développer ses compétences, le maintien de la capacité professionnelle fait l'objet d'un devoir de *veille*. Que recouvre exactement ce devoir de veille? Dans un contexte différent, le code civil dispose que

> L'obligation de veiller à la conservation de la chose, soit que la convention n'ait pour objet que l'utilité de l'une des parties, soit qu'elle ait pour objet leur utilité commune, soumet celui qui en est chargé à y apporter tous les soins d'un bon père de famille. Cette obligation est plus ou moins étendue relativement à certains contrats . . .[6]

Par analogie, on peut sans trop d'audace affirmer qu'en droit français l'employeur doit apporter au maintien de la capacité professionnelle de ses salariés tous les soins d'un bon père de famille, et que son obligation est plus ou moins étendue, non selon le type de contrat, mais selon la taille de son entreprise et la capacité de celle-ci à anticiper l'évolution des emplois, des technologies et des organisations. En droit allemand aussi, veiller au maintien de la capacité professionnelle des salariés fait aujourd'hui partie des devoirs d'un bon chef d'entreprise, comme le montre Wiebke Brose dans son analyse des dispositions relatives aux mesures de reclassement dans le cadre des procédures de licenciement économique. Et là aussi, il s'agit d'une obligation de portée relative, dont l'intensité dépend des ressources et de la situation de l'entreprise.

Ce n'est pas seulement dans le contrat de travail que la sauvegarde ou la restauration de la capacité professionnelle s'affirme comme objet possible d'une obligation, mais aussi dans les relations entre le demandeur d'emploi avec l'assurance-chômage ou avec les opérateurs chargés de l'aider à retrouver un emploi. Le processus de contractualisation de ces relations, engagé sur le modèle britannique du *Jobseeker's Agreement*, a connu des destins divers sur le continent,[7] mais l'idée

5 C trav art L 6321-1 (ex 930-1) introduit par la loi du 4 mai 2004.

6 C civ art 1137, définissant l'obligation de donner.

7 En France toute référence à l'idée de contrat entre le demandeur d'emploi et l'assurance chômage a été supprimée après que cette dernière a été condamnée par certains tribunaux à respecter les engagements individuels qu'elle avait pris à l'égard de certains chômeurs. V sur cette affaire: A Supiot, 'La valeur de la parole donnée [à propos des chômeurs "recalculés"]' [2004] *Droit social* 541; X Prétot, 'Le contentieux de l'assurance-chômage entre le juge administratif et le juge civil' [2004] *Droit social* 766; Ph Martin, 'Assurance chômage: hasards et nécessité de la contractualisation des engagements' [2004] *Droit ouvrier* 397. La convention d'assurance chômage signée en 2006 a abandonné la terminologie juridique contractuelle de

d'activation des dépenses de l'assurance chômage a conduit partout à l'instauration d'une obligation pour le chômeur, non seulement de rechercher un emploi, mais aussi de faire évoluer ses capacités professionnelles pour améliorer ses chances d'en trouver un. A cette fin, l'assurance chômage finance 'des actions de formation renforçant les capacités professionnelles des allocataires pour répondre à des besoins de qualification identifiés au niveau territorial ou professionnel'.[8]

La capacité professionnelle est donc source d'obligations aussi bien pour le salarié que pour l'employeur. L'ambivalence de la notion se révèle aussi dans le fait que l'employeur, s'il doit veiller à maintenir la capacité de ses salariés, a en revanche le droit de privilégier les plus capables. C'est ce que montre par exemple les dispositions du droit allemand relative à l'ordre des licenciements économiques, ou celles du droit français relatives aux discriminations prohibées.[9]

Une troisième facette de la notion de capacité en droit du travail est mise en lumière par Renée-Claude Drouin dans son analyse de l'évolution récente des activités normatives de l'Organisation internationale du travail (OIT): il s'agit des capacités collectives. Marginalisée sur la scène internationale depuis le triomphe des thèses néolibérales et des politiques de déréglementation du travail, l'OIT est tiraillée entre une politique d'accompagnement de ce mouvement néolibéral et l'obligation où elle se trouve, sauf à se renier elle-même, de réaffirmer les principes fondamentaux qui la fondent. La Déclaration des principes et droits fondamentaux au travail qu'elle a adoptée en 1998 témoigne de ces tiraillements, ce qui lui a valu des critiques acerbes et souvent pertinentes. On lui a notamment reproché à bon droit d'ignorer ce qui forme partout la base de la capacité de travail, c'est-à-dire la capacité physique et le principe de santé et de sécurité au travail. Mais cela ne doit pas conduire à mésestimer le fait que cette Déclaration place en tête des quatre principes et droits fondamentaux qu'elle proclame 'la liberté d'association et la reconnaissance effective du droit de négociation collective'. Donner une telle place à la capacité collective, c'est-à-dire au droit des salariés de s'organiser, d'agir et de négocier ensemble, est sans

la convention de 2001 au profit d'une terminologie de type médical qui objective la personne du chômeur (engagé dans un 'parcours de retour à l'emploi', comme le malade dans un 'parcours coordonné de soins'). De son côté la Cour de cassation a décidé que le Plan d'aide au retour à l'emploi n'engageait pas juridiquement l'assurance chômage ([2007] *Droit social* 403, obs X Prétot).

[8] Convention du 18 janvier 2006 relative au retour à l'emploi et à l'indemnisation du chômage, art 1er, §.3.

[9] Cf les dispositions de l'art L 122-35 C trav '(Le règlement intérieur) ne peut comporter de dispositions lésant les salariés dans leur emploi ou leur travail, en raison de leur sexe, de leurs moeurs, de leur orientation sexuelle, de leur âge, de leur situation de famille, de leurs origines, de leurs opinions ou confessions, de leur apparence physique, de leur patronyme, ou de leur handicap, *à capacité professionnelle égale*'.

doute l'apport le plus incontestable et le mieux venu de cette Déclaration. Car la grande singularité, et la modernité inentamée du droit du travail, consiste justement à reconnaître que la capacité des individus s'ancre nécessairement dans celle des groupes auxquels ils appartiennent et que la société n'est pas et ne peut être cette poussière de particules contractantes à quoi voudraient la réduire les intégristes du Marché.

Les termes de la Déclaration de 1998 mettent en lumière les deux versants de la capacité collective: d'un côté la capacité reconnue aux individus de s'organiser librement et d'agir collectivement pour défendre leurs intérêts économiques et sociaux (liberté d'association); et de l'autre la capacité des organisations de conclure des conventions collectives (droit de négociation collective). Sous le premier sens il s'agit plutôt d'une capacité de fait, qui connaît des degrés selon les conditions concrètes d'exercice des libertés de s'organiser et d'agir collectivement. Sous le second sens il s'agit au contraire d'une véritable capacité de droit, qui conditionne l'opposabilité des accords conclus. Le régime de cette capacité juridique s'est sensiblement durci à partir du moment où le domaine des conventions collectives s'est étendu à des domaines antérieurement réservés à la loi ou au règlement. Le droit européen a joué ici un rôle pionnier. La possibilité conférée aux partenaires sociaux par l'Accord social de Maastricht de négocier le contenu des directives en matière sociale a conduit le juge communautaire à décider que de tels accords ne pouvaient être valablement conclus que par des organisations ayant une 'représentativité cumulée suffisante'.[10] Cette jurisprudence a été la première à introduire une distinction entre la représentativité d'un syndicat et sa capacité à conclure des conventions collectives. Cette distinction s'installe aujourd'hui dans les droits nationaux, comme le montre l'introduction en droit français par loi du 4 mai 2004 d'un principe majoritaire applicable à toute espèce de convention collective. Dans son sens le plus général, il résulte de ce principe que la validité d'un accord collectif 'est subordonnée à l'absence d'opposition de la majorité des organisations syndicales de salariés représentatives dans le champ d'application de l'accord'.[11] L'écart ne cesse donc de se creuser entre la capacité civile, qui est reconnue de droit à tout syndicat,[12] et la capacité

[10] TPE 17 juin 1998 (aff T–135/96) *Union européenne de l'artisanat et des petites et moyennes entreprises*. Aux termes de ce jugement (point 90), il incombe à la Commission et au Conseil 'de vérifier si, au regard du contenu de l'accord en cause, les partenaires sociaux signataires de ce dernier ont une représentativité cumulée suffisante. Toute représentativité cumulée déficiente doit (les) conduire . . . à refuser de mettre en oeuvre l'accord conclu au niveau communautaire'.

[11] C trav art L 2232-2 (anc L 132-2-2). Cette exigence de consensus peut sous certaines conditions être remplacée par une exigence de consentement majoritaire: v J Pélissier, A Supiot et A Jeammaud, *Droit du travail* (Paris, Dalloz, 24 éd, 2006) n°780 et suiv p 905 et suiv.

[12] C trav art L 411-10. On sait que ce n'est pas le cas dans tous les pays européens, le syndicats n'étant dans certains d'entre eux, comme la Belgique, que des associations de fait.

de conclure des conventions collectives, qui dépend de la constatation d'une représentativité suffisante au moment de cette conclusion.

La démonstration semble donc faite, non seulement que la notion de capacité connaît un réel *risorgimento* en droit positif, mais aussi qu'elle se fragmente en admettant des degrés (entre la pleine capacité et la totale incapacité) et des types différents (capacité de droit ou de fait, individuelle ou collective). Alain Wijffels montre dans sa contribution que ce processus de fragmentation affecte également d'autres notions de base, comme la propriété et la responsabilité. Un tel processus marque non seulement un reflux du mouvement de 'rationalisation' du Droit théorisé par l'Ecole du *Vernunftrecht*, mais aussi un démenti pour la sociologie wébérienne qui avait cru pouvoir identifier ce mouvement à une loi de l'histoire. Plus précisément, il rappelle à nos esprits modernes, très enclins à l'oublier, que la raison ne s'identifie pas au calcul, car elle oblige à tenir compte aussi, et peut-être d'abord, de ce qui ne se calcule pas. L'échange contractuel est bien une affaire de calcul, mais il ne peut advenir qu'entre des personnes qui ne sont pas réductibles à des machines à calculer. Parmi les différentes conditions de validité du contrat, la capacité est la seule (avec l'erreur sur la personne) qui oblige à tenir compte de *qui* contracte et à s'interroger sur l'aptitude réelle des parties à s'engager et (dans le cas de la capacité collective) à engager autrui. Cette question des aptitudes concrètes à conclure et exécuter un contrat se pose avec une acuité nouvelle dans le contexte dit de la 'société en réseaux',[13] qui engendre foule de contrats de facture féodale, ayant moins pour objet d'échanger des quantités que de lier des personnes.

Ceci devrait conduire, ainsi que le recommande Martijn Hesselink dans sa contribution, à faire place à la capacité dans le droit commun des contrats qui se dessine aujourd'hui en Europe. Dès lors qu'elle vise à se doter d'un instrument de protection de la partie vulnérable, une telle reconnaissance de la capacité à l'échelle européenne pourrait s'inspirer des développements récents que la notion a connu en droit du travail. La contribution de ce dernier au droit commun des contrats a été très important au niveau national[14] et il n'y a donc pas de raison qu'il en aille différemment au niveau communautaire. D'autant que le droit commun

[13] V M Castells, *The Rise of the Network Society* (Oxford, Blackwell, 1996) trad fr *La société en réseaux* (Paris, Fayard, 1998); G Teubner, 'The Many-headed Hydra: Networks as Higher-order Collective Actors' in J McCahery, S Picciotto and C Scott (eds), *Corporate Control and Accountability* (Oxford, Oxford University Press, 1993) 41 *et seq*; F Ost et M van de Kerchove, *De la pyramide au réseau? Pour une théorie dialectique du droit* (Bruxelles, Pub Des Facultés universitaires Saint-Louis, 2002) 587 *et seq*.

[14] Cf J Mestre, 'L'influence des relations de travail sur le droit commun des contrats' (1988) *Droit social* 405; PY Gautier, 'Les interactions du droit civil et du droit du travail' in B Teyssié (dir), *Les sources du droit du travail* (Paris, PUF, 1998) 129 *et seq*; M Fabre-Magnan, 'Le droit du travail vu du droit civil: l'unité du droit des obligations' in *Regards croisés sur le droit social, Semaine sociale*, éd Lamy, n° spéc, Supt n°1095 du 28 oct 2002, pp 32 *et seq*.

qui se construit aujourd'hui en Europe ne se découvre plus dans un code mais se construit dans un patient travail doctrinal et jurisprudentiel.[15]

Ainsi que le souligne Aurora Vimercati dans sa contribution sur le droit italien, recourir au concept de capacité permettrait, sinon de juguler, du moins d'endiguer la tendance au renversement des moyens (économiques) et des fins (humaines). Ce renversement est particulièrement visible dans la *novlangue* en usage dans les institutions européennes, qui illustre particulièrement bien ce que Bruno Romano appelle le fondamentalisme fonctionnel[16]: on n'y parle plus d'êtres humains, de capacités professionnelles ou de libertés, mais de capital humain,[17] d'employabilité ou de flexibilité. Ces déplacements terminologiques appréhendent les personnes comme des choses et substituent aux catégories juridiques des manières de pensée importées de la physique ou de la biologie. Popularisée par Staline,[18] l'idée de capital humain a servi d'équivalent communiste à la notion nazie de 'matériel humain'. Contraire au principe de dignité humaine, elle procède d'une vision scientiste du monde qui réduit l'homme à l'état de ressource économique.[19] Il en va de même de l'employabilité, qui consiste, au sens étymologique à *plier* les hommes *dans* les besoins des marchés[20] au lieu de partir de leur intelligence et de leur créativité, c'est-à-dire de leur capacités professionnelles pour atteindre les objectifs que l'Union européenne s'est donnée au début du millénaire à Lisbonne.[21] Quant à la notion de flexibilité, elle permet de mettre dans le même sac les travailleurs et les machines, là où raisonner en terme de liberté obligerait à concilier la liberté d'entreprendre et la liberté du travail et à se confronter avec ce qu'il y a toujours d'inattendu et d'imprévisible, non

15 Cf A Wijffels (dir), *Le Code civil entre ius commune et droit privé européen* (Bruxelles, Bruylant, 2005).

16 B Romano, *Fondalismo funzionale e nichilismo giuridico. Postumanesimo 'noia' globalizzatione* (Torino, Giappichelli, 2000).

17 Cf La décision du Conseil européen relative aux lignes directrices adoptées pour les politiques de l'emploi des États membres (2006/544/CE, JO L 215 du 5.8.2006, pp 26–7), qui leur fixe comme priorité d'*investir davantage dans le capital humain* en améliorant l'éducation et les compétences.

18 J Staline, *L'homme le capital le plus précieux. Pour une formation bolchévik* (Paris, Editions Sociales, 1945).

19 Au sens précis du terme, le capital humain désigne l'actif inscrit au bilan d'un propriétaire d'esclaves. V CS McWatters et Y Lemarchand, 'Comptabilité et traite négrière. Le Guide du commerce de Gaignat de l'Aulnais (1718–1791)' in JG Degos et S Trébucq (dir), *L'entreprise, le chiffre et le droit* (Bordeaux, 2005) 209–36.

20 C'est la définition qu'en donne la Commission européenne 'A person is employable when he or she has the marketable skills, competence or features which are regarded by labour market demand as necessary conditions for hiring' (citée par P Pochet et M Paternotre, *'Employabilité' dans le contexte des lignes directrices de l'Union européenne sur l'emploi* (Brussels, Observatoire social européen, 1998).

21 'Faire en sorte que l'Europe devienne l'économie de la connaissance la plus compétitive et la plus dynamique du monde, capable d'une croissance économique durable accompagnée d'une amélioration quantitative et qualitative de l'emploi et d'une plus grande cohésion sociale'. Conclusions de la présidence, Conseil européen de Lisbonne, 23 et 24 mars 2000.

seulement dans la circulation marchande et monétaire, mais aussi dans l'esprit et le travail des hommes.

Malgré la séduction du pessimisme qu'elle ne peut manquer d'exercer, l'hypothèse d'une dissolution inéluctable des catégories juridiques dans la pensée cybernétique et gestionnaire est sans doute infondée. L'utopie du remplacement du gouvernement des hommes par l'administration des choses travaille l'Occident depuis deux siècles, et le fait qu'elle triomphe aujourd'hui dans la communauté européenne ne signifie pas qu'elle cesse d'être une utopie, appelée comme toutes les utopies à se heurter un jour au principe de réalité. La 'flexisécurité' mise en avant aujourd'hui par la Commission est une bonne illustration de ce rappel à la réalité du temps long de la vie humaine, et des sécurités qu'implique sa préservation et sa continuation. Il semblait entendu que, dans le domaine économique, la sécurité n'était plus un bien que s'agissant des choses (sécurité monétaire, sécurité des affaires, sécurité juridique), mais que s'agissant des hommes la sécurité économique, dont la Déclaration de Philadelphie avait fait à l'issue de la 2nde guerre mondiale le but des politiques commerciales et financières, était condamnée à disparaître au profit d'une précarité de principe, propre à rendre les hommes flexibles et aptes à s'adapter aux besoins des marchés. C'est ce qu'enjoint de faire l'article 125 du Traité CE et c'est ce que recommande la Commission européenne comme du reste toutes les organisations économiques internationales.[22] En 2005, dans une déclaration remarquée, la présidente du Mouvement des entreprises de France (Medef) pouvait s'interroger ainsi à voix haute 'La vie, la santé, l'amour sont précaires, pourquoi le travail échapperait-il à cette loi?'.[23] Cette politique se heurte toutefois à la réalité des hommes, qui sont d'autant plus aptes à s'adapter qu'ils jouissent d'une réelle sécurité économique et de solides capacités professionnelles. D'où l'apparition dans le vocabulaire communautaire de cet hybride qu'est la flexisécurité.[24] Il faut bien sûr saluer cette redécouverte des besoins humains fondamentaux. Mais coller ainsi dans un même mot des notions différentes donne plus sûrement le jour à une chimère qu'à un concept opératoire.

Le concept de capacité au contraire combine et hiérarchise d'une part la sécurité de l'état des personnes, et d'autre part leur aptitude à agir librement. La dimension biophysique de l'être humain (sa 'contenance', son utilité) s'y trouve associée à la reconnaissance de ses aptitudes

[22] 'Workers need to be more flexible and adaptable to cope with constant technological change, rapidly eroding skills and increasing global competition' peut-on lire sur son site à la rubrique Growth and Jobs: http://ec.europa.eu/growthandjobs/areas/fiche09_en.htm.

[23] *Le Figaro Economie*, 30 août 2005.

[24] Aujourd'hui portée sur les fonds baptismaux par la commission européenne: cf sa communication du 27 juin 2007 'Towards Common Principles of Flexicurity: More and Better Jobs through Flexibility And Security', COM(2007) 359 final.

particulières et de sa liberté. C'est du reste ce qui explique l'intérêt durable qu'elle n'a cessé d'exercer sur la pensée économique et sociale depuis les débuts du capitalisme, de Saint-Simon[25] à Amartya Sen. Comme du temps de Saint-Simon, elle peut constituer une référence commune à des banquiers et à des syndicalistes, et son enracinement dans l'histoire longue du droit des pays européens lui donne de chances raisonnables de porter de nouveaux fruits.

[25] La devise des saint-simoniens était 'Tous les privilèges de naissance, sans exception, seront abolis. A chacun selon ses capacités, à chaque capacité selon ses œuvres'. Pierre Musso a montré récemment la place nodale occupée par la notion de capacité chez Saint-Simon, 'Avec la vertueuse combinaison de capacités, la société industrielle peut être assimilée à une association, à une entreprise dans laquelle la hiérarchie disparaît et où tous coopèrent à la production . . . A la centralité de l'État dominateur doit se substituer celle de l'entreprise organisatrice', P Musso, *La religion du monde industriel. Analyse de la pensée de Saint-Simon* (La Tour d'Aigues, Éditions de l'Aube, 2006) 190. Sur la fortune politique de la notion de capacité au XIXème siècle, notamment dans les professions qualifiées, voir aussi Y Le Marec, *Le temps des capacités: les diplômés nantais à la conquête du pouvoir dans la ville* (Paris, Belin, 2000) 335.